HOME
MANAGEMENT

PLAIN & SIMPLE

KIM BRENNEMAN

Dedicated to my children
and all the future generations of parents raising
their children to the glory of God.

CONTENTS

CONTENTS

Home Is Where Each Lives for the Other
and All Live for Christ

—from a plaque hanging on the wall
of my childhood home

WHY I WROTE THIS BOOK

We all live in a home of some sort, we all have laundry, and we all eat food. It's universal. All this living can be messy. I struggled with my first attempts at being responsible for a house, laundry, food, and then a baby. I didn't automatically know how to keep a house. This book is a how-to for taking care of life's daily tasks. My goal for the reader is that you will be able to progress faster and jump ahead in home management so that even your best days will be better.

If you have children, you will find a lot of information here on how I manage the home with children. We also homeschool our children and live on a farm. You have your own variables, but the bottom line is that we all live in a home and have the work that comes with it.

This is the second version to a book I wrote a few years ago, titled *Large Family Logistics: The Art and Science of Managing the Large Family.* The book went out of print, but while it was still in print, I found that many people without my family dynamics found the book helpful.

My hope and prayer is that the home management tips and tricks that you learn in this book will allow you to enjoy your life more, breathe easier, sleep better, and have more time for things that count in the long run. Be encouraged; you will learn methods and systems that will help you in better managing your home.

HOW TO USE
THIS BOOK

This book is designed so that you can flip to a particular topic and read for inspiration or start at the beginning and methodically implement each skill as it is presented. Part One is philosophical and gives encouragement for our lives as women, homekeepers, wives, and mothers. It includes faith foundations and overarching methods that will help you implement Part Two, which offers the nitty-gritty particulars for how to keep the home.

If you are in dire straits, then you will want to go to the two appendixes, and start with a detailed strategy on how to climb out of a big mess. Don't stop there though. Later, come back to the beginning and nail down the details of homekeeping and attitude management.

PART ONE

REALITY

Today as I write this, I am in my 40s, and have nine children, plus a daughter-in-law. I have had the experience of running businesses, and am currently in nursing school, working towards certification as a nurse-midwife. Looking back though, I remember myself as a young wife: pregnant and living in a tiny little box of a rental house that boasted ancient avocado green carpet that matched the kitchen stove, and a fireplace that sucked all the heat straight up the chimney. To top it off, it was furnished and decorated with a somewhat awkward combination of hand-me-downs and wedding presents.

Each day, I looked around at this strange new life, wondering what I was supposed to do. I have always been a visionary sort of person, but this new reality was not matching up with what I had dreamed of as a girl. My dreams were of a home, not just a house, and a home for me smelled like lemon furniture polish, fresh baked cookies and pumpkin pie. The home in my mind was decorated with thought and care, and things were in order like the clean and folded laundry. Home meant everything had a place and everything was in its place... and my place looked just like a beautiful mixture of my mother, grandmother, and every other great woman I knew.

My new reality was something different. My previous life of childhood, school and activities, followed by the scandalous freedom of college life, had left me both unequipped and ill-prepared for the daily requirements of making a house into a home. While I had been taught how to clean, my activity-filled adolescent life had left me naively unaware as to the what, when, and how often of keeping a home. I had to learn a new daily routine beyond that of school and friends. I knew that homes were supposed to look, feel, and smell warm and welcoming, and not in a vintage avocado green kind of way.

This whole new life of having my own home and my own family was quickly becoming overwhelming and not living up to my expectations of wedded bliss and starting a home.

How was clean and tidy supposed to happen when I was already so tired from being a college student, a wife, working part-time, and being pregnant? What was I supposed to buy at the grocery store with the little money we had? How much food was I even supposed to make? What if the food in the cupboards didn't match the recipes in the two cookbooks I had gotten for wedding presents? Why was the house always dusty when I had just cleaned? And the dishes... the dishes piled up because I had eczema on my hands so bad. The skin always peeled right off of my fingers and it was so painful to touch anything, and water only made it worse. Even folding laundry hurt. This whole new life of having my own home and my own family was quickly becoming overwhelming and not living up to my expectations of wedded bliss and starting a home.

I knew this was getting out of hand when I started dreaming of becoming sucked into mud. I realized I needed to access some help to figure this out. I talked to new friends from church about how I hated to wash dishes. One told me that she only made herself wash dishes if there were more than ten items to wash, and that she even counted utensils. If there were less than ten things she walked on by the sink and did something else, but if there were ten or more then she had to quickly wash up the dishes. This kept them from building up, and gave her permission to walk on by. My grandma taught me to think ahead about what I was going to have for meals, and to prepare food early in the day, not twenty minutes beforehand. This builds in some preplanning, plus takes some of the last minute stress out, making mealtime more enjoyable. My mom told me to dust once a week, and that yes, it will get dusty in between.

This gave me a plan, and made it okay to have midweek dust. Another new friend told me where to get the best prices for groceries, which left a little bit of extra money in the budget. I made myself a rule that if I saved more than a certain amount, I could buy one new book, something that I couldn't already get from the library. From the library I chose cookbooks, gardening, organization, and even business management books. So I learned bit by bit, here and there, to manage and create this new chapter of my life.

Through that experience I discovered some things about myself. Life is like that, each new chapter or turn in the road has fresh lessons. I learned that I was living in a box of expectations that I built around myself. I had to give sincere thought to which items in this box were real and true expressions of who I was as a person, and which represented who I thought I was supposed to be. I learned what type of work I enjoyed and how to quickly get through those tasks that I didn't. I learned to ask questions and seek knowledge from all kinds of sources, then choose things that were meaningful and useful for me at the time, setting aside the rest. I learned that there were other ventures in life that I would rather be doing than cleaning, cooking, and laundry (such as reading books and learning new skills), yet also that I appreciated a tidy house, good food, and clean laundry, and so I learned self-discipline.

Finally, I found that it all became rather automatic. Over time, I no longer had to think about what to do, how to do it, or when to do it, it was just happening, somewhat naturally. Day by day, bit by bit, with a little nudge here and a push there, plus the wisdom gleaned from others and the abiding grace of God, I learned the art of home management. And somewhere along the line, I figured out where I fit and where I didn't, and eventually found my place.

If you have picked up this book, you are likely looking for practical advice on how to be a better manager of the responsibilities that come with a house and family. I've been in your shoes—looking for ideas from whatever helpful sources I could find on how to be more effective in guiding the affairs of the home.

But before we can delve into all the details, we must have our priorities straight. We start with a solid foundation for life, or our efforts will fall short. Our goal is not to merely gain knowledge on all of the issues related to keeping house, though knowledge is a good and helpful thing, but our goal is to seek wisdom in making our house a home.

To be wise, we must seek Jesus, for we will not find wisdom apart from him.

In my own story of home management, I had to realize that if I wanted my house and home life to match my imagination and goals, then I had to set some roots. We lived in rentals for the first several years of marriage and that made it hard for me to want to invest in home management; each place really wasn't my house or property. I couldn't physically set roots down. I had God, my husband, and my babies. I used those years in learning to know God, learning to know my husband and how to be a better partner for him, and in loving and nurturing my little children. I worked hard at seeking wisdom and learning how to manage home and life for my family and me.

To be wise, we must seek Jesus, for we will not find wisdom apart from him. As the writer of Proverbs explains: "There is no wisdom nor understanding nor counsel against the Lord" (Proverbs 21:30, KJV).

Thankfully, God has not left us in the dark but has imparted great wisdom to us in his Word which serves as a "lamp unto [our] feet, and a light unto [our] path" (Psalms 119:105 , KJV).

In reading the whole of the Bible we learn who God is, what God has done and why. There will always be some things that are outside our realm of understanding in this lifetime, but in learning to know God, we establish a firm foundation, a reference point, a security that can come only from seeking God first, learning to know Jesus and following him, and being empowered by the Spirit.

WHAT DOES THIS HAVE TO DO WITH HOME MANAGEMENT?

No matter our living circumstances, our living space is a place of ministry to family and friends. The attitude we have in keeping our home, in how we relate to our family and friends, and in caring for others reflects God's love to us. When we take care of our spiritual health and seek wisdom from God's Word in how to love others, that outpouring of love appears in our homes.

GOALS

I sat on the porch steps in the afternoon sunshine with a battered notebook, and wrote down everything that was bothering me. I'm not sure where the idea came from, but it was a good one, because the relief was sweet. Just getting the thoughts out of my head and onto the paper was freedom. After the first words came out, they flowed like a river. Little bothers, big troubles, irritations, and the impossible, all of it spilled out onto the lines and filling the pages.

Every day I loved my little boys, I made their meals, did the laundry, washed the dishes, played and read stories. I put them down for naps, did my Bible study, and read books for my brain. One by one the days flowed by, and they were good days but... but what?

All of the swirling thoughts, ideas, pictures, and feelings erupted onto the paper. Looking at these pages of problems—the things that bothered me, both large and small—I saw that there were answers available, there were things I could do. Beside each line I wrote an answer, a solution. The big, the little, the practical, and even the impossible, writing the answer doubled the feeling of freedom I had gotten from just naming the trouble. Even if the answer wasn't attainable, I was able to release it to God. Sometimes I just wrote, 'Thy will be done.'

By giving myself tasks, tangible steps to resolve my little and big problems, I learned to take myself seriously. I could step outside of myself, gain some perspective and make sense of things, and find rest in the act of doing. I made action plans addressing a path toward resolution for the thoughts and feelings inside of me. There was value in placing forward movement to these thoughts and ideas that kept resurfacing inside of me.

Later, I learned the value of putting a timeline to a goal, and the importance of identifying long term goals as well. From his work in the corporate world, my husband brought home the concept of SMART goals. SMART is an acronym for Specific, Measurable, Achievable, Realistic, and Time. From my mother, I had learned to plan backwards when preparing a holiday meal, and I began to apply that thinking to everything.

Twenty-some years later, you can still find me out in the sunshine with a notebook on my lap, sitting on the steps and spilling my thoughts out onto paper, ultimately to become an action plan.

Setting clearly-defined goals is an important first step toward faithful stewardship of our time and resources. Careful planning identifies our key goals for our families and makes the most of our opportunities. It helps us to know what to deliberately aim for, rather than haphazardly reacting to our circumstances. We move forward instead of settling for a fatalistic attitude.

When we prepare our way, reaching toward specific goals, we move towards victorious living. Our effectiveness in our personal and family lives will substantially increase. This is especially true when we take the time to establish long-term goals. A vision for the future keeps us moving forward with focus rather than getting bogged down in the here and now. Without a vision, chaos ensues:

Where there is no vision, the people perish.

—Proverbs 29:18a (KJV)

FOUNDATIONAL GOALS

As Christians, our ultimate goal is to love God with all our heart, soul, and mind (the *Shema*, Deuteronomy 6), and to love our neighbor as ourselves (Mark 12:29-31). All the goals we set our hands to do should flow from these two core commitments. Love God. Love others.

If we love God, we will desire to "keep [his] commandments" (John 14:15)—to understand what he would have us to do and then do it with the help of the Holy Spirit. This brings us to the "one anothers," all the verses in which Jesus tells us how to love each other. The focus of these verses are what make us stand apart as Christians and are what bring real change in our world. When our goals center around the "one another" verses, we bless others with our goals.

MAKE GOALS TOGETHER

Goals made with your husband will be more realistic and aid both of you to better reach those goals because the two of you will be on the same page. Making goals together is important for unity and cohesiveness. Dad and mom should move in the *same* direction as a family; otherwise, you will create confusion for your kids and your family as a whole.

Goal areas to plan for include:

☐ Personal

☐ Family

☐ Spiritual

☐ Home

☐ Community Outreach

☐ Educational

- ☐ Physical

- ☐ Recreational

- ☐ Financial.

You and your husband might think of more areas, you might want to break these up into smaller areas, or you might want to group areas together. You each have strengths and weaknesses that reflect in these goal areas and they may present challenges. Some will be personal goal areas for each of you and some as a couple and some as a family.

Do not get bogged down in too many details if this is all new to you. It is easier to make changes in one area at a time. Success breeds success, so build upon the areas in which your family makes positive progress. Make little steps forward when setting goals in weak areas. Baby steps build strength, and soon you will have reached goals and need to set larger ones.

Our goals reflect our vision of the future, and, as Christians, our goals must align with Scripture. Don't make your goal to be like another family, beautiful as that family may be. Study the Scriptures and create your own family vision in accordance with it. God calls us each to different things; pray about your goals and the steps forward.

Make long-term goals, short-term goals, and immediate goals. Where you will be in three months is determined by what you do today. Make your actions today count towards the future. The immediate daily and weekly goals will be the stepping stones to the short-term goals. The short-term goals are the steps taken to reach the long-term goals.

WRITE DOWN YOUR GOALS

I have found that whatever I'm trying to change about my life, writing it out is very fruitful. Rather than just having a goal in my head, writing it gives further *commitment* to a thought. In writing down goals, I prioritize them more effectively and can better evaluate my progress in reaching or falling short of them. I've written prayers, goal sheets, resolutions, and goals on my calendar, in addition to my daily list of things to do, and formalizing these in writing has been essential in getting my act together. It seems that the more detailed I write goals, the more quickly I reach them. It is also helpful to keep reviewing them and working on the steps to reach the goals.

Don't just talk about your goals; write them down. Talking about goals is helpful though because it forces a commitment and accountability to keep working towards them. Organize your goals, prioritize them, post them and take action. Then regularly compare your progress against what you have committed in writing, and make adjustments to your list of goals as necessary. Be flexible because reality certainly can get in the way of a goal. Just readjust, realign, change the time frame, and don't give up.

A PLAN FOR VICTORY: ONE STEP AT A TIME

Put your goals a step beyond writing them and closer to actually getting them done by breaking them down into specific steps. Sometimes we need small steps, even baby steps. With this in mind, I'm going to walk you through how to set a specific goal and the steps to take to reach that goal.

EXAMPLE ONE: AN EXERCISE PLAN

You probably have made some sort of New Year's resolutions. For ease, I'll use the classic "I'm going to exercise more this year." This is a pretty big and broad goal, so let's break it down a bit.

First, examine why you have this as a goal and write down the whys:

☐ The body is the temple of the Holy Spirit and I need to be a good steward for the temple.

☐ A strong back and strong arms will make me able to play with my kids, have energy for work and fun, and have a healthy productive life.

☐ I need to be physically fit to take care of my children and grandchildren, I can't love and care for them if I don't love and care for my health first.

☐ I want my future to be filled with good health and that means taking care of my body now. What I do now will have an influence on what I am in twenty years.

With your goals, you need to be more *specific* about the end and choose a goal that will prove your results both now and in the future. With the "exercise more" goal, pick the end point, such as "run the local 5k in September." Now *plan backwards*. You have eight months to be able to run the 5k. Then, establish monthly goals, planning backwards:

- **MONTH 8** 5k

- **MONTH 7** run most of 5k, walk the rest

- **MONTH 6** run half of 5k, walk half—run, walk, run

- **MONTH 5** run ¼ of 5k, walk ¾—run, walk, run

- **MONTH 4** run, walk, run 5k as able

- **MONTH 3** run, walk, run 4k as able

- **MONTH 2** run, walk, run 3k as able; research supplements that may help my body work better

- **MONTH 1** run, walk, run 2k as able; research better methods of walking and running stretches and form

I find it helpful to have some sort of tangible reward for meeting each monthly goal. Some "rewards" for meeting a specific goals in your quest to run the 5k might include a new running T-shirt, a subscription to a running magazine, or weights to wear while running. Of course, there are real physical rewards—increased energy, strength, and the ability to do more than sit on the old duff—that you will benefit from along the way as you persevere!

Here are more pertinent questions to consider as you plan backwards for the 5k. You know that the summer months are hot, so what time of day will you run: morning or evening? Who will watch the children when you engage in this exercise? How will this affect your schedule? How about your wake time? Will you need to go to sleep earlier?

Write out a new schedule that includes your running time and shower. Then, write on the calendar at the end of each month the reward you will give yourself for meeting the goal.

Now you are at the starting point. Get some good running shoes and look through your closet for running clothes. Consult the new schedule and set out your running things. Then go do it!

EXAMPLE TWO: A HOSPITALITY CALENDAR

Let's plan backwards again with a new goal: to open your home and show more active hospitality as a family.

First examine the why:

☐ The Bible says so!

☐ We have a need to be social.

☐ We enjoy getting together with friends and family.

☐ Having people over is a reward for our family when we get some extra work done around the house and yard.

Why aren't we more hospitable? Examine your personal reasons that get in the way of your goals. Naming the obstacles helps to overcome them.

By setting goals and putting planning exercises in place, we can learn to be more self-disciplined and effective in the hospitality.

If our end goal is to be able and willing to have people over any time, to welcome drop-in guests, and to spontaneously invite others over after church, how do we get there? Let's plan backwards again.

Let's say that next holiday season you want your home to be an Open House—not just for one evening, but the whole month. That's eleven months away. What do we need to work on to be more hospitable? A hospitable attitude, a presentable house, as well as appetizing food and drink.

Food and drink are easy because fruit and cheese are beautiful when placed on a clean plate and served with a glass of cool water. The home being presentable can be a problem if regular chore time is not a part of the day. Things get messy quickly and it can be embarrassing. Lastly, there's our attitude. A hospitable attitude should be one of love. It's an attitude that makes the guest feel special. When a guest is over, the normal household routine stops and centers around making guests feel welcome. Hospitality is not "show and tell time" for our family.

Let's set up monthly goals to get us to the place of having a hospitable home. Start with the end result you desire and work backwards:

DECEMBER The house is open for guests. There are meals and appetizers in the freezer (even if you bought them at the grocery store). House chores are done regularly throughout the day. Any Christmas craft activities are welcome for guests to participate in also. Invite all the people you had over during the year for a variety of hospitality events. Have families over for a craft day and potluck supper. Hold a Christmas tea party. Gather friends for caroling and then a snack supper. Plan to have guests after an event (such as a music program).

NOVEMBER Invite guests over on the spur-of-the moment twice this month. Be prepared for anything. Maybe have your husband do the inviting so you don't chicken out.

OCTOBER Pick a Sunday and prepare for guests. Plan a good slow-cooker dish that's tried and true. Make all the Sunday food the day before. After church, look around for strangers or visitors and invite them to join you for Sunday dinner. Practice makes perfect.

SEPTEMBER Look around your church: who are the lonely? Invite a grandma for an afternoon tea or a college student for an evening meal and table game. These people will bless our lives just as you are blessing them with warm hospitality.

AUGUST Do you have neighbors you don't know? Invite them over for an evening. What do you do when new neighbors move in? Make a plan for when that happens. A fresh pie or cookies would be a great treat on moving day. Don't get so caught up in your own life that you miss these opportunities to spread good cheer.

JULY Plan an outdoor party. Prepare ahead. Send out invitations or phone a couple of weeks ahead of time. Make a frozen dessert. How will you serve the food? Where will everyone sit? How will the small children manage eating outside? How will you keep things safe for guest's children? What group games everyone can play? Think ahead and write down your ideas, plan for them, and have fun making it a great day for your guests! Do a yard clean-up, as you don't want a guest to trip on a hoe while playing kickball and end up at the ER. Put some fresh planters out or make some flower arrangements with your children for the tables. Don't forget a back-up plan if the weather turns bad. Is your garage a Plan B option?

JUNE Does your church ever have visiting missionaries who need a home to stay in? Prepare your home for this type of opportunity. Create a plan for having overnight guests. What will you serve for food and drink? Where will they sleep? Will this displace your children, and where will they sleep? Prepare your children for overnight guests by talking over these plans and teaching manners (treat others like you would like to be treated). Let your church leaders know that your home is open for missionary guests.

MAY Invite an older couple from church or neighborhood that you would like to get to know better. Instruct your children ahead of time that there is much to be learned from your guests and that they should stay near to them, serve them, ask questions, and converse with them. Your children should not ignore them or run off to do their own thing until permission is granted. Instruct and role play for this ahead of time, making it part of your school time.

APRIL Invite a family for dinner that you would like to get to know better. Have your children plan activities or games to do with the guest children. Work on having a play area that guest children will enjoy also. Discuss with your children how to handle sharing or putting away very special dolls or objects. Encourage your children to play group activities such as games. Make a notebook or folder of game ideas and their instructions.

MARCH Plan a tea party with your girlfriends and their daughters. In the room where you are having your tea party, do extra cleaning and decorating. Set the date for the end of the month and then plan backwards for it. Spend time on your Office Days, Cooking Days, and Cleaning Days to plan and prepare for the event. Do this every month with the thought, "I'm working on being more hospitable this year; therefore, I need to improve our attitudes, chore time, cleaning, and food prep."

FEBRUARY Invite friends over, the ones you have over when the house is a mess. Only this time, pull out all stops, set the table beautifully and then serve them your best food and drink.

JANUARY Prepare your household management skills for being hospitable. Regular chore times and a weekly cleaning day are a strong start. Pray for help in your new goal area.

As you start doing hospitality events, you will grow more and more able to be hospitable, and soon it will become old hat. Hospitality will become an automatic function of your home. You and your family will learn systems that work best for serving people outdoors and inside, planned and spur-of-the-moment.

Be real, be comfortable, and accept the imperfections of life. What people need is to be loved.

Practice makes perfect: The more you host events, the easier it with get. Remember, the most important thing is not you, your home, or the food. The most important thing is the guest and making the guest feel comfortable and welcome. Take your eyes off yourself (and your home) and put them on the guest. Usually guests don't feel comfortable doing nothing or having their hands empty, so either put something like a drink in their hands or let them help you with preparations. Ask them questions about themselves to get the conversation rolling. Relax and your guests will be relaxed. Smile and laugh. You and your home do not need to be perfect. Perfect people and homes make others feel uncomfortable, as if they themselves don't measure up to be present, and as though they could never invite you to their imperfect home. Perfection is pretentious. We all know that only Jesus was perfect. Be real, be comfortable, and accept the imperfections of life. What people need is to be loved.

Being prepared for guests helps you to focus on guests rather than on work. With this plan, you are working at preparation skills one month at a time.

Keep your hospitality ideas, systems, recipe and drink lists, and conversation starters in your Home Management Book (make a tab for Hospitality). When you get a little befuddled, you can pull it out and remember "Oh, yes, this recipe looks great and is simple; it will be easy to serve for ____."

If you enjoy a reward system, then reward yourself with a décor item, a table service item, a book about hostessing or recipes, or a special tea blend for the next event. It doesn't have to be expensive, just something that helps you feel like a more competent hostess.

This goal planning system can be applied to any goal. Running a 5k or having regular hospitality are just two examples.

Planning out your goals and resolutions puts feet under them. Soon, if you put your step-by-step plans into practice, you will be so improved that your New Year's resolutions will not be the same-old, same-old ones. You will not give up on setting them, and you will be reaching higher.

SYSTEMS

I didn't know where to start. What should I do first? Then what? And when will it ever get done? What if the top of the list needs to be done again before I get to the bottom? This was house cleaning for me in our first little home. It was seriously small. I spent more time thinking about cleaning than it took to actually do it. And my thinking wasn't organized, it was more like a weak pep talk or pathetic un-motivational speech, trying to get myself to do the work.

Every time I cleaned I simply mustered up the gumption, dove in and started. I didn't know how long a task would take and I didn't keep track of time. I got distracted with other cleaning chores every time I walked to a different area of the house. I had no method or plan. I just went about cleaning like a crazy woman. Then all of sudden it was time to eat and I wouldn't have prepared anything for supper, because I'd been caught up in cleaning.

A couple of houses and babies later, I suddenly had little people toting toys from room to room. I still didn't have a real plan and I still cleaned in a random way, now with the additional distraction of little people and toys. And I still became startled when it was suddenly time to feed my people again. Didn't we just eat?

Then one day, I read of a method that said to start cleaning in one corner of a room and move with focus left to right, top to bottom. It was an aha moment! That helped me so much with efficiency, and I was learning quickly that I needed my house cleaning time to be effective, because there were little people that needed me. I knew by then that it wasn't something I particularly enjoyed anyway, and I would much rather read stories, take the children outside to play, work in my garden, or browse a magazine any day. I also had grown to like the structure of having our meals ready at a certain time, and found it unduly stressful to be surprised by mealtime!

Bit by bit, I brought order to other parts of the house. I broke the tasks into steps and gave methods to my previous madness. I was learning that for me at least, systems created freedom.

Systems are essential for the right functioning of any endeavor. But not all systems work well. Some are good systems; some are bad. The family that doesn't clean a table until right before the next meal has a system. The family that piles up mail but never sorts it has a system. These are, of course, bad systems. A good system is one in which the work is done completely and efficiently.

In our house, some systems get implemented *some* of the time by *some* of the people, but not all systems are properly implemented by *all* of the people *all* of the time. Like any family, we have system breakdowns. This is natural in a home full of flesh-and-blood people of different stages of growth and development. Add in a bad cold that takes a month to work through a family and there are a lot of system breakdowns!

A system may be good, but if you don't use it, it will be ineffective, so work to not only establish effective systems in your home, but to diligently implement them.

A system breakdown that I have happen is when older children get outside employment. We will have a meal, but the person responsible for unloading the dishwasher isn't present. What happens next is that nobody does their chore because the dishwasher is full of clean dishes, the dirty dishes can't be put in so they are sitting on the counter, the counter can't be washed because there are dirty dishes on it, and the rest of the crew doesn't think they need to do their chores because other people aren't doing their chores. One person absent has caused a snowball effect, resulting in a dirty kitchen and frustrated people.

The answer is that everyone learns a lesson in flexibility and picking up the slack. If the problem continues, then we have to reassign chores and the missing person is reassigned a chore that does not cause a snowball effect, such as taking out the kitchen trash which can be done at any time and doesn't delay others from completing their meal chores.

Good systems throughout the home are a blessing to all. From dishwashing to laundry, from cleaning the toilets to bedtime routines, each system plays an important part in a family's routine. This does not mean that there is no room for creativity in our life; it simply means that when we do something, we follow an order of events or use a prescribed method for doing a task. If we have strong, well-working systems, they improve efficiency and give us more time for creativity. I think we all want more time for doing the projects that are really interesting to us.

When improving a system, identify its components and write them down. Then put them in an order that improves the speed of the system. For some systems, you will want to post the completed order of events at the place where the task is performed as a reminder of what needs to be done. I have posted instructions for hand washing dishes and cleaning the kitchen sink area. I have also posted laundry instructions. At one time I put instructions in each room for steps in cleaning that room. Once these things are learned and done a few times, the instructions are unnecessary because the work gets done from memory and becomes automatic muscle memory motions. It's amazing!

Each system that is reordered must be taught to the family. Explain to them that the new way of doing things will be a better and faster way. That means that they will get more time to play or read a book! Explain also that God wants us to do our work heartily as unto him (Colossians 3:23). Heartily, with the heart, with our full effort and attention.

Systems don't work if you don't work the systems.

I know from experience to start slowly if I want to make a system stick. Focus on one new system at a time. Work through this method while teaching family members a new thing:

1. Show them how to do it. Demonstrate the protocol.

2. Watch them do it, giving correction.

3. Let them do it unsupervised with you checking later, and give further instruction if needed.

4. Require independent work with occasional checks; if they begin to be sloppy (they are human), then start over.

When you want to add a new system or task to your day, add it to something that is already working well. For example, if your family does a great job of cleaning the kitchen after breakfast then add to that success by "attaching" a new system to it. As soon as cleaning the kitchen after breakfast is done, then move right in to the next system that you are attaching to it. This is building on your success. Do this throughout your day whenever you feel the need to improve a time period or you need to add some tasks.

"Systems don't work if you don't work the systems" is a quote that my husband brought home from the corporate world. A system may be good, but if you don't use it, it will be ineffective, so work to not only establish effective systems in your home, but to diligently implement them. When you do this, you and your family will be blessed with more time and less chaos.

SELF-DISCIPLINE AND MAKING NEW HABITS

just thought I was lazy. After growing up in a culture that valued work and being busy, I felt shame because I didn't want to do work that didn't interest me. I thought that I must be a slacker, a lazy and undisciplined person. I loved to read, to learn, to try new things. What I saw as busywork bored me quickly. I appreciated clean, I loved what clean was, but I didn't like spending that much time on something so dull. Anything was more interesting than that. My goal was to have a beautiful, clean, orderly and pleasant home, but I couldn't figure out how to get myself to make my home that way.

That felt like failure, so I took action. I studied how to be a more disciplined person. I underlined verses in my Bible, I read books, I observed other people, and I sought out information for any source I could find, everywhere. I tried to implement what I learned and make myself be a busier person whose house was always clean, with good food cooking, a tidy garden, the laundry folded and put away. That's what I wanted, truly. I could do some of it some of the time, but I couldn't keep up with it all of the time because then I didn't have time for my other pursuits, which meant I was losing me in the process.

But one day I realized that I had strung together a number of individual habits that allowed me the freedom to do life my way. Habits were my key to learning self-discipline. So I applied that thought to other areas and discovered even more efficiency and order.

Because I had freed up time in my day, I was able to pursue other interests. My days were better, I wasn't beating myself up; and that inner-voice bully—usually so quick to call me a lazy slacker—was suddenly uncharacteristically quiet. I looked around and thought about what else I could apply the idea of habits to. I started building in rewards for completing the mundane work. I learned to stand back and appreciate what had been accomplished, instead of berating myself for not doing more.

That which we persist in doing becomes easier—not that the nature of the task has changed, but our ability to do has increased.

— Ralph Waldo Emerson

These strings of habits added up and over time, clean became more effortless, tidy was close at hand, and good meals were consistently ready at orderly times. Achieving self-discipline for me was a process of working with who I am and using the tool of habits to build the life I wanted. I learned to be more kind to myself, acknowledge who I am as a person, identify how I think and do things, and to step out of the box that I put myself in. Once I began to find ways to get the work done (without sacrificing time for my other pursuits) I was able to see things more clearly, because the filter of shame that I had viewed it all through was removed and the self-fulfilling cycle of defeat was broken.

Getting from goal to execution requires self-discipline. Self-discipline is making yourself do something that you don't want to presently do. This starts by saying no to yourself and then resolving to do the hard thing—to finish the work you've laid before you, to do what you say you are going to do, and to be timely and orderly. Our sin nature groans at this thought! It is so easy to give in to the flesh and do what it wants to do right now.

Chocolate fudge brownies with ice cream won't help us wear those clothes that used to fit. Not cleaning the kitchen means that there will be a mess to clean up before preparing the next meal. If the laundry piles up, we won't have clothes to put on. Saying things that shouldn't have been said, acting without thinking, self-discipline affects a lot of areas of life. Self-discipline means delaying gratification. When we have a goal, we must delay the gratification for the present desire in order to achieve long-term reward and blessing.

Learning self-discipline starts with keeping our eyes constantly on the goal. We first must be seeking God's kingdom, and we do that by studying his will for our lives. We learn about kingdom living in the Bible and by praying for his help through the Holy Spirit. Guided by God's Word and the Holy Spirit, we can overcome our weaknesses and live disciplined lives for Christ.

It helps to know and understand ourselves and what gets in our way. I wrote about how mundane busywork bores me, it even feels like torture to me to see somebody do a repetitive task. Some people enjoy repetitive work. It's OK that we are different. We are all different with our personalities, gifts, faults, backgrounds, families, and a hundred other variables. It is helpful to examine these things, know them, and understand them. Then we face them, name them and prayerfully challenge them in ourselves.

Slowly but surely, as we fix our eyes on Christ and put aside our selfishness, delay gratification, and pray for help, we will become more like Jesus in our thoughts and actions. Sometimes we will move forward quickly in one area of the Christian life while, at the same time, being blind to sins in another area. That is why we must be so gracious with each other; God is working on us all in different ways. None of us have arrived yet. We will not "arrive" until we are made complete in Heaven. This said, when we keep our eyes on God's will for us and regularly seek his wisdom, we will gain his character over time. The "one anothers" will come out in our actions. We will begin to see the people of the world, including those we live with, as God does and respond with loving kindness, patience, justice, mercy, and all the rest. Being Christ-like is the goal and while we move towards that goal, we gain self-discipline.

When we have God's Word in our minds and are sensitive to the Holy Spirit, we will gain control over our selfish desires. We surrender to God daily through a life of prayer. God tells us to pray without ceasing for a reason. It is hard to give in to temptation and pray at the same time! It hard to lose our temper while praying. Our God helps us overcome our indulgences with the power of the Spirit. Maybe not everything at once. Maybe some things will be easy and some things not, but we keep on fighting the good fight.

Gaining self-control is found through the renewing of the mind. We renew our mind by learning who God is and how he wants us to love others. I am not saying that self-discipline is shutting down our feelings but gaining control so that we aren't hurting others with our emotions. Take your anger, sadness, frustration, hurt, and everything else to God and talk to him about it. When we hide God's Word in our heart, God will replace our thoughts with his thoughts, helping us overcome the lack of discipline by discipling us through his Word and with the Spirit.

I have found help in memorizing Scripture relevant to my thoughts and emotion and praying for wisdom in using my tongue. Bad thoughts need to be replaced with good. For example, when we understand that God gives us trials and that we are to count them as joy, our outlook will improve and we will learn to see the good in trials (James 1:2). Our perspective will be righted when we embrace a heart of gratitude. Being thankful conquers a self-pitying spirit (1 Thessalonians 5:18), so make a list of thanksgivings! It is about opening our eyes and learning to see a bigger world, a larger vision, and greater purpose in life.

Gaining self-control in different areas happens with small steps and small victories. When we need to discipline ourselves to overcome a large thing, it can help to start out with small steps. These little steps become habits, habits that become automatic and done without thought. Choose something for which you need more discipline, and once you have conquered it, add a related thing. Soon the small things will add up to be a big thing that you are disciplined about.

Forming good habits make self-discipline easier to learn. A habit is something that you regularly do. Choose a small thing such as keeping your bedside table tidy, and do it every night before lying down. Make it a habit. Then add to it. Put a prayer list on your bedside table, and every night after you tidy your bedside table, pray over the list. Once that is a habit, add another task before tidying the bedside table, such as tidying that part of the room. When you have strong habits, it becomes easier to deny self-gratifying impulses. The habits just happen because your brain isn't doing the energy and work of thinking of the thing. A habit is successful self-discipline. A string of habits becomes a good working routine that you can do automatically. Think of when you drive regularly a certain route, you can arrive at your destination and not remember how you got there because you were busy thinking about something other than driving the car and how to get to the place. The same thing happens when you have established a new habit or routine.

Take your anger, sadness, frustration, hurt, and everything else to God and talk to him about it.

These things can sound huge to an overwhelmed mom who is drowning in work. I know—I've been there—and you can get past your discouragement! Start with small things and add to them. Practice makes perfect. Someday, when you fail to be disciplined in an area (sometimes life events interfere with our good habits!); it will be easier to regain that discipline. You did it once; you can do it again! You can do it with God's strength and the joy of the Lord is your strength.

The same principle applies to our children, and it is critical to teach them self-discipline while they are little. For example, require them to do small chores when they are small, and as they grow, increase their responsibility. When they are required to be faithful in small things and know the importance and value of their work, they will gradually learn the skill of self-discipline. When they are self-disciplined in one area of life, it will carry over to other areas. It requires faithfulness on your part as a parent to check on your children's work and require it to be done right. Just remember to guide and correct them with an attitude of loving encouragement. Give them freedom in their work so that they learn further self-discipline skills. If it fits the task, let the child choose when they start or finish. Self-discipline is not something that can be forced upon a person, it is learned within freedom. If we want our home to be characterized by order and tranquility, we must lead by example. It starts with us. May we be more like Jesus in the example of self-discipline we show our children!

ATTITUDE

I wanted to create a happy life for myself and my family. That was my goal from the beginning and it still is. I gave it intentional thought, I aimed for it, and I put deliberate effort into creating happy days. I still do. I learned that attitude is action, and action is movement towards a sunny day.

There were certainly ho-hum days, monotony, and just flat out bad days. Waking up with a migraine, that's a bad day. Some days even require a call for help from others. There are days where half the family is sick with the stomach flu already, I think I'm feeling nauseous too, and am waiting with great trepidation for the rest of the family to get it. Or those days when a child is teething and it upsets the whole house, and ruins the day for everyone. Days when the toilet mysteriously doesn't flush. Did somebody flush a stuffed animal or does the septic tank need to be pumped? Or when a storm takes out the electricity for a week. How about when you step on a Lego on the way to the coffee pot? Have you ever hit your shin on an open dishwasher door? Or maybe the sky has been cloudy for weeks, and everyone is edgy and housebound. Sometimes it's the seemingly small, irritating or painful things that make for a bad day. I could fill a book of the things that can bring me down, and I'm sure it would look a lot like yours.

I discovered one that thing that helps is to simply turn around, walk back to my bedroom, and restart the day. Just taking a five-minute restart can help. I take a deep breath, say a prayer, make my bed or straighten something in the bedroom, brush my teeth, wash my face and get dressed (maybe for the second time), force a smile, and start it all again. It doesn't matter what time of day I do a restart. After lunch is a great time for it. Put everyone to a nap or quiet time and then restart, just like I have to restart the computer at an inopportune time. Inconvenient timing perhaps, but just as the computer sometimes functions better after a reboot, I do as well.

Putting my eyes on that one clean spot can make a big difference in a disruptive day. Action is a choice towards a better day.

I put on some happy music or perhaps something calming. That's a trick I learned from my mother and my mother-in-law; it actually changes the attitude of the people in the house, including myself. Then light a candle or two. I think of some things to be grateful for and share them with the rest of the family.

Next up, I wash the dishes and clean the kitchen. The original plan for my day may be in shambles, and if there are other problems going on, such as the need for rocking a sick baby, cleaning the sink might take a couple of hours, but it certainly helped to give focus to the bare necessities when I caught a break. Five minutes here and there in the day on the simple tasks helps to keep on the bright side of things. Putting my eyes on that one clean spot can make a big difference in a disruptive day. Action is a choice towards a better day.

I still haven't arrived, acting towards better days is a life-long pursuit of movement. It's examining myself, my choices, my actions and re-actions. It is cutting out the negative influences and adding in the good.

SELF-EXAMINATION

You've met them: The family that appears to have it all together. You've admired their example; you've even learned important lessons from them that have helped you in your journey to be a better person. In key areas, they've been a benchmark for you to measure your progress on how a together-family operates. And then you've lamented the unexpected when this outwardly-exemplary family fizzled out or blew up.

Maybe we shouldn't have had our eyes on that family for our example but on Jesus.

When we follow a set of prescribed man-made rules or when we look to a certain family and pattern our lives after theirs, we become poster children for the hypocrites Christ identified during his earthly ministry. The focus is wrong. This is parenting for a stage and we are actors. Or we are parenting out of fear of some wickedness coming out of our children. Someone else looks like they are getting the results we want so we'll copy them. Well, guess what, we are humans. We cannot force others to be like Jesus with rules and we cannot teach them to love others while we also teach them to look with judgment on anyone not following a prescribed set of rules.

Following a human standard lasts only so long. When our hearts drift from being rooted in Jesus, we set ourselves up for a potentially disastrous fall. When we parent without Jesus we can't expect the children to be like Jesus. They will be either hypocrites following a set of rules or they will leave your social club, one way or another.

Guard your hearts against this by daily confessing your sins, keeping your eyes on Jesus, being like him, loving others, and staying sensitive to the working of the Holy Spirit in your life. Don't become callous in your heart toward God.

PERFECTION

Do you see others as perfect? Your friends or people you admire seem to have it all together and are such godly people? Is perfection your goal?

I *know* that others aren't perfect, that only Jesus was perfect. I know that in my head, but a big part of me wants life to go according to *my* standards of perfection.

My idea of perfection centers around the perfect day, my perfectly respectful and obedient children, being the perfect wife, having the perfect home, perfect meals, the perfect landscape design, and a perfectly weed-free garden with perfect fruits and vegetables. I even stretch that ideal of perfection into my service in the church. Of course, all this is because I am the perfect person. I want to be perfectly kind, perfectly gracious, perfectly patient, perfectly everything. Is this wrong to aim for?

We must first recognize that all our attempts to attain perfection in our own strength will fall short. "All our righteousness are as filthy rags" (Isaiah 64:6, KJV). Even Job, who was one of the most faithful, godly person who ever lived, did not measure up to God's perfections, and when he compared himself to God, he proclaimed, "I abhor myself, and repent in dust and ashes" (Job 42:6, KJV). It is only by God's grace and mercy that we can do anything right, and we should give glory to him whenever we excel at any pursuit.

Your salvation does not depend upon your perfection; the Scriptures refute this thought. (See Romans 1:16-17, for example.) Jesus, the perfect Lamb of God, is our righteousness, and his covering over of us is the only way we can stand before God. Yet if you are a Christian, you are to seek to be like Jesus. Paul instructs us to put off our old life and put on the new (Ephesians 4:24).

While perfection in human terms will not happen in this world, we as Christians are to seek after God's perfect character. We *are* to work towards that goal, not just give up and say, "I guess I won't even try," "I could never do that," "Why bother," or "I can't." We are not to walk around with our heads hanging with defeat; yes, we are defeated when we do it by pulling up our own bootstraps. We must continue to strive depending on the power of the Holy Spirit.

Seeking to be like Christ involves many important character traits. Our God is a God of love (1 John 4:7-8), for example, and I certainly don't love others like God does. I love Self: Me, Myself, and I—me, me, me. But I am to take my eyes off myself, see others with his eyes, and love them as he sees them.

Our God is slow to anger (Numbers 14:18). Not so with me, as I can get irate pretty quickly and sin in my anger, which the Scriptures condemns. Our anger does not produce God's righteousness (James 1:20).

I can also be a lazy parent because discipline is hard work. It seems easier to avoid conflict. I must persevere in doing what God has called me to do and keep on keeping on with God's help.

Love God, love others; but do not love perfection.

I could go on all the day looking at each way that God is perfect and I am not. Just a little bit of this exercise brings me to repentance. Jesus is our righteousness; everything we do apart from him, even the things that go perfect, are as filthy rags (Isaiah 64:6). We are to repent of it all, be filled with the Spirit, and reach for the goal (Philippians 3:14). He is perfection, and we are called to be like him (2 Corinthians 13:11). Perfection because of the sacrificial blood of Jesus and the power of the Holy Spirit.

Yes, we are to be perfectionists. We are to perfect imitating Christ in all areas of life. We can look around us and learn from others, but the goal is not to be like our imperfect friend. Our goal in perfection is being like Jesus. Love God; love others.

This world tells us to let go of perfection; don't even try; you're hurting yourself and those around you through your quest for perfection. There is a grain of truth to this. If your goal in perfection is your *own* glory rather than God's glory, then you *will* hurt those around you. Love God, love others; but do not love perfection.

Pleasant and beautiful homes, and healthy, gourmet meals are things which are not bad goals if they are pursued to bring glory to God through serving others rather than Self. Aim for perfection according to God's goals for us.

I CAN

We don't say, "I can't." We say, "I can do all things through Christ which strengtheneth me" (Philippians 4:13, KJV).

In our family, we don't permit our children to say, "I can't." This is a habit that we deal with early on with them.

Last night I had to have a talk with one of my little daughters. In this situation, she was simply being stubborn and willful about a normal daily routine task. This was not a problem with the task; it was a tired and whiny problem. She was refusing to do it by whining, "I can't."

Sensing the opportunity for a teaching moment replied, "In this house, we do not say, 'I can't.' We say, 'I'll try my hardest' or 'I'll do my best,' but we do *not* say, 'I can't.'

The situation last night reminded me of a recent conversation that my husband, Matt, and I had with another mom of a big family. The setting was mealtime with a lot of people present, and we were discussing large families. The mother asked us if, in response to a hectic mealtime, we ever said, "I just can't do this anymore. I can't do one more meal."

Without thought, we both responded, "No," and I added that sometimes we have to get really firm, requiring everybody to sit down at the table and be quiet. After being firm and even sometimes saying, "No more talking," then it's okay, and peace and order returns. But saying, "I can't" is something we don't say. "I can't" gets replaced with praying without ceasing. "Lord, have mercy. Lord, grant me strength. Lord, bring peace."

When I have to have the "I can't" talk with an older child, we also discuss our thought life. I tell them that it's a mind habit to quit, and that they need to replace the "I can't" thought with an "I'll try my hardest" thought. Usually the child then says the verse or starts singing the song, "I can do all things through Christ who strengthens me." A defeatist attitude is replaced with an attitude of determination and calling on God for help. This is grit.

Even if the end result of the child's effort is not perfect, doing the best job possible is worthy of great praise and usually is rewarded in some way or another. Satisfaction in learning or even trying a new skill is also a reward. Skill builds on skill and soon the struggle of trying new things and the determination for success that goes along with it results in a confident, can-do person. But it starts with those little conversations with little people who let those "I can't" words slip out with a whine.

FOLLOW ME

I once heard a speaker at a mother-daughter retreat tell us mothers to get in line with Jesus and that our children would follow our lead. If our children see us being Sunday Christians, then they won't take Christianity seriously, and church will just be a Sunday social club. By contrast, if they see us confessing, repenting, reading the Bible, and living according to its precepts, then they will do the same. We must live a life that says, "Follow me, girls!"

It's a big responsibility, but it is our calling. We are mothers and must live a life of following Jesus, leading the way for our daughters. Of course, this applies to our sons as well.

The scary thing is that our children will follow us or react to us whether we want them to or not. That is why we need to follow Jesus and not the prevailing wind of the day. We must put out of our lives those things that influence us and our daughters away from being people of God. Ouch.

What we watch, listen to, and read has a great pull not only on us but on our children as well. Given this fact, it's important to ask: What magazines do you have lying around your house? What books are on your shelves? What music do you listen to? What shows and movies do you watch? What websites do you visit on the internet? We might think that such things don't influence us, but they do, as advertisers know well!

OUCH, OUCH, OUCH!

These influences change our attitudes, our thoughts, and in turn what comes out of our mouth. They are watching and imitating us.

Are you talking to them about things that will draw them closer to the Father? Are you whining and complaining through your pity party? Are you showing them a fence-riding Christian who lives a double life? Do you say one thing and do another? Do you threaten to leave your husband or family or even joke about it? If you're a homeschooling mom, maybe you threaten to send them off to school?

Do you use the TV to keep your children out of the way? Do you act and talk as if your children were burdens? Is the law of kindness on your tongue? How often do you sigh?

Oh, these are hard-hitting questions, and we are all guilty of sinful thoughts that are further expressed in actions!

Don't quit! Don't give up! Get into God's Word. Make it part of your daily life, apply it, and set the example for others. You don't need to say, "Follow me," just live in a way that you would want your children to go, and they will follow. Let's not lose sight of the fact that our attitude is critical in our efforts to reach our goals.

TIME, WHERE DOES IT GO?

My time had always been managed for me. The school bus arrived at a 7:20 and let us off at 4:10. Buzzers signaled us to move from room to room. Any job I ever held started at a certain hour. My college professors began and ended their lectures on the minute. Tests and assignments had deadlines. Suddenly things were different and I was on my own. I was there with a little house to manage and no parent, teacher, or boss to tell me what to do and when to do it.

My husband's work schedule and the feeding and napping of a new baby were my only parameters. My goal for each day was to have supper ready soon after my husband came home, which unfortunately conflicted with the Oprah show in the late afternoon.

If I didn't have something started during the Oprah hour supper would be later than I liked it to be. In those early days I sat and watched Oprah and wondered what to make for supper.

I didn't like that feeling of pressure. The Oprah hour was one of my first lessons in managing my own time, motivating me to keep my eye on the clock and to organize my day.

As the children came along, more parameters came with them. Regular meals, naps, and bedtimes made for happier babies and children. Intentionally planning for specific activities or tasks at certain times of the day gave us a nice balance of fun spots to look forward to and quiet, peaceful times enjoy. Critics might suggest that all this planning creates a rigid environment with no room for spontaneity, but I found the opposite to be true. By creating structure in our day, we had level of order in our home that allowed for and even encouraged more impulsive fun family activities.

I didn't set out to be a better time manager, my goal was a happy home. I discovered along the way to be creative, and that planning and building time periods into the day were keys to making better days for all of us.

So teach us to number our days, that we may apply our hearts unto wisdom.

—Psalm 90:12 (KJV)

Fourteen hundred and forty minutes are yours in each day.

Have you ever wondered where the time goes? We say it when we see our children grow quickly and leap milestones. But have you ever asked yourself, "What did I do all day? What did I accomplish?"

Do you sometimes feel like you are sitting and spinning? Do you keep trying to make progress but it does not come very quickly?

Here is a helpful exercise that will expose the minutes of your day and get you on track. Write down everything that you do and an approximate length of time for each task. Start right now and continue this for a couple of days. The longer you do this, the more you will see progress in getting to where you want to be, but do this for a minimum of two days. If you journal, you can record your exercise there, and if not, just use a standard notebook and pen.

It will help to keep a watch or clock right beside your time log. Do not write only the big things but write down interruptions— *everything.* If you change a diaper, write down how long it took. If you helped somebody with a math problem or three pages of math, write it down. If you stop at the sink and drink a glass of water, write that down. Tonight when you go to bed, review it and commit to doing the same exercise tomorrow.

This will show you where your time goes and what you are doing with it. It will show you places in the day where you can be more efficient. You might see that if you lined up your day a little better, you will be able to save time and do more. You will see opportunities where you can multitask. You might also find that you are trying to put too many things into your day, and that is why you cannot get anything done. That is my current time-use problem. Are there things that you can delegate? Maybe you need to excuse you and your family from some outside activities. There are so many good things to do, and sometimes I find it easy to overcommit our family and ourselves.

Take a step back and revisit your priorities and goals. How does reality fall in line with your primary priorities? This exercise can be enlightening and expose things that need cut out of your life. When you cut something out, it doesn't mean that you can never do it again, but rather that this is not the season for it. If you streamline your daily routines better, will there be more time for what you need to do *and* what you desire to do?

Continue this activity for a few days and start writing down notes to yourself about places in the day that can be improved and how you will improve them. Watch your children, and write down what each is doing during the day. Just take a quick glance around and quickly write down who is doing what. Are they wasting their time and yours with bickering about chores? Write down the time their bickering takes and show them how they are using the minutes.

This exercise will also help you to see a child who is taking lots of your time and determine whether this is truly necessary or not. I am not suggesting that you cut your children short on love and affection. Different children need support in different ways. Writing down what happens each day gives us clarity.

Think about what you can do in changing your reaction, your disciplining of this child, or restructuring this child's day so that the dilemma is overcome. Maybe you *do* need to keep on doing what you are doing with this child. Writing down what is happening and journaling about it will bring things to light about you and your children that otherwise would go unnoticed except in your ever-increasing frustration at the situation or child.

Think about what you can do in changing your reaction, your disciplining of this child, or restructuring this child's day so that the dilemma is overcome.

Another very helpful thing to do with this time-logging exercise is to write down everything that you eat and drink. Patterns will emerge in your days that you see are unhealthy. You will not want to write down that you ate six spoons of cookie dough at 4:30 p.m. Begin to brainstorm and journal about what you can do to ward off your hungry belly at 4:30. A handful of raw almonds would be healthier. Write down how *much* you are eating. The last time I did the exercise, I was amazed at the amount of food that I was eating. Did I really need that much? I discovered that I did not. I started to pay attention to my body and learn to recognize again the sense of being full. I began to serve myself smaller portions and eat more slowly.

Journaling minute-by-minute exposes reality. When you think you have done enough itemizing of your days and thought about what is truly happening, write a *realistic* plan for your days. Match up what you want to happen with what is really happening. If it takes you ten minutes for a diaper change, then that is reality. Leave enough time in the events of your day to encompass diaper changes, settling of disputes, switching laundry loads, and wiping up spilled milk. Plan for interruptions.

Some of us tend to be idealistic and think that we can do everything, do it all well, and do it superfast. Others among us don't attempt to do as much as we could. Every person can find value in taking stock of what really truly happens with their day. The overachievers will see that they are letting first priorities suffer. The underachievers will see that they can step it up a notch and be more helpful in the broader community.

Everyone benefits when exposing the reality of our days. We all learn where we are weak, where we are strong, and how we can further bring glory to God in our homes and families.

THE INTERRUPTED DAY

I remember an occasion when I was cooking something, or maybe washing dishes, and a little person came in wanting something from me. Perhaps it was just a request for cup of water, a snack, or some comfort for a hurt, but for me it was the umpteenth interruption of my day. I was shocked when my reaction caused the child to shrink back away from me.

Interruptions were the underlying current of my days.

That particular incident was a wake-up call to me that I was full of irritation, frustration, and perhaps even anger, and I didn't like that feeling one bit. I loved my children and our family deeply, so the last thing I wanted to do was to injure or disrespect them with an impatient action, a frown, or an eye roll. I'd been around people like that in my life and my natural inclination was always to avoid that person. I believe it to be a passive aggressive method of chasing people away, and I didn't want to run off my children with my surly attitude.

I was the mother, and had been entrusted with the responsibility for these precious children. I was aiming for and focused on creating a happy home and a healthy family, but in the process I had become an annoyed mom.

I took a step back from my situation and intentionally tried to see the forest for the trees. I attempted to identify why I was aggravated and realized that it was the million little interruptions I experienced day in and day out. I had to make a deliberate decision to let go of my expectations, stop watching the clock so zealously, breathe a little deeper and ultimately, change my attitude. To that end, I taped bible verses to the window over my sink that inspired me. I initially hadn't thought I was angry, but after seeing the situation through a wider perspective and taking a hard look at myself, I think maybe I was.

I was able to improve my reaction to interruptions and I give thanks to God for continually working on me from the inside out. Though improved, I'm not a finished person. There have been and will continue to be days when we are all better served if I set aside my plans and just choose love. The resulting peace and joy allows other aspects of my attitude to emerge and is a blessing to all.

The world will not end because the current Laundry Day does not go according to your wishes.

Days do not always go as planned. The constant barrage of interruptions have the ability to upend a day. Sometimes you can recover. Sometimes you need to spread a task out through the week to get back on track. And sometimes it's one thing after the other, and life spirals into chaos. You lose. Or at least it appears that you lose, but in reality God gives many lessons in trials.

The key thing is attitude. Keep in mind that you should focus on doing something that you *can* do something about, and let the rest be. There is always next week. *Next week*, Monday is Laundry Day again. *Next week*, you can clean the laundry room, work on the ironing and mending, and clean the top of the equipment. The world will not end because the current Laundry Day does not go according to your wishes.

By planning a routine for your work, you can rest assured that you have inadvertently also *planned* for these interruptions. "So Laundry Day isn't working out this week, next week we will get to it." Later this week we will make an extra effort to make sure that we do "Four Loads by four." These are the things we say to ourselves and our families when the day doesn't go well. Cycling through different tasks each day and every week assures that all things get done eventually. Some weeks will be stellar, some not. A routine brings peace of mind. You can say with confidence, "We'll get back to this."

In looking at my calendar, I can see ahead of time when a week is full of events that may hinder our daily work. Thus, by looking ahead, I can plan to do extra work the week before, and I can also knowingly try to work extra fast during that busy week to make up for time lost. When those two things fail, I can still relax inside and say, "We *will* get to it later." Getting uptight and upset accomplishes nothing but damages relationships.

Interrupted schoolwork goes the same way. It's part of the beauty of homeschooling that we can double up the day before or the day after. The children can take their work along in the van. They can work in a waiting room. They can do it on Saturday. We can add weeks to our school year. It's good to make goals; they give us direction and a target, but our plan to reach a goal should not turn into a whip for us or for our children.

Plans are a guide, not a master. A plan serves you; you do not serve the plan. A plan helps to get the work done in an efficient way. It gives you time and freedom to do things you might think that you can't do. When an opportunity that will disrupt your day presents itself, you can say with confidence, "We'll do five loads of laundry by five the rest of the week." Or, "I have enough things stocked in the freezer, and we'll clean the frig next week when Kitchen Day comes around again. Let's go have fun!" A plan gives you confidence. You know how to plan ahead, and you know how to recover from an event.

We cannot know what God wills for us and for our children ahead of time. But when interruptions come, we can say with confidence, "This is God's will. He must have something to teach me or the children, or maybe God is blessing me and the children with this." Or "Somehow, God is being glorified in this event, I need to live obediently and not grump about it or fight it."

Being upset about interrupted plans is, in essence, fighting with God. Yes, a season in life can be really awful. Sometimes it's a full-blown trial. It stinks; it hurts; it always seems so inconvenient. A lot of times the interruption causes more work.

The key is for us to remove Self from the center of our world and put God there instead. Serving him is the most important thing. When we depend on him for strength, our merciful God equips us with the grace to deal with interruptions.

WORK ETHIC

What I remember most about my grandma is working with her. Not that I didn't do work at home, and not that I didn't do fun things with my grandma, but I remember truly enjoying just being with her as she did her work.

On laundry day, Grandma let me help her with the wringer washer which was so much more fun than the modern machine at home. I handed her the clothes as she hung them on the line, right beside her strawberry patch. She taught me to use her iron and I got to iron her pretty handkerchiefs. I helped pick tomatoes from her garden. She washed and I dried the dishes after meals. She sent me to the shelves in her basement for pickles to have along with supper.

As my babies grew up into little children, I wanted them to enjoy work like I had with Grandma. To know that this is just what we do, no need to fuss about it, we just keep on moving to the next task.

I either procrastinated about my work or did it super-quick. I'd generally rather be doing something else. I thought about how the older and wiser people in my life approached their work and realized that I should take enjoyment from the rhythm of it. It might make for better days if I would appreciate the process and steadiness of the work.

I learned to look for new sights and then to share the view with the children. I slowed myself down enough to look up at the sky, into the trees, and at the plants in the garden. I took in the scents of the baking and the fresh air coming in the windows and talked about it with the children. I listened for the good morning songs of the birds and taught them to listen for them as well. Again in the evening, we listened to the goodnight sounds.

Just like Grandma, I included the children in the work I did and gave them pint-sized jobs to do. As time went on, my work became more enjoyable, my children learned life skills, the lessons and memories of my Grandma enriched another generation, and the work became a blessing.

Our children learn household habits at an early age. Our children will live in a house their whole lives. More than likely, they will be living with other people. It is necessary to know the routines that need to happen in every household. It should not be a hugely taxing effort to know what it is they are to do next. It is a valuable skill to *see* the work and have the ability to dive in and do it. This happens when household habits are ingrained into their early life. I'm not advocating the creation of household slavery of children, but rather simple chores for little children—chores big enough that the children feel like important contributors to the good of the family.

Just like brushing teeth before bed is a habit that you teach, also teach them to spend a couple of minutes tidying their room. Small routine tasks taught throughout the day to your little children become part of them, and when they are grown, they will carry them into whatever living circumstances they are in.

Move beyond taking the trash out and give your children some character-building work. Start when they are two, three, and four with little things like moving the laundry from the washer to the dryer, by carrying a little basket or dishpan of folded laundry to be put away, and by using a wet sponge to wipe the table. Little children love to help, and they want to do what you are doing. Let them.

Do not swish your children away to be entertained by the television or toys; include them in your work instead. Give them a broom or a wet washcloth. Talk to them while you work, and tell them why you are doing what you are doing. Explain to them the value of work and the joy that comes from a job well done. Praise them and brag about your busy little workers to the family and grandparents. Do not allow them to whine! If a new chore is hard, we say, "I'll try my hardest."

As your children grow, give them more difficult jobs, and grow those little muscles. Encourage them and tell them to do their best. Do not expect children to do the quality of work an adult can perform, but do encourage them to do excellent work. Watch their spirit and gauge whether it needs inspired and bolstered or whether they are starting to cheat and slack. Usually a word of warning is all that is needed to turn a slacker around, if you nip this tendency in the bud early on.

Do not swish your children away to be entertained by the television or toys; include them in your work instead.

Everyone appreciates hearing encouraging words and receiving thanks for the work that they do. Be liberal with your praise and thanks. Maybe the work you gave is truly too hard for the child and you need to let it go for a year or two. Be sensitive to the individual. Sometimes you will need to examine how you can make a chore more efficient and enjoyable. For instance, a poorly sized or broken tool is disheartening. Do your best to improve poor work environments. Is the child truly tired, or does she just simply dislike physical effort?

If a child slips on a job that you know he is capable of, then have him return to do the work again. Set a goal such as going for a treat when hard work is done well. Perhaps an end of the week special dinner or dessert. Take breaks, but do not let your children lie down on the job. Lying or sitting down while work is being done around them is unacceptable. "If you do not know what to do, then ask" is a phrase frequently heard at our house.

Teaching the children never ends. Just as soon as a character shortcoming is addressed in one child, a different one will crop up in another. Each child will need to learn each task. The good news is that the older children will help teach the younger children attitude, character traits, and the chore. Be sure to teach the older children well!

When the children are done with a task, teach them to come to you and ask, "What can I do next for you, Mom?" You should reply, "Oh! Are you done with _____ already? Good job! And thank you for coming to me and offering more help! I sure am glad to have a good helper like you!" Always be encouraging, inspiring, and thankful.

Everyone likes to be thanked for their help. When you visit others or you're at a social event, teach your children to be helpful there also. Teach them to ask the hostess, "Is there anything I can do to help you?" and hopefully the hostess will have them set the table or get chairs or at least thank them. Teach the children that when somebody else asks them for help at church or an event, they should willingly and cheerfully hop to it. Better yet, train them too *see* work and begin helping *without* being asked. This is teaching them to love others through serving. It starts with you and your example to them.

I have heard it said, "Children should not be required to work because they will be working the rest of their lives"; that "Childhood is the one time in life that they can just play and be children." If children aren't taught to work when they are young, then they will find it hard to work the rest of their lives. They will grow up with an entitlement mentality. They will expect everybody around them to take care of their every need. We've all seen the entitlement attitude up close and personal, and it's destructive. Besides that, there are plenty of hours in the day for work and play. Work is what we were created for, way back when God set Adam and Eve in the Garden and told them to take care of it. Work is a joy when done with the right attitude. This is the ethic we must encourage in ourselves and our children.

This said, my family and I are not perfectly willing workers all the time. We are *always* working on something with someone. Even when we think something was taken care of years ago, it might crop up again. God is still working on *me* in different areas of my life. Sometimes I'm a slow learner, and sometimes I have to relearn lessons that I thought were conquered! But I can't quit. In teaching my children his ways, God teaches me.

WE WORK BEFORE WE PLAY

A quote from my grandma that we often use in our home is: "We work before we play." For our family, playing includes building tree houses, playing educational games, and reading books and magazines. Chores need to be done either at the designated chore time or before any playtime happens. This is not so much of a problem with little children as it is with older ones. I often write this quote on their chore charts and schoolwork assignments. The middle part of the day when a lot of the chores and schoolwork are completed is when they start to slip away to their play and I have to herd them up to be sure that our work is done first.

Establishing a solid worth ethic in yourself and your family takes focus, but the reward is great—we use our time more deliberately and have more time for other things. Also, our children are prepared to take on the responsibilities of adulthood and have the ability to care for their own homes and families someday.

REPEATING

As young parents, Matt and I parented using a formula uniquely our own. A mixture containing elements of the way we each were raised, elements that were a reaction to how we each were raised, and elements from a conglomeration of parenting books and para-church classes. Our goal was a happy family, knowing that we were operating in an imperfect world. Our culture is performance based and so was our parenting.

Every day I messed up, right along with my husband and our little children. I had enough early childhood education to understand that babies and children are like strangers on this planet. They can't be expected to know what they don't know. But I really liked my days to run smoothly. My parenting in the early days was *if this, then that.*

The children grew older and we discovered what didn't work and what did, recognizing the now glaring fact that every single child is unique. We were able to recognize that a performance based culture and parenting style does not build healthy people or healthy relationships with others. Communication and connecting with others doesn't happen in a real way when people aren't acknowledged for the individual person they are, and I realized I didn't do enough of that when they were young.

Homeschooling made it easier to allow each child to have the freedom to be their own person. I tailored the education for each one individually, considering their unique interests, and allowing them freedom in the day to explore and develop their passions.

But we aren't perfect people and in retrospect, we certainly imposed our own personalities and ideals on them too much. Freedom to communicate requires a safe environment, without pressure to conform, or condemnation for thoughts and ideas. We learned to say, "I'm sorry" to our children. Not "I'm sorry, but..." We learned to repent, to apologize, and to acknowledge when we were wrong. Pride destroys, and healthy relationships are built with honest communication and true connections with each other.

With adult and teen children, we quickly learned to facilitate conversation, allow freedom, and provide safety in our relationships. Now, we encourage each other in the process of knowing our own selves, to seek out information on how each individual thinks, makes decisions, and communicates. When we fully understand ourselves, we can have greater respect and understanding for others.

Each of our children has a story inside, reasons for why they are the way they are, the choices they've made, the environment that has shaped them, to this point, and beyond. Our environments are dynamic, changing as people come and go, bring new ones along and creating different combinations. Each of their stories is who they are so far, part of the shaping of a person, and as parents we are key players in that tale. I love to hear the stories of my children. They make me laugh, feel sadness and joy, and ultimately... give me hope. Hope that in spite of all the errant realities of our humanity, we can still be with each other, love each other, offer mercy and grace to each other, and continue on this journey that is life. We stand alone as unique individuals, and come together... as a family.

We're great at multitasking. But teaching our children isn't something that can be multitasked.

It is hard to do anything with uncooperative children. They aren't fun to play with, they won't help with the work, and they are impossible to teach. Plus, have fun getting a sitter! Work on the character trait of obedience in your child before trying to teach him a chore or anything.

We all fall into the repeating habit without even realizing it. "Put the cushions back on the couch."

I say it a bit louder, "Put the cushions back on the couch."

Louder yet (maybe he didn't hear), "Put the cushions back on the couch!"

We often don't even hear ourselves say it the first three times. Then at the fourth time we lose it and realize that we have been repeating ourselves. "How many times did I say that?"

Is this a kid problem or a mom problem? We moms are busy people. We're great at multitasking. But teaching our children isn't something that can be multitasked. We need to stop and focus. We need to train ourselves to hear ourselves. It's hard—no doubt about it.

Pray for wisdom as you address this problem. Ask God to help you hear yourself. Ask God to show you how to focus and train each child. Each is unique, and each responds differently to discipline. When we are teaching obedience, we must combine it with a strong loving relationship. Know your child, respect your child's uniqueness, and love your child unconditionally with your actions, not just your words.

Train the children that when you give them an instruction, they are to respond, "Yes, Mom." That signals to you that they have heard and will obey. If they didn't respond, then be sure that you are looking at them with the instruction, that eye contact is made, and that they really do hear. I have often seen little children so focused on their play that they are unaware of the world around them. Be sensitive and respect them as human beings when you see this happening.

These are the children that need a gentle touch to the shoulder and eye contact.

One approach I've used is to role-play first-time obedience in a fun way with variations on games such as Mother May I?, Red Light Green Light, and Simon Says. This said, be sure to explain to your children that obedience is not a game, but serious—sometimes even a matter of life and death. Give examples so that they can understand danger such as talking about "what if" scenarios.

As mothers, we can find ourselves in a poor situation when we are multitasking while instructing a child. Our "mother ears" are picking up what is going on with other children, or we're hearing the pot bubbling on the stove at the same time that we are having a conversation with a child. Again, it is learning to focus.

Part of the solution with disobedient children is in teaching the children manners. Teaching them how to properly interrupt is one solution to frustrating situations. They are not to demand your attention from another room; that is rude. If they need you, they should come to you (unless someone is burning down the house). When they come and you are busy with somebody else, they should lay their hand on your arm as a sign that they need you and wait patiently until you can give them your full attention, just like they should do when you're at church or a party and you are talking to your friend. This is something you need to deliberately work at training. Role-play it over and over for several days. As the children grow, the little ones will usually pick it up from the older children, but you may find that if you haven't deliberately given the lesson for a few years, that you will need to teach this lesson to the next set of children coming up.

Perhaps you are instructing one child and there is bickering going on in the next room. Assuming there's not a major crisis, focus and finish with the first child. Then go to the bickering children and give instruction and discipline there.

It's often hard to discern who is at fault with bickering. I find it helpful to get each child's perspective, including the ones who weren't involved. Typically, they are all at some fault and get a consequence. My favorite for bickering is to assign work for the bickering children to do together as a team. It doesn't take long for them to learn how to work together to get the thing done. Sometimes though the children just need some space from each other. Having a quiet time for a set number of minutes can make a difference in the atmosphere of the home.

When we're discouraged, it's harder to discipline with love and grace. We end up sounding pretty ugly. Keep your spirits up with proper nourishment. If you can make it work with your schedule, get up before the children and spend some time reading the Word and in prayer. Fill your head with good things. Deliberately choose to keep junk out, for it will drag you down and steal your inspiration and joy.

If you have a friend whose child-rearing standards are different, and who contributes to your pity party or brings you down in any way, then it's time to get some space from her. Misery loves company; choose encouragers to be with, not the miserable. Once you and your children are stronger, then spend limited time with those needing your encouragement. I say "limited time" because bad influences will undo you and your children (Proverbs 13:20b). Also, don't be the one who drags others down; be an encourager!

Keep the fun, love, and cheerful workers in your home by spending focused time on teaching manners and obedience.

TEACHING A NEW CHORE

They stood around the toilet, gloves on, cleaning wipes at hand. Ready, set, go! I hit the start button. One at a time, we were racing time. How much time does it really take to clean a toilet? We were going to find out.

Wipe top to bottom, swish the bowl, wipe the floor. We all took a turn in the competition. Afterwards, while sitting around a plate of cookies, we laughed at ourselves.

My mom goal that day was to demonstrate two things. One, that unpleasant work can be made fun by turning it into a game such as "Beat the Clock," and two, that work can be fast if we plan to move quickly, then do it.

Chores , work, tasks, service to others—they're all part of life. We just have to do them over and over; the variables are efficiency, tools, skills, attitude, and delegation. The people that live in a house can help with the work it takes to keep the house. It's for everyone's benefit.

There are five classic steps for teaching a new chore to children:

1. Tell them.

2. Show them.

3. Do it with them.

4. Supervise their practice.

5. Trust them to do it without supervision.

I would encourage you to put these things on a sticky note and place it above your kitchen sink for a season until you have the steps down.

Do not expect children to do a chore well when you have only done the first two steps with them. It can take a short or long time to get from Step One to Step Five, depending on the child and the specific chore.

Make it a fun time by gathering all the kids for the telling and showing steps; then use the timer to see how fast each person can do the new task. My children loved to have contests against the clock. Celebrate improvement with a happy dance or a treat!

After telling, showing, and doing, write the steps on a card and tape it near the job site. This aids in supervised practice for the reader. If you are teaching a nonreader, you will have to spend more time supervising. Teaching chores will be work for you in the short run, but in the end, you will have a team of cheerful, diligent workers cleaning the house in no time flat.

"Inspect what you expect" is an often-quoted saying for those in management and very handy for moms to keep in their heads! If I get busy and lax about inspecting, then things start to slide. Inspecting is best done cheerfully with lots of praise along, with suggestions for improvement sandwiched in.

This brings me to the most important point: attitude—yours and theirs.

Do not treat your children like slaves, your personal minions, or property. These little people are human beings created in the image of God. They have things that are important to them, feelings, personalities, and a million other things that make each of them unique. Be respectful, kind, and loving to your children.

"And whatsoever ye do, do it heartily, as to the Lord, and not unto men."

—Colossians 3:23, KJV

If you complain about your work, your children will complain with you; it's contagious. If you're having a bad day, then acknowledge it; own it. Be honest with your family and then do something about it. Put on some happy music, read something encouraging, make a plan, take a walk, take a shower, pack everybody up and go to the park. Show them how to change your attitude. Then get back to work with a renewed attitude. Don't complain about your children and the work that comes with parenting; that is the biggest joy-squisher of all! It is terribly demoralizing and will destroy your relationships with them. Don't complain to your friends about your children, don't complain online about your children. It can become a bad habit. When you catch yourself complaining, turn it around into a praise for something about your children. Live gratefully and find something to be thankful for.

"And whatsoever ye do, do it heartily, as to the Lord, and not unto men" (Colossians 3:23, KJV). If you are working "as to the Lord," your children will notice your cheerful and grateful attitude! You can't be grumpy and whiny when you are doing your work as if Jesus were right there beside you and you were doing it for him. Keep the words, "as to the Lord," in mind. What a good habit to replace grumbling!

When you work cheerfully with your children, your demeanor is contagious and spreads joy among your family! Laugh and be silly while you do tasks. Enjoy the time together.

Do not wound the spirit of your children. Take care of them with your words, your smile, your singing, your stories, and your joy. You take care of their minds with education; you take care of their bodies with good food and medical care. Take care of their spirit too!

Do more than the minimum required. When we do a task, we want to do it wholly and completely. It is one thing to be short on time for one reason or another and to give a chore "a lick and a promise." It is another thing to consistently not do a job in a complete and thorough manner. Teach your children to do a job from start to finish, left to right, top to bottom, inside to outside.

If you have a child always rushing through work and not doing a complete job, require them to do it again—not in a way that picks on him or is mean, but for their own sake. Be calm and matter-of-fact about it. If you allow him to get away with incomplete work, you are setting him up to be a lazy worker for his whole life. You really do not want your child to struggle with employment or with keeping a home and caring for your grandchildren! Bring him back to the job and help him to see what didn't get done. Some people easily see the big picture but not the details; they simply don't notice details. Others see details that seem imperceptible to the eye. Most fall in the middle. Don't be too hard on those who fall on either side of the spectrum; embrace the uniqueness of each person and give work that is suitable to that person.

Train them to love work. Show them by your actions and attitude how to work with a good attitude. Work brings satisfaction in a job well done. Talk about these things as you work together. Work is serving God, and little ones learn this when they learn to do their first chores. Love God; love others with your work.

REFRESHMENT

I just wanted a shower. I had a needy baby that wouldn't settle down in the evening, and was up and ready to eat every morning at the crack of dawn. During the day I had two-handfuls of children going five different directions. I was in a hard place in the all-consuming journey of motherhood. I had been in this spot before a time or two, and thankfully I recognized it and knew it was just for a season, but that didn't help with my immediate need for a shower.

The mad rush of each day made it hard to figure out just when I was supposed to get a shower, let alone any of the other things I needed in order to keep my sanity.

Over the years, I had become a list maker and a planner, so I did some self-examination and writing in snatched moments in an effort to identify my specific needs. I am an introvert, and as such I need alone time to recharge. I like to learn and read. I wanted to connect with friends. I needed the basics like sleep and a hot shower.

I had to learn to be deliberate, to plan for healthy activities, to identify coping mechanisms and schedule them into my life. I learned to be flexible, to adapt to both challenge and opportunity. To abandon the schedule at times and do what made the most sense. I learned that it was okay to seize the moment and take a shower... even in the middle of the day.

Being a parent is a huge responsibility. It is an immeasurable honor and duty to receive this little bundle of personhood and to protect, nurture, lead, cultivate, nurse, shield, teach, and provide for her numerous needs and give account to God for it all in the end.

Children are not a burden to escape or endure; they are a blessing that drives us to Christ because we are incapable of parenting well without him.

Motherhood is a life of sacrifice; it is a life poured out for our children. So what are we to do to get some space from it all? Every mom knows the feeling of just wanting to go to the bathroom alone in peace and quiet, of wanting quiet time for reading just one chapter of a book, or just to be alone to think. It's not our children whom we love that we want to escape, it's the 24/7/365 that can wear on us. It's our unique personalities that can challenge us in the everyday-and-all-day of being with children.

Children are not a burden to escape or endure; they are a blessing that drives us to Christ because we are incapable of parenting well without him. God is who we need. While there are helpful strategies we can employ in order to have a more peaceful day with our children, and we can strategize to find a quiet and peaceful hour or two, the number one thing we must do is to cling to Jesus. We need the Helper, the Spirit, living inside of us and giving us strength for the days and wisdom for the work.

MORNING

Disruptions can set me on edge. Just like little children, I like routine. Some variety is fun; it adds spice to life. But when I have a pattern to the days, a certain order of events, a way of doing things, peace reigns in the home. The interruptions of children during the day are to be expected of course. "Mom I need ____." "Mom how do I do ____?"

Settling squabbles, correcting behavior, giving instructions, kissing the boo-boos—these are part of the routine. But when my morning routine gets severely disrupted, it can wreck my day. If things don't go the way I want them to early on, I can quickly get a stinky attitude. Some days I can go back to my room and start all over and that helps. But others start off like a shot out of the cannon, and the battle rages on all day long. I need to check my attitude on the fly. I think this is where that verse "Pray without ceasing" (1Thessalonians 5:17, KJV) comes into especially good use. These are the days when the Scripture verses stuck above the sink or on the mirror help tremendously.

I love mornings. I love to see the sun rise; it's one of my Top Ten Things in Life. I love the morning routines that I create as the seasons change. In the winter, I like a cozy time by the fire with my coffee and Bible, having breakfast with Matt, the house silent. That early morning silence is a balm to my soul. In the warm seasons, I like to do that on the deck, watching the sun come up. It is time with God, time with my husband, time to breathe and think. It becomes "me time" when my attitude gets bad and when I don't get that time and take it out on the world. I can't make an idol of my early mornings.

God doesn't give us a beautiful start to every single day. When the children are up too early for my tastes, I read the Bible aloud to whomever is present. That is a beautiful thing! To read the Bible aloud in the early morning to your children is living the Shema (Deuteronomy 6). It is good to appreciate God's gift of beauty and quiet in the morning. My personal quiet time may be gone but it is still redeemed time.

AFTERNOON

Naptime is a good opportunity for everyone in the house to have a quiet time. We use it here for reading alone, doing a quiet craft or project alone. I personally have a hard time napping during the day unless I'm completely exhausted. I prefer to have a longer night by going to bed early. After I have a baby, my mother-in-law comes over in the afternoon to sit with the children and insists that I lie down. I protest but do it anyway and sure enough, I collapse for a couple for hours. If you're an afternoon napper, go with it!

If you aren't a napper, a quiet hour is a good time to do those things that you need a quiet house for. Each of us is different and needs quiet for different tasks. I generally like quiet when I'm doing something that I need to really think about. If we have a project that we need to do without any interference from little children, we do it during naptime. As soon as the little ones are down, we race the clock until they get up.

Maybe you love to sew, paint, write, garden, study a subject, or have a home business or some other creative activity. Schedule a quiet time in the house for your family, and use this time for your interest. We need to do these things so that we don't lose ourselves in the business of life with children and our home management work. Plan and prepare for this valuable time of day so that you can have this inspiring time that allows you to express who you are as a person.

There are seasons of life that fit different things that you want to accomplish. Don't get hung up on a time or a method. Go with the seasons of life. Be flexible.

EVENING

Your bedside table is a place to keep those most important things to rejuvenate your life. Your Bible and a prayer journal should be there and ready for late evening and early morning routines. The key is in being ready for the opportunity for some quiet devotional time.

The key is in a routine that is started early enough to allow you and your husband some alone time before exhaustion hits.

Do your best to keep regular bedtime routines for the benefit of everyone's health. Doing the same thing every night with the children helps them to settle down and relax. Children love to know what is going to happen next; it makes them feel safe and secure. Structure makes for peaceful evenings. A pleasantly-structured evening with the children means that you and your husband will more likely have the opportunity to have a quiet alone time together later on. When the chaos at bedtime drags on and on, the evenings becomes a big source of irritation. Following the same evening routine lends to a peaceful bedtime.

We have done different things over the years, such as taking time before bed to Read-aloud altogether, read a story in each bedroom, make up stories on spot, sing a song, or eat a simple bedtime snack with everyone around the table. Be creative in creating your bedtime routine; do what works for your family. The key is in a routine that is started early enough to allow you and your husband some alone time before exhaustion hits.

RELATIONSHIPS

Being home alone with children can be lonely at times. As a young mom, I missed the daily interaction of friends that I had experienced from kindergarten through college. It felt strange to be alone. I remember that the highlight of my week was going to a Bible study with other moms. I learned to make Jesus my best friend. He was faithful and present for me. That said, I also succumbed to entertaining myself every afternoon with the soap "All My Children" and dreamt more than once that I was part of the stories. Erica Kane was my best friend. It was a double life and I eventually overcame my soap addiction by taping Bible verses to the television.

Once Erica left my life, and I replaced the bad habit with a good one—studying God's word—I became more content with the relationships I did have. It was not easy to give up Erica, I learned that I could watch her once a month and still keep up, and then I gradually got so disgusted with the show that it became easy to not watch it anymore. There truly is victory in Jesus.

Who did God put in my life to be in relationship with? First, my husband and children—I could do my best to be a blessing to them. Second, I had a lot of extended family around. Third, I had the people in my church, Bible study group, and later a homeschool community. I had to learn that relationships aren't about me—that's a selfish love—but about loving others and seeing them as Jesus does. God gives us strength and wisdom when we are willing to work with him and helps us to give others our best. Studying who Jesus is and developing a relationship with him and loving others with his help became a far richer life than serving my desire for the entertainment value of friendship.

My husband is God's gift to me for a best friend. We balance each other. Together we create a family that will impact the future in tremendous ways. The trials that life brings us can draw us together if we keep our eyes on Jesus and are committed to bless each other with loving actions. We are unique individuals and when we live in awareness of that, we are healthier and happier people. I just read a sweet story of a couple happily married sixty-four years who died within four hours of each other. That is what being best friends is. Relationships require time and it's easy to simply do the work of living, taking care of the kids, and live exhausted. We have to say no to some things in order to say yes to others and that includes the relationship we have with our spouse. What gets in the way? What can you do to shift the focus from surviving the hecticness and back to supporting your relationship?

As the years go by and our children grow up, they too become our friends. You will love to listen to them, talk with them, and do things together as friends do. They will be the ones you think of when you want to share an experience you've had, when you see a sight, discover something, or want to hash over an issue with. That is the reward of respecting them as little children, helping them develop their unique gifts, teaching them thinking skills, and spending time developing loving relationships with them.

> ## As the years go by and our children grow up, they too become our friends.

The family is the most important earthly relationship to develop, and it starts in the early days of marriage and bringing up children. What you do with each day, how you react to each other, how you talk to your children, whether you see them as unique individuals created in the image of God, and what you teach them will be your family legacy. When hard times come for any of the members of your family, it will be family that draws near and gives the care and support.

You can't let the days go by willy-nilly with no direction. You must give thought to your actions and how those actions will change the relationships you are involved in.

FRIENDSHIPS

The Bible has plenty to say about friendships and gives us multiple examples of good and bad ones. God intends for us to interact with each other in the Body of Christ. As a mom of young children, I found it difficult to contribute to the church body. I was busy and exhausted! If I tried to help with something, I felt like I wasn't giving my best and that I was divided between my little children and my church work. I didn't quite get it that my work of raising up little children was church work. Little children do require a lot of physical and mental labor. It's good work, and we shouldn't discount what we do as unimportant. Caring for little children is much more than feeding, watering, and sleeping them. You are their first teacher and much of what they will be is determined by their care in those first crucial years.

When the children were small, I would get together with another mom or two and all of our children. Of course, the children loved these times, and even though it was a bit hard to have a lengthy conversation when there were constant interruptions, the encouragement and fellowship was very precious. It becomes easier for conversation when little children grow older because they organize games, kiss ouchies, and keep the peace. These are good times for all. Our children learn to interact with others not in their family, and moms have an opportunity to visit face-to-face.

I had a long season of meeting a friend for lunch on a monthly basis. That might not sound very often but, believe me, the month flies by and it's time to have a lunch date again. The children had a special lunch at home under the watchful eye of an older sibling, while I slipped out for a short time with my friend at a local restaurant. Those days were refreshing.

Moms Night Out events that our local homeschool group organizes are also great fellowship times. Coffee, tea, and conversation are balm to other moms. As our girls grew older, they started coming along and having their own separate fellowship time.

Good intentions don't accomplish anything. That's why planning a certain day every month helps a lot in actually getting a hospitality event accomplished. Before I *planned* for friendship, long periods of time were going by without seeing local friends face-to-face! It's not an intentional dropping of friends; it simply requires thought and planning to either host or show up at an event. When we are busy with children, work, and kid activities, it is effort to plan for a friend-event but so worth it.

At one time our family held a family Hospitality Night. I scheduled an evening or a Sunday afternoon to invite another family over. Getting together as families is a rich time for relationships and growth as families together.

After God, husbands, and family comes the church.

Friendships are important. They warm the heart; we rejoice in victories, and give empathy, understanding and support in trials. Friends are wonderful but my best friend is God and after that, my husband; nurturing my children comes next. These are the priority relationships that the Lord has given us, and these are the ones that we will have with us all of our lives. After God, husbands, and family comes the church. The Bible teaches that we are to extend hospitality to other believers, edifying each other. If our friendships are taking away from those priorities, then we have adjustments to make. Don't let other people take precedence over your husband and children. Sometimes we get caught up in a relationship with a toxic friend; if someone is trying to control your life, then it's time to break that friendship off.

On the flip side, if you are so alone that you have no fellowship with other Christian moms then you need to work on finding like-minded sisters in Christ and building relationships with them. We need the support of other women, especially older ones.

Be content with what God has given you and use it to his glory!

Seek out wise godly women and invite them over, ask them for advice in the stage of life you are in. As you grow in maturity, do the same for the younger moms coming behind you. There is a lot of support for moms on the Internet, but nothing takes the place of real live local friendships. Look for these women in your local church, homeschool support group, or book club, or seek out other moms involved in the same activities your children are in; be creative in places for reaching out and connecting with local people. Be wise and discerning in the friends you choose and the places you find them.

God might have you in a season of aloneness as he did with me in the early days of my marriage. Be content with what God has given you and use it to his glory! He is the potter and we are the clay; he is shaping and molding us into his image. Jesus is your best friend, and, in his time and way, will supply your every need. Pray and tell him what you need, and he will be gracious to you and answer in his good time.

TIME TO READ

Books allow us to visit with those knowledgeable on a subject that we want to know more about. They teach us and take us on travels around the world and through time. Books can build us up, inspire us, encourage us, and mentor us. They can also cause us to grow discontent with our husband, family, friends, home, finances, and more. We can escape our own reality through reading. Be wise with book choices and read with discernment. Even Christian literature can have wrong teachings or feed desires that are destructive. If you find yourself reading to escape reality, it might be helpful for you to do some self-examination and ask yourself some questions about that. Our time as mothers is limited; use that time to the benefit of the lives we serve. Constantly seeking knowledge is not always a good thing either (It hurts me to say that!). We need to take care of our work and relationships with those around us first. Then read for knowledge. Read great books aloud to your children and inspire your mind along with theirs.

I love to read and learn new things. When my children were little, I would read a chapter and then work, read, work, read, work. I liked to think about what I had just read while I worked. This system was useful for a long time until the workload grew larger, the homeschooling hours grew longer, and the accumulated chatter of children drowned out the voice I was reading; that slowed me down for a season! Reading a bit before sleeping and while nursing the baby feeds the brain. A little bit at a time, and I find that I've read quite a stack of books. Because the time for reading is limited, I have become very choosy about what I read.

Being a mother is an awesome responsibility and an incredible experience. The blessings that come with motherhood far outweigh the trials small and large that come along with it. By keeping our focus on Jesus, ordering our days in peaceful ways, and building relationships with others that bless the whole family, we can find refreshment in ways that honor him.

ALONE TIME FOR CHILDREN

What about "alone time" for children? What is the alone time used for? Think about the child who is seeking alone time. Is it a need for quiet reading or study? If the child needs alone time to calm her spirit in a healthy way, then help that child carve out a niche somewhere in the home to have that quiet time. There are introverts in every family. Alone time doesn't *need* to be in a bedroom, although it can be. The space can be a workshop, a reading chair, a walk or run, or a bubble bath. Be perceptive of your children's needs and help them learn to know themselves and how to calm themselves.

LIFE WITH LITTLES

Many years ago, I had three children under the age of four. Another time I had five children under the age of ten, and then six under the age of eleven. The day before our oldest son turned sixteen we had our ninth baby. It has been exhilarating and exhausting. Each day is a delightful adventure in learning for each stage of development. It is fun, exciting, and challenging at every level.

The hardest days were when we had three under the age of four... because it was all on me. A four-year-old can run little errands for mom, such as getting diapers and such, but those days and nights were hard. I became a minimalist before it was trendy, and simplicity was my mission. If I were going to keep up, I needed organization.

All of a sudden they were six months older which made all the difference. Suddenly, I could look around and take a deep breath. Life with children is like that, six month increments of significant change. I can look back and see how far each one has come and how they have developed and grown. It's a beautiful thing.

Over time I learned to stay calm and see that even a two-week time period can sometimes make a big difference. I could look back and ask myself what the biggest problem was two weeks ago? But, whatever it was, we got through it. Seeing such beautiful and amazing growth builds hope for the future.

The children each grew and took on more responsibility, and we all learned new skills. Their vocabulary and conversation abilities grew as well. The day came when life wasn't so much physically exhausting as mentally arduous, because of the constant conversation. Life with Littles can seem to go by slowly, yet suddenly the independent, strong-willed little girl who wore dress-up clothes all day-every day is leaving the nest.

How little is little? That depends on your family. If you have nobody over the age of six, then your oldest children, even though in another family they would be the Littles, are the Bigs in your family. I have a friend whose oldest child is the same age as one of my children. Her child, as the oldest, is very mature and a mother hen towards her younger siblings. My same-aged child does not have the same sense of responsibility, in part because of the older siblings' catering, and in part because of my failure to give that child chores that encourage responsibility. We're working on that. Each family will be different and each child's place in the birth order will shape who they are. Always be sensitive to the uniqueness of each child and sensitive to personality and needs. Doing otherwise will cause emotional, mental, and spiritual damage.

"How little is little?" depends on how you are training your Littles. Children don't instantly become helpful when they hit a certain age; it is a result of the developmental training process that you employ at each age. Make work fun, do it with a right attitude, as unto the Lord, and as children grow, they will gradually pick up new skills and slowly become more helpful. Every six-month passage means a huge difference in the ability of a child.

A two-year-old can help unload the dishwasher with your encouraging help, help you switch laundry loads and fold wash clothes, and stand on a chair at the sink with you and wash dishes. It might look more like play, and you might trip over their efforts, but they are learning through watching and doing with you. Two-year-olds cannot stay on task long or be held responsible for regular chores. Two-, three-, and four-year-olds are in the preparatory stage for doing regular chores. They love to help do work; they love to accomplish something; they love praise; they love to do things with you.

Enjoy this time of life with them, include them in your work, and teach them how to work. Encourage them to be helpers by saying things like, "Come help me mop," and give them a little mop rag. Then thank them for their wonderful help. Say, "See how fast it went when we worked together?" and "The family will be so happy to see a clean floor and know how hard you worked to make our house clean; look how clean it is!"

Little children can learn to work much more easily if their day follows a routine.

When somebody spills something on the clean floor, teach the children to handle a spill *with grace* as you hand them a little wet towel to quick-mop it with a smile and not a sigh. A good attitude on the part of mom, who teaches that good attitude to her children, makes for a happy home.

Little children can learn to work much more easily if their day follows a routine. If you train them, through doing it with them, to make their bed every morning, it will become a work habit. They aren't coordinated enough to make a bed to look beautiful, but encourage them to do their best. Teach them, "If you pull the sheet tight at the top, it makes a neater line." And "When you are done washing your face, grab a paper towel and wipe down the counter." Say little phrases such as these to them while you do the work together, and they will learn. When these little children are big, you will hear them saying the same things to the next set of little children in your home. This is your reward for training your oldest children well. Little children can learn helpful work habits and learn to do them with excellence!

After they make the bed, have them go to the bathroom, wash, and brush with you there beside them or with your direction. They will get into the habit of doing that little chore. If they are accustomed to rising and sitting in front of the television, then that will become their habit. Isn't it much better for them to rise, make their bed, dress, and do personal grooming for their early morning routine? Little children can do this if we help them do it.

Now, let's be real. Let's say you were up with the baby four times in the night and you are still in bed when the little children get up. Maybe they did their routine and maybe they didn't. What are you going to do? Chill. Tomorrow is another day. No matter what time it is that you get out of bed, you can restart. Do the morning routine even if it's three hours later than normal.

EASE INTO EDUCATION

When the little children are accustomed to routine and order and taught basic chores and skills with your encouragement, then the next step of teaching them life skills becomes easy. It becomes easier to teach a new skill by simply adding it on to another thing you are already doing during the daily routine.

Do you have a time of day when you read to the children? Tack on a few minutes of phonics and numbers. While reading aloud, have the children narrate back to you a little bit at a time. Gradually increase what they narrate. Does your preschooler help set the table? Show him on paper what 5 plates plus 1 plate reads like. Do you already play outside? Get down and find a bug, and then look it up and read about it.

Learning is found everywhere. Teach your children to teach themselves by providing them toys, activities, and experiences that foster curiosity, imagination, creativity, and a love for life and learning. This can be done with a baby, toddlers, and preschoolers before they ever enter traditional school age. These life skills can be introduced by you right now in how you structure their day and the things you encourage your children to do in their day. You are not passing the time babysitting; you are mothering. Do not think of the preschool years as merely entertaining them, but as years when you can help them to be people who love learning, who love God, creation, and people who love others.

HEALTHY BRAIN FOOD FOR PARENTS

Life with Littles involves a fair amount of physically hard work. It can lack a certain mental stimulation that we adults crave. We feel that lack and will look to fill it with something.

My oldest children were little before the days of the Internet, so I didn't have to battle getting caught up in online discussions, rabbit trails, and looking through Pinterest. If you are looking to online friends for encouragement, tread carefully and wisely. The women of old got in trouble going from house to house gossiping. Today we don't need to leave our houses to fall into the same sins. I would suggest using a timer so that you don't fall into the Internet abyss. It's a little scary how fast time flies when you are engrossed in something online. You do not want your children to have their only memories of you in front of a screen.

For safer, better mental stimulation, I recommend reading books. Not necessarily fiction, but how-to, theology, philosophy, Bible study, history, science, business, gardening, health or other topics you find intellectually stimulating. These types of books can be read one chapter at a time and then thought about while doing physical work. How-to books can also promote creative action. Of course, you can find helpful articles on the Internet, too, but you have to watch out for the ensnaring web which can sap your time as well as your emotional and spiritual energy. I recently unfollowed a couple of magazines whose articles I love to read because I realized that they were sucking too much out of my day.

What you put in comes out. If you sow into your mind things that promote discontent—argumentative online debates, television sitcoms or irrelevant reality shows, romance novels, and Hollywood magazines—then you will reap discontent in your life. This can happen online or offline as well. Examine your heart to see if it is focused on God and serving him or if it creates discontent in your life. Do not allow yourself to be discontent, but look at all things with thanksgiving and challenge yourself to overcome trials with biblical responses. Starting a gratitude journal is very instrumental in overcoming discontent. Try making a list of ten things that bring joy and happiness to life and seek how you can incorporate them into life.

HIDE GOD'S WORD IN YOUR HEART

List the good things that come about through each trial and do what you can to improve each hard thing. Improve your attitude towards it by choosing to see it as a growth opportunity. Look and see how God's Word instructs us about that particular trial, learn how to handle the situation better, ask for help, and try to understand what God is teaching you through it. Look at the trial as a challenge to be overcome, and the next time that trial or one similar comes around, you will be better equipped to handle it. You will have the rewarding *aha* moment of recognizing a situation and know better how to do it again.

As the years go by and you become stronger, things that were trials at one time become easy. The physically hard work of this stage of life is making us strong for the future. We learn to rest in God and depend on him for the strength we need for each day. We learn to seek him for wisdom in how to handle all the things that wear on us.

We learn to pray without ceasing and make God our best friend in the lonely days of little adult interaction.

As you learn to lean upon the Lord through Scripture and prayer, be sure to train your little ones to do the same. The everyday choices we make affect the lives of our little children. What do you want them to have stored in their heads from these days?

The everyday choices we make affect the lives of our little children.

We can work on this daily with our little children. They are like sponges and can memorize easily. Add a time of day when you do memory work with your Littles. Do it after a meal, or make a little circle with them on the floor, and spend a few minutes reciting a verse. Another easy way to learn Scripture is through song. Place into your day a time when you listen to Scripture music. This can be when you are folding laundry together or washing dishes. Sing along with it while you work. Little children can learn hymns. Hymns are rich stories of the Christian faith that will help your children throughout their lives. Choose a time of day when you practice singing a hymn and teach them great truths of God in this easy way. Hide the Word in their hearts!

I CAN'T GET ANYTHING DONE!

Now, you ask, how am I to add all these things into the day when I already can't get anything done? Do you currently have a plan? If not, that's your problem. Without a plan for the day, you are aiming at nothing and hitting it every day. If you have a plan that's not working, then your plan needs modified. There are times in life that certain things do not fit in and must be let go for a season. Saying yes to a thing may mean saying no to something else.

What are the most important priorities to your family? These are the things that must be emphasized in your daily plan. Examine your days and see how the many activities that must happen can be made more efficient, more streamlined, and better organized.

A very successful way of examining your day is by writing down every single little thing that you and the children do from the moment of rising until you fall asleep at night. It is an inconvenience to do this, but it will help you become better at managing your home in the long run. What this exercise will do is expose areas of the day when you and the children are wandering aimlessly. I'm not saying that there is no place for wandering aimlessly but let's do it in the yard on a lazy summer afternoon, not while going about the daily routine of life with Littles.

Efficiency sometimes gets a bad rap in the creative crowd, but what being efficient does, in its proper place, is allow you *more* time for creative endeavors. Sometimes being efficient in this stage of life means letting some things go. Paper plates, paper napkins and plastic silverware might be the answer for a season or hiring or bartering for a cleaning service. Staying home instead of being on the go, go, go improves efficiency and contributes greatly to a healthy and happy home life. There is a place for going out and experiencing new things with the children but try to make it the exception to the at-home life and a small part of the daily and weekly routine.

Is the tyranny of the urgent ruining your days? Try to identify what the tyrant is so that you can manage it better. Sometimes it is an especially needy child. What can you do to meet this child's needs better? The needs for sleep and food are typical culprits for irritable Littles. Or does this child need to learn respect and obedience? Identify the need and address it. Maybe it's a child with high energy or a special need? Think through how to help this child with unique needs so that the day can be more effective for everyone in the home. Sometimes the tyrant is a time of day. Does your lunch need to be earlier? Are you waiting too long before having nap time? Do you need to schedule a snack time? Is there a part of the house (bedrooms, playroom, bathroom, kitchen) that is a problem? Spend a day or two studying the problem and thinking about what would make it more pleasing to your home life. Interruptions are part of life, but you must be diligent so that the interruptions do not take over and become the tyrant.

LESS IS MORE

Less is more with Littles. They do not need every toy under the sun. What will be most helpful to them—and you—are open-ended imaginative toys and activities. Aim for classic toys that will stand up to use and can be passed down through all your children. These teach their brains to grow and think. Minimize the sheer amount by decluttering the toys that don't get played with, the flashy, noisy toys that give you a headache (mom doesn't need that!), and of course all toys with missing or broken pieces.

Place some toys or activities in storage and rotate them by week, month, or season to further pare down the volume. Keep the remaining toys in a way that the children know where they are kept and can put them away with ease when told to. Teach them, "Everything has a place and everything in its place." You will need to help them put away their toys to train them how to do it and to train them in work. As parents, we need to help them learn self-discipline and a work ethic. It starts with teaching the littlest ones to put away their toys. What you will see happen with less toys but perhaps higher quality toys is that they will play longer and with more imagination as their brain grows and stretches. Instead of a toy being interesting for ten minutes and laid aside, they will often play with it for hours or days in untold ways.

Toys for little ones should be kept near to where you are working. Then you can keep on top of mishandling and disagreements. A playroom that is too far away from the kitchen or main part of the house will leave the children unsupervised. Been there, done that. Toys in bedrooms contribute to disastrous bedrooms. Been there, done that too. If you keep the bedroom chores to the minimum of making the bed and clothing storage, cleaning maintenance will be far easier on you and the children.

Before lunch and naptime, hold a ten-minute-tidy session. Sing a silly song about picking up toys and make it fun and quick. Once again, have a ten-minute-tidy time before supper and the evening time. If the toys come out again before bedtime, have another pickup before the bedtime routine. Pickup times should be able to happen in ten minutes or less. If it takes longer than that, then it's time to have another declutter session or box up more for the toy rotation. If a child has an especially interesting toy project that he doesn't want disturbed, then be kind and respectful, and store it out of the way or pick up everything but that spot where his project is.

BABY BALANCE

After nine babies, I think I've done every schedule, non-schedule, and modified version. Our ninth baby was born at twenty-six weeks gestation age, and when he came home from the neonatal intensive care unit (NICU), my singular goal was to get as much nutrition and as many antibodies into his body as I could. I let him nurse whenever he was interested and for as long as he wanted to eat. This was typically every three hours except for a session in the early morning when he ate every thirty minutes for about two hours. The rest of the day he slept in our arms. I wanted him to sleep because babies grow when they sleep. If it was in my arms, so be it.

While in NICU, I read all the literature on premature babies I could get my hands on, and I learned that in study after study babies who are held skin to skin become more physiologically stable and grow better. In the NICU, I held him as much as I possibly could. When we came home, he slept with me and my body was in tune with him. When he stirred, I turned to nurse him. During the day we held him all day long. Our baby grew and was healthy, and that's what was most important.

Caring for my youngest reminded me of the days of my first baby. With our first I nursed on demand as I was taught at the hospital and through the literature of the La Leche League. When you have one baby and are home alone, you have no extra arms to hold the baby or other little children to entertain the baby! It is a unique situation that normally only happens once in a lifetime. Our first baby was, in retrospect, a very easy baby. He quickly settled down into a routine of his own. He took naps without sleep props. He weaned himself at fourteen months.

The second baby was the same, although he was a big hungry boy. He did not settle into a routine as predictable as the first baby. He did take two naps a day and slept well at night but also preferred to eat every two to three hours. As an older baby, he was too busy playing all day to eat and did his nursing during the night. When he finally started eating food, he quickly dropped nursing which happened at fourteen months.

We did the early '90s version of a popular parent-directed feeding method with the next three babies. I had plenty of milk for these babies until nine months, and then I had to supplement and eventually switched them to the bottle. I was a slow learner. With our sixth, seventh, and eighth babies, I nursed on demand for the first several weeks, never tried to cut out any nighttime feedings, and never went to a four-hour schedule. Instead of putting them off in the late afternoon and evening, I fed them every two hours. These three babies nursed exclusively for the first year and I never had a problem with my milk supply.

In the second year, I nursed before meals and offered them food until they weaned themselves which was eighteen months with Baby #6, twenty-six months with Baby #7, and twenty-four months with Baby #8. All of these babies took a late afternoon nap until six to nine months, a morning nap until about fifteen months, and an afternoon nap for years. They all slept about twelve hours at night. Baby #9, ate every three hours, had a morning nap, afternoon nap, and late afternoon nap. In the late afternoon and evening, I fed him every two hours or however he cued. He nursed more than two years.

The biggest value in the parent-directed method is the sleep-eat-wake cycle. Learning to see the baby's cues for being tired, which happen approximately one-and-half hours after waking from the last nap, is a benefit for mom and baby. Then the baby takes an hour-

and-half nap, which I found that they easily do, which allows Mom to attend to the things she can't do while the baby is awake. After a nap, the baby is well-rested, hungry, and will have a good nursing session. It is good to have days when you know what to expect, and a well-rested baby is a happy baby.

The biggest value in the parent-directed method is the sleep-eat-wake cycle.

When the baby is awake, there is plenty of time for holding and playing with them. If you use the same routine for laying a tired baby down to sleep by himself from day one, he will learn to go to sleep by himself. It is key to put him down before he is overtired. Watch the clock for that hour-and-a-half mark and for cues, such as rubbing the head, ear, or eyes, and tired eyes along with grumpy vocalization. Very early in life establish a go-to-sleep routine (for example, a song, prayer, or story) which becomes a signal to the baby for sleep. Swaddle a new baby for their comfort and sleep but allow access to hands if they want. Some babies suck on their hands to go to sleep; some do not care.

If a baby wakes during his nap, it is probably a burp. Pick him up quietly, pat his back until he burps, lay him back down, and he will normally go back to sleep. When the baby wakes up after his hour-and-a-half nap, go to him immediately with a happy face; change his diaper and, feed him. Then he can play. In the late afternoon, the nap will be shorter. A schedule is only a tool for you and your baby. Do not be a slave to the schedule or to the baby. This is parenting with grace.

Learning your baby's communication signals takes a bit of practice, but if you watch and listen, you will learn the cues. This learning process with each baby is one of the joys and challenges of mothering. Babies talk with their eyes, facial expressions, their hand and arm movements, along with vocalizations. Babies will grunt, squirm, search for you, suck on their hands and root when they are hungry. Do not put off a tiny tummy that digests breast milk quickly; it will disturb the child's health and development.

Pray for wisdom and be discerning about the cries of the baby. There is a cry that babies will make in a nap that we do not need to run to, and that is the little cry they make when they are disturbed and will go back to sleep. I have had babies do this almost exactly forty-five minutes into the nap. If this cry is immediately run to and the baby is further awakened, then he will miss out on sleep. Babies grow when they sleep. Quietly check on the baby to see how awake he is. If he looks uncomfortable, try to ascertain why. Often the wakening is a burp. Quietly put him up to your shoulder, burp him gently, and lay him back down. He will often sleep another half an hour or more.

Pray for wisdom in understanding the needs of each baby and reading cues.

If your baby consistently wakes up while sleeping—and it's not because he's hungry—raise one end of his bed to aid in digestion. Reflux hurts! Letting a baby cry is potentially ignoring hunger, reflux, apnea, teething pain, and the unknown. It also disturbs the development of trust and attachment. Pray for wisdom in understanding the needs of each baby and reading cues. If you're unsure about recognizing cues for sleep or hunger, there are plenty of YouTube videos that demonstrate these universal signs. This would have been really handy to have when I had my first babies. When we miss the little one's communication signals, we get an unhappy baby. In my experience of both having babies in my room and not (#s 3 and 4 were in the nursery with a monitor), it is easier to get to know your babies cues when the baby is nearby. This is a walk of grace with each child; they are each different, and that is what makes them uniquely loved.

MOTHER'S MILK

Studies show, and it is my personal experience, that mom's milk supply is lower in the late afternoon. If your baby is hungry, then feed him; don't put him off if you can help it. You will know when he is hungry due to his cues, look at YouTube videos on baby cues. It is their language, how they communicate. Learn to read your particular baby. If he is still hungry, then you need to learn how to increase your milk production. If he has trouble nursing, talk to a lactation consultant. They provide a boon of educational information on a vast number of problems. A good one will be well worth the effort to find.

Breast milk is very valuable in myriad ways. It is the perfect food created just for babies. Breast milk is full of nutrients and antibodies to support everything in the mother and baby's environment. If at all possible, do what you can to make your milk nutritious by eating good food and taking supplements. I learned in the NICU that different moms have different fat concentrations in their milk. Some nursing mothers need to feed their babies more frequently due to a calorie difference—that is how their particular breasts work. Keep your production as high as you can so that you will have enough milk for as long as you can. Your baby still needs all the complex nutrients and immunological factors in breast milk as he grows older and into his toddler years.

Factors that affect milk supply and ways to increase it that I learned about while pumping in the NICU include the following:

☐ Herbal teas such as More Milk Plus and Mother's Milk.

☐ Fenugreek capsules.

☐ Alfalfa tablets or liquid.

☐ Brewer's yeast tablets.

☐ Oats and/or rice in the diet.

☐ A tall glass of water or herbal tea each time you sit down with the baby.

☐ Nutrients that you might be low on include protein, zinc, essential fatty acids (primrose oil, flax oil, cod liver oil, borage oil, walnut oil).

☐ Nurse/pump every two hours, nurse and then pump.

☐ Power Pumping, which means to pump for ten minutes, rest for ten minutes, on and off for one hour once a day

☐ Pharmaceuticals may help; ask your prescriber.

☐ Going longer than three hours between nursings or pumping is detrimental to milk production and may even affect how much milk you will produce in the future for an older baby.

☐ Babies may need to eat more frequently in the very early morning hours and again late in the afternoon.

THE FAMILY DYNAMIC

Back in the days of lots of little children, I was stretched too far, like a rubber-band about to break. Home management was not going well and I simply could not physically do it all. Not to a standard I could feel satisfied with.

My daily goals back then were to cover the basics: food, dishes, floors, bathrooms. I was happy to get my daily goal done, but it was exhausting and I was acutely aware I hadn't even done any real cleaning.

I happened upon the teaching of Maria Montessori. Among other things in her methodology, Maria taught that little children should be allowed practical life play. Her philosophy made perfect sense to me because of my own great experiences as a little girl, working alongside my grandma. I remembered my mother giving me a dust cloth and having me wipe down anything and everything. My children were at home, not in a Montessori school, so why play at life when life is real? Why not make every day a play day-work day combination?

I promptly bought child-sized tools for everything and let the children help out more than they had in the past. It became the job of the preschool age children to pour drinks and wipe the table. They used pint sized pitchers, a little bucket, sponges, and small wash cloths. Using a little broom and dust pan, a small child was assigned to sweep the floor under the table after lunch. Dish tubs became small laundry baskets so little children could put away their own clothes. Small baskets were used to walk around and gather up toys and put them away. I made more of an effort to teach them the habit of putting a toy away as soon as they were done playing with it. A positive environment complete with singing was a key factor in pulling this off. I had happy helpers and work was fun!

We're a family, we love each other, we take care of each other, we help each other.

The value of teamwork in home management became readily apparent. We divided up the areas of the house for each person to take care of. Everyone was on board because we talked about it as a family with a positive attitude, and each person, regardless of age, was made to feel a part of the family team.

Our encouraging words to each other were, "We're a family, we love each other, we take care of each other, we help each other." Family defined.

Many moms of today grew up with childhoods of simply busywork. We got up, rode the bus, went to school, rode the bus, did homework, ate supper, watched TV, went to bed, and did the same routine every day for years and years. Some of us led even more busy lives by being involved in every activity possible that took us away from home every evening and weekends—sports, dance, clubs, youth group, drama. Some of us had chores before and/or after school and on Saturdays. Some of us had moms who did all the work while we were gone. If the family is not at home, the house doesn't get messy and, honestly, the cleaning just doesn't take that long.

We tend to raise our children as we were raised and clean like our mothers cleaned. In my case it took only a few years for that system to fall apart at the seams; throw several more children with homeschooling into the mix, and the old system of mom doing all the housework breaks the system and breaks the mom. Are you burned out with school or housework? If so, don't throw in the towel! You can do this! Your family is a dynamic group of people with different strengths and weaknesses. You need to put all these people on the same team—the family team.

PLANNING

First, identify what is working and what is not in your home. Think through each aspect of your home life and schedule. If you need to, take a sample of three to four days, writing down what each member of the family is doing each hour during the day. Talk through, as a team, what is going on and what is needed. Brainstorm ideas on how to make a healthier, vibrant home where each person has reasonable responsibilities that contribute to the good of all.

THE FAMILY MEETING

Next, gather the whole family. Then, have your children help you make a list, perhaps on a white board or a large piece of paper, of all the responsibilities and duties necessary for taking care of the needs of the family. Some of these would include laundry, ironing, cooking, dishes, mopping, cleaning bathrooms, and so on. Make a pie chart or a graph or a similar visual aid to show the children that if everyone in the family takes some of the responsibility, everyone has a lighter load than if one person would try to do the whole thing.

You can even have a test run. Pick a section of the house and divide up the cleaning. Set the timer for five minutes. Have four people work for five minutes (one dusts, one sweeps or vacuums, one puts away odd items, and one wipes surfaces). When the timer goes off, everyone will marvel at what was accomplished in five minutes by four people instead of one person spending twenty minutes alone! When the children see how this works practically, their heads will be brimming with ideas!

Next, have ready a list of all the things that need done in each room of the house: daily, weekly, and monthly. Have each room's list on its own laminated paper or sheet in a protected sleeve. To start, you want the lists fairly simple, so that the tasks don't seem overwhelming.

Talk through the lists with the family so they understand what is expected. Let everyone know that each person needs to carry their own weight, and then ask for volunteers. When the volunteers are exhausted, you will cheerfully assign the rest of the duties.

Babies and toddlers of course, cannot clean by themselves, but they can learn by watching. Assign them to a buddy who can include the little ones in his work and have them do little, but important, things like pick up trash. Preschoolers can work very hard when supervised by cheerful older siblings. If the preschoolers are the oldest children in the house, then it is best that your preschoolers tag along with you in whatever you are doing. Show them what to do, and let them do the work with you. It will take longer to do the work, but it will pay big dividends down the road.

When you go into each room, show the children the paper that has listed the things that need done. Assign each item to the smallest person capable of doing each item. Teach this method to your big children that form a mini-team with little children. It might be easier for you or the big kids to do the work, but if you keep that up, the younger set will grow up being slackers, expecting everyone to do things for them. You don't want that!

It probably won't all sink in to them until you are actually coaching them through the work. The first few days and weeks will be challenging. Praise and reward children as you go. Challenge and motivate those who are struggling. Remember: this is a long-term investment!

Working alongside children of any age, encouraging and teaching them, is a wonderful way to get to know them better and makes them want to work harder and more diligently. They get a better picture of why they are doing what they are doing. Working alongside a loved one is fun, enjoyable, and doesn't seem like work at all. When work is done alone, it can be lonely and dull. Of course a lot of times work does need to be done alone and this is when they need to be taught to enjoy work for work's sake, to do it for the family, to do it heartily as to the Lord, to sing or whistle while they work, and to work quickly and efficiently in order to get it done. You can teach these things to them when you are working side-by-side. Start this when the children are little, and they will teach it to the next set of little children.

Some people like to work alone and are more productive and at peace with their work. Let them do it. In a family there are many variables and situations that give us options; be flexible.

JUST DO IT

Just Do It! Coined by Nike to sell shoes, this advertising slogan is so familiar that its message has almost become lost. But, really, that is what a lot of work boils down to. It's another thing that we need to teach our children.

Try not to yell, "Just do it!" Teach them that it's an attitude. It's determination and perseverance. Demonstrate it for them. No pity parties allowed. Set a good example. When you sigh while washing dishes, they will learn to do it also. Sometimes it takes great effort: you have to force yourself to defrost the deep freeze or gather the supplies to paint. Then once you're actually doing it, it flows and goes forward, and soon you're done and you realize that getting up the momentum to do it was far greater than the effort to do the task! The "Just Do It" attitude is what got the job started and gets it done.

FLEXIBILITY

Some days things just don't go according to plan. Sickness, weather, a late night, and unexpected needs are some of the things which call for an extra measure of flexibility. When this happens, just adjust! Change your plan, or take a break. Gather everyone together, offer some encouraging words, pray, take a nap, get a drink, have a snack, or read a story. Take the time needed to get everyone back on track physically, emotionally, and mentally!

Sometimes one person's area needs quick cleaning, such as when you see unexpected company driving down the lane. Then everybody must pitch in to do a quick tidy of the public area of the house, starting with the front door. We don't want the guests to trip over the accumulation that happens in everyday life. And then our guest needs a clean place to sit down. A quick tidy is something to practice so when it happens in reality, everybody knows what to do and how to do it fast. Whining, "But it's not my job" is unacceptable at any time because everybody should help each other but when doing a quick tidy, it's especially unacceptable. You don't have time when company is walking up to the house to go discipline the whiner, so prepare ahead of time with practice runs so that there is no whiner. A helpful saying that we have around our house is "We are a family, we love each other, we take care of each other, and we help each other."

YOUR
PERSONAL SPA

My neighbor and I were laughing about the odd and crazy things that life throws at a person. She made the comment that if she had to be committed to an institution, she wanted the one with a spa. We laughed even harder, but that comment got me thinking.

Everyday life is tough on a person. Why put off the spa for special occasions? We ought to be taking care of ourselves on a regular basis. Even the thought of a spa can evoke a dreaminess in our minds. A relaxing and peaceful environment, soothing sounds and music, soft and low voices, a fluffy robe, body and skin treatments, deep renewal and wholeness. Health, beauty, and refreshment for body and soul.

Having the ability to indulge in such a thing on any kind of regular basis was out of reach for me for a variety of reasons, but I could create it at home. I looked around and saw that it was definitely possible. I planned and gathered what I needed, investing in a new robe and bath salts. It wasn't a big effort, but more about the desire and determination to create an experience. To identify an issue and find a resolution.

After the creation of my in-home spa, I found I got better sleep and had a renewed energy for life. Just as I enjoyed the sunrise each morning, I now looked forward to a soothing experience at the end of each day. It became an evening ritual for me... a ritual of peace and renewal.

If you are like me, you probably leave your bedroom first thing in the morning and often don't return until you are ready to fall into bed at night! Maybe your bedroom has even become the storage area for all those things you have not had time to put away. But this is the sanctuary for you, a marital retreat where you are restored, refreshed, and re-energized to serve your family again. So, let's get going and turn your bedroom and bath into a personal, restorative spa!

We ought to be taking care of ourselves on a regular basis.

First up, your bathroom. Even if it's one you share with the rest of the family, you can claim it as a mom-retreat once a day and decorate for that. Collect ideas online or in magazines. I like to be creative but I'm not innovative. I use somebody else's ideas. Collect ideas, match them to your space and budget, and create your own personal spa.

HOW TO CLEAN A BATHROOM SUPER FAST!

First, take a big drink of water and maybe even a snack for energy—something healthy and energizing like a banana or apple. This is also an exercise workout, by the way.

Next, grab your kitchen timer. We're going to do a series of five-minute jobs.

While you're getting the timer, grab the dish soap and a rag. Next, get your window cleaner and a couple of paper towels, the toilet bowl cleaner, and the broom and dust pan. Ask one of your children to help carry the load. Ready, set, go! Fast as you can, complete this ugly task and never let the bathroom get this messy and dirty again!

1. First, fill the bathroom sink with hot water and squirt in your dish soap.

2. Squirt the toilet bowl with the cleaner, but don't swish it yet; let it soak.

3. Toss the dry rag up into corners of the bathroom to catch any cobwebs.

4. Pick up all the dirty laundry, the bath rugs, pull off the curtains and take it all to your laundry room. While you're there, throw the curtains in the washing machine.

5. Collect the trash, including any empty shampoo containers in your shower.

6. Sweep the floor and empty that into the trash, and then haul it out.

7. The five minutes should be up, and you might be panting with exertion. Open the window and take a big breath of fresh air.

8. Set the timer again for five minutes. Next is the second set.

9. Put away all the things that you have sitting around. And say to yourself five times, "I will put things where they belong. I will not leave them out to make a mess." (Next time you catch your children not putting something away, say it to them too.)

10. Take your wet rag and wipe the counters and any other level surfaces that have been collecting that sticky bathroom dust.

11. The third five-minute set will help the light shine in and around your bathroom.

12. Wet the rag and wipe around the windowsill, the casing, and the window.

13. Grab your window cleaner and wipe the window and mirrors.

14. That was easy, wasn't it? And doesn't it look brighter?

15. Rest for five minutes. Set the timer again for five minutes.

16. Does your sink water need changing? If so, do it.

17. Rinse out your rag well and give it a good wringing. You're going to spend this set dusting. Yes, you are going to use a wet rag to dust. That bathroom grime can be sticky, and it sometimes needs some help to get it off.

18. Wipe off nick-knacks and anything hanging on the walls (maybe remove them for your new decor plan?). Then move down and wipe the cabinets and the floorboards.

19. Rest for five minutes. This is the fifth five-minute set. Can you believe you let the bathroom get this bad? Yuck! Never again! This five-minute workout is for the shower and tub. You do not need a special cleaner.

20. What's on your shower walls? Soap. Get it wet and give it some elbow grease.

21. Five more minutes for the sink, toilet, and floor and then you're done!

22. The sink should be pretty clean by now, just wipe the faucets and the bowl so that no toothpaste is left glued on.

23. Next is the toilet. Swish and flush. Then wipe it from top to bottom. When you get to the bottom, keep on wiping, moving to the floor.

24. Wipe the floor all around the toilet, working your way backwards out towards the door.

You have just had an interval workout. There is no need to exercise today! Do some stretching and thinking now. How could this job be easier?

For starters, when things are not very dirty, they are easy to clean. It takes more time to clean up an ugly job than it does to maintain. Now I know your time is valuable to you. You would probably rather get your exercise some other way than cleaning the bathroom, wouldn't you? And walking into your clean and pretty bathroom would be like having your own personal spa, wouldn't it? Start thinking of this bathroom as if it were a spa made just for you.

To maintain it, do one cleaning job every time you go into your bathroom. Make it a lifelong habit.

Here are a couple more.

Every time you wash your hands, wipe down the sink and counter. Keep a towel for this purpose under the sink. When you take a shower, do a quick wipe of the shower walls. It's an easy thing; the hard part is *starting* the habit. To help you with the thinking process of starting the new habit of keeping your bathroom clean, write down every task that we just did. Post this list on your mirror and every time you are in the bathroom, do one task. Pretty soon, you won't have to look at the list on the mirror; you'll just automatically be doing the work.

Remember all the things I had you grab and carry to your bathroom? Put those in a bucket under the sink. Put a small broom and dustpan in a nearby closet or cupboard. Put together one set of cleaning tools for each bathroom. If the tools are accessible, you will be more apt to use them.

CREATE A SPA ATMOSPHERE

Take an honest look at your spa. You're going to be spending time in there every day anyway, so make it a place where you will be able to unwind from the day. There is something about sitting in warm water that causes your muscles to relax. When the house is quiet and we are relaxed, we can contemplate, dream, reflect, and just be.

How can you make this room be that place you go to at the end of the day to unwind? How can you make this room more beautiful? What is your favorite color? What color would you like to be surrounded by while taking a leisurely bath? Think about bathrooms you've seen and appreciated and ask, "Can I do something similar here?" Make a list and a plan to make your bathroom more personal and spa-like. It can be as simple as a bud vase and some new bath soap. Do you have a pretty nightgown to wear after you've lathered your skin with lotion?

So you think a spa bath sounds like a luxury you can't manage in this stage of parenting life? You're wrong. You can do it every night. Let me tell you how. First, tuck your children into bed (Remember: you've been working on a consistent bedtime routine.), feed the baby and put him to bed.

- ☐ Start the tub.

- ☐ Straighten the bathroom, do a quick cleaning job, and light the candles.

- ☐ Lay out your night clothes and your clothes for tomorrow.

- ☐ Get a drink to sip while you soak: a glass of water or wine, a cup of herbal tea or whatever suits your fancy.

- ☐ Wash and soak until the water starts to cool and get out before you get cold (fifteen minutes or so).

- ☐ Drain the water; comb hair, brush teeth, apply lotion, put on nightclothes.

- ☐ Rinse the tub and straighten the bathroom.

- ☐ Go to bed.

Do you see that it doesn't take much longer to add a bath to your bedtime routine? I promise that you will go to bed much more relaxed, you will fall asleep more quickly, and sleep better.

If you're a morning shower person, then keep on with that if you want. The nighttime bath is about more than getting clean. Its purpose is to relax and rejuvenate.

Now you will never be embarrassed about your bathroom again because you keep it nice with one cleaning job each time you go in. It has become a retreat where you will want to spend time. During the day when you get tired or frustrated, you will remember that tonight you will return to your spa and enjoy a soak in your tub, surrounded by candles. A fresh and fluffy towel is waiting for you as well as some lotion to rub onto your tired feet.

You no longer have a grungy mess—you have a spa. Enjoy!

YOUR BEDROOM

In a perfect world our bedrooms are only for parents; they are not also the home office, storage room, laundry station, or sewing room. So first let's do some thinking: are there other places in the home for these things? Fix that problem first, unless you just have to accept that it is what it is and make the best of it. Remove and find places for items that don't belong in the bedroom.

Clean the bedding and move the bed to the best place in the room for it. It is the largest piece of furniture so placing it and making it beautiful will be the most dramatic change. Perhaps it is time for new bedding—something new and different.

Deep clean around the bedroom, moving left to right and top to bottom. Take a good look and think about paint. Would that freshen up your room? Or perhaps you love the color it is right now. Look at Pinterest pictures and identify what you like best and how you can recreate the look you like in your own room.

If you have a baby in your room, put the baby things in order and where they are easy to get to at night.

If you have older children who come in for late night talks, set a comfy chair in an appropriate place.

Place bedside tables, lamps, and the things you like best to do before sleep on your nightstand. Bible, books, magazines, music? Nothing at all? Think about things that help you to relax and give you a restful time before sleep and create your bedroom to reflect you and your needs.

DRESS FOR SUCCESS

It was Sunday morning and again, I didn't know what to wear. Everyone was fed and dressed but me, and I was standing in my closet crying. What I wanted to wear didn't fit, and I was sick to death of wearing the things that did fit. There was a really cute sweater but nothing to match it.

I needed a plan, a better strategy. I was sick and tired of the same dilemma every week; sick of the dilemma, but especially how it made me feel. I decided I needed to go to the mall come what may, even with my little flock of children along.

Going to the mall with children called for its own strategy, so I needed to increase my efficiency and determine which stores could potentially help with my Sunday morning problem. That thought led me to the knowledge that some stores were more suitable for everyday wear for my lifestyle, and that really, only a couple would be helpful for my Sunday morning clothes.

All of these thoughts had me running to my closet and throwing clothes into a trash bag or a give-away box. I set a day for my shopping time and made a list of needs. Somehow I had been shopping for my fast-growing children but not myself, for far too long. What size did I need to buy? I gritted my teeth and tried on clothes from my closet, further paring down my wardrobe or putting items in storage for another season.

Working through my closet before my shopping trip gave me the idea of having clothes for certain days. Then I wouldn't have to think about what to wear, but it would still look nice and be appropriate. I was done with the everyday frumpy and the Sunday morning distress.

With my little children in tow, I landed in a couple of stores for suitable everyday clothes that would stand up to my life, and another that gave me options for Sundays. I learned to stop in at these stores every month or so, because the things I liked at the front of the store would generally be on sale in the back within weeks, and it made my shopping fast, easy, and affordable. Having an organized closet and shopping plan made all the difference, and resolved an ongoing problem that was dragging me down.

FIRST, GET DRESSED

Every mom has had them—those days when you don't get dressed until the baby goes down for his morning nap. Or a day when one mess or mini-crisis after another results in your realizing that it is two o'clock and you haven't brushed your teeth yet.

Yes, some days just stink. Put everybody in a safe place, go back to your bedroom, and start the day over. Get dressed, wash your face, brush your teeth, brush your hair, make yourself look presentable. Look in the mirror and smile; laugh a little at yourself—there are worse things! Pray for wisdom, strength, and courage.

Gather your children, smile at them, and read a story. Put on some cheerful music, then sit them at the table to color, and put supper together. Help the children put away their coloring projects, and straighten the house together.

Tonight, take a bath and go to bed early, but before you go to bed, lay out your clothes for the next day. Get dressed as soon as your feet hit the floor in the morning. You'll have a better day!

WHAT NOT TO WEAR

Moms bend over a lot to help their little children zip a jacket, pick up a pacifier, whisper instructions in a small ear, and do a hundred other things. There are a few clothing items that just won't work with those kind of situations. Wide neck blouses are out for you. Everything stays in place just fine until a squirmy baby starts to climb up your neck using the neckline of your shirt for a toe hold. Get the picture? And midline shirts creep up when you bend over, exposing your backside and climb up when you redo your pony tail. Avoid snap-up shirts; that's right: the children will unsnap them. And the same with zipper sweaters. Lord, have mercy. Here's a good rule of thumb: always wear camisoles.

Not all skirts are created equal. When shopping, choose longer skirts. On a windy day a loose swishy skirt that might have been long enough without a breeze will certainly blow up while you are holding little hands, and God didn't give us a hold-the-skirt-down hand. Wrap-around skirts fall open when you sit down, as do skirts with a walking slit up the front. This is not a huge problem if your hands are free to deftly pull yourself together, but when you are also handling a couple of little children, frustration mounts. For your life with little children, it's just best to leave those skirts on the NO list. Keep it simple, easy, and avoid clothing frustrations.

Save yourself some grief and get sensible shoes.

Heels can be dangerous to wear while carrying babies and children, are not good for your feet or back, and really what is their practical purpose? Save yourself some grief and get sensible shoes. Check the tread of the shoes you buy; slick-bottomed shoes are . . . slick. You will fall on your bum and drop your baby. There are plenty of stylish shoes that will not damage your body or cause you to accidentally hurt your children. The key is deliberate thought into clothing for real life.

WHAT TO WEAR

When I was a young mom, I wore whatever was comfortable or whatever looked cute on the mannequin. The mannequin or catalog model was not shown bending over picking up a toddler. When you are trying clothes on, move around and make sure that you can maneuver in different positions and not show the whole world what you'd rather not show them.

Mom-smart clothes should be easily cleaned. The blouse that has to be dry-cleaned is better suited for a night out with your husband than for Sunday. It seems that Sunday, when you want to look your best, is the day that you get spit up on, snot rubbed on your shoulder, and the baby has the biggest blow-out diaper of the week. Clothing that does not let your skin breathe is a poor choice, for motherhood is often hard, sweaty work. Long sleeves get wet and in the way while you bathe children, wash dishes, and wipe counters. An apron is very handy in the kitchen.

Clothes to wear while nursing can be tricky to find. Button-down shirts or dresses paired with a camisole work well and were my go-to. Cut strategically-placed, lengthwise nursing slits in the camisole so that you don't need to pull it up.

Nursing covers are handy in certain situations. Numerous styles can be found online or you can make your own. Choose lightweight fabric for the summer and warm flannel for the winter. When the baby starts to wave his hands around and be grabby, tuck the bottom of the cover between his head and your arm to keep his arm inside. Social babies don't nurse well, if their view is covered they will eat fast and efficiently.

I am of the camp that thinks that a baby should be able to matter-of-factly eat anywhere. Our over-sexed society is sick and wrong to be offended at a nursing mom. Breasts were made to feed babies the perfect food. Nursing babies are a fact of life. It is sad that people have not grown up around and are not accustomed to babies or, specifically, breastfed babies. Historically speaking, the last fifty years of objectifying breasts is offensive. That said, we need to be kind when we are obviously causing someone to be uncomfortable. You can choose a part of the room that is not front and center, you can use a nursing cover, and your clothing choices should enable you to nurse your baby anywhere. I found the newborn to be the most difficult to nurse in public. They need extra support and help and it's tricky to find a comfortable spot to make it easy for mom and baby. It is best for the newborn and post-partum mom to simply stay home as much as possible to bond, connect, and live stress-free. I love the idea of a baby-moon.

Breast pads are essential to avoid milk spots on your clothes. Keep a hefty supply on hand. Washable pads are a good investment. My favorite kind are a special soft wool. For a really inexpensive nursing pad, take panty liners and cut them in half.

AVOIDING FRUMP

We all detest the idea of being frumpy. Clothing style is a very personal choice. It is an expression of our unique personalities, whether they are casual, sophisticated, artsy, sporty, or scholarly. Some love the details of trims and appliqués; others prefer belts, bags, and shoes. Frumpy happens to moms because their body size goes up and down with pregnancy and nursing without their clothing sizes being updated accordingly.

At any given time, we have four sizes of clothes in our closet and know better than to purge them because we are going to wear one of those sizes sometime in the next year. When we have four sizes of clothing in our closet, we inadvertently wear the wrong size with another piece that may or may not be the wrong size, producing a sloppy look. Add to that the fact that an item doesn't look quite as good as it did before being stretched out with pregnancy, a small spit up stain on the shoulder, and an old jelly stain on the sleeve.

Fact: Our bodies change and they are not the bodies of models. But they are AMAZING!

Don't cry! We can plan for this and avoid frustration. It starts with being honest about our bodies. Yes, your size goes up and down with pregnancy, post-partum, nursing to nine months, nursing beyond nine months, nursing the toddler, and nursing the toddler and being pregnant.

Fact: Our bodies change and they are not the bodies of models. But they are AMAZING! Think about what your body does in bringing life into the world!

Fact: We each have our personal clothing style.

Fact: Our life at home is hard on clothes.

Dresses are more forgiving in sizes, going up and down and still looking good. Ill-fitting knit clothes that twist are bad news and cling in places we don't want them to cling. Tunic-type shirts and peasant blouses hide the mommy tummy and let it grow when you are pregnant, prolonging the need to get out the maternity shirts. Yes, ill-mannered people will assume or ask if you are pregnant, but after having a baby every other year, don't they do that anyway? Let them be and carry on. Just be sure your blouse is attractive and fits your shoulders. When you wear something flowy on the top, pair it with something slimming on the bottom to avoid the frumpy look.

Small print causes large people to look larger. Dark colors make a person look slimmer. Long skirts and dresses make a person look taller and thinner. Only the very thin can wear gathered waists, as they make the midsection look bulky. To help avoid the problem of wearing the wrong size, keep clothes that do not fit you in storage or in the back of your closet so that they are not within your easy reach. Perhaps use different colored hangers or turn the hanger around backwards for the clothes that are not your current size.

If you are unsure what style expresses yourself best, then order a selection of catalogs and/or window shop brand stores at an outlet mall. Take note of brand names, and pick one that suits your unique taste. We're all different, so what you like, your girlfriend or sister might not. You will probably find your tastes change over time or your favorite stores might change their styles away from what you appreciated. By choosing a store or brand name or signature line of clothes to shop from, you will find your closet getting a unified look where items coordinate and work together in a pleasing manner. It makes shopping more efficient and simplifies life.

Buy good quality fabrics with strong seams to stand the test of time. When buying knit shirts, get ones with seams on the sides to avoid twisting. When working at home, wear clothes that hide stains and are easy to clean. Whites are a mistake unless you buy them for your under layer. And if you are wearing clothes you are afraid of staining, you will avoid cleaning or kitchen work. Prints hide stains. Denim, of course, is heavy duty but not often feminine. Workout clothes or yoga pants are comfortable but are typically not made to stand up to the test of time and look bad fast. Sweaters are warm but sometimes the bulk can be confining. Cardigans open easily and are thus handy for nursing, and are easier to slip on and off. Lightweight cardigans with three-quarter sleeves are my personal favorite. Wool is warm but needs special care, and whatever requires special care doesn't usually get it when life gets busy. Matching shoe, belt and handbag colors gives a together look to your outfit.

Good posture makes anything look better so walk tall; lift your shoulders up, pull them back, and relax to down, still keeping the shoulders back. And smile from the eyes. Spread God's love to all you meet. Each person you meet is a human being, a person created in the image of God. Look past the fact that they are different than you; their story is not yours, their style is not yours. Be full of grace and love for those you meet that do not look like you.

CLOSET ORGANIZATION

Your closet probably contains the following categories of items: winter, summer, everyday clothes, going-out clothes, workout clothes, Sunday clothes, maternity clothes, post-partum clothes, nursing-baby clothes, losing-the-baby-weight clothes, lost-the-nursing-bosom clothes, early pregnancy clothes (which might be the same as the post-partum clothes). Whew!

The task of organizing this mess involves five steps:

1. Collect all the clothes in season that fit you right now. Put the things you hate and never wear into the give-away box. Put the rest in the main part of your closet.

2. If Step 1 did not involve maternity clothes, collect them and put them into a box. Do not keep the maternity clothes you never wear, put them into the give-away box.

3. Sort the rest of the clothes by size and put them in boxes, one box for each size.

4. Sort through the socks, underwear, and nightclothes, discarding what you never wear.

5. Each time the season changes or your size goes up or down, do this task again keeping only what fits in your closet.

PLANNING WHAT TO WEAR

A large part of this book is about planning, organizing, and making your life more efficient so that you can spend more time loving your family and doing things that bless those around you. I am going to propose an idea that free spirits might not appreciate. That's OK, you don't have to do it, and the world will still go around. Some of you will really appreciate it and find it an effective tool to make your days go better. I'm sure that there will be people in the middle who will take this task partway but not fully, and that's OK too. We are unique and have different personalities and styles. This task will help you with your week's work and make your mornings flow better. You will sleep better knowing that you have a plan for the first part of the morning that will make your day go more smoothly. Yes, you can do this task and it will bring peace not only to your mornings, but to your Laundry Day. And not only your Laundry Day but also your closet. Organized clothes make for more orderly laundry days and a thinned-down closet.

Here's what I suggest that you do: plan each day's clothes for the day of the week. An outfit for Laundry Day, Kitchen Day, Town Day, Office Day, Cleaning Day, Gardening Day, and the Lord's Day.

If you think about it, you might already have clothes that you wear for cleaning, when you leave the house, when you go out for dinner, or to church. Take it a step further and choose an outfit for each day of the week. If you really enjoy clothes or are a free spirit, then you might want to choose two or three outfits for each day.

Match the clothes for the day's work. For Cleaning Day choose clothes that will work well for cleaning: clothes that are comfortable to move in, that won't show dirt. For Kitchen Day choose an outfit that goes well with your favorite heavy duty apron. For Office Day, choose clothes that make you feel business-like, something that will put you in the frame of mind for taking care of expenses, numbers, pencil pushing, and phone calls. Think about your week, look at your clothes, and organize them by what you do each day of the week.

Make them complete with accessories and an idea of what shoes to wear with each if you have to leave the house. This is your signature look.

This task should have pruned out more of your clothes to put in the give-away box. Now you know what you are wearing each morning when you get up. You will avoid the frumpy look by having given thought and planning to your clothes. You will be mentally prepared for the work of the day by knowing what you will wear.

PART TWO

YOUR HOME MANAGEMENT BOOK

The purpose of creating a Home Management Book is to help you manage your new life of habits. When you don't know what to do next, check your Home Management Book; it will tell you. It is for those days when you are learning new habits, it is for the day after a sleepless night, and it is for your husband and children when you are unavailable. It is the protocol for how your house functions. It helps you know what to do next.

Each component of the day listed here is detailed in further chapters. This chapter provides a broad overview of the system.

THE TOOLS AND HOW TO USE THEM

You will need the following items:

- ☐ A three-ring-binder

- ☐ 8 ½ x 11 inch paper

- ☐ Page protectors

- ☐ Sticky notes

- ☐ A pencil

If you want to build this with a day planner that you're already using or with an unused planner sitting on your shelf, that is great. However, I think it is best to make your own. You can be far more creative and will be better able to personalize it for your life, your family, and your home. Your life is not like my life, give thought to how you live, how you desire to live, and then start moving in that direction, one step at a time.

When we move carefully and methodically, one-step at a time, our new habits become stronger parts of our lives.

If your current life is crazy-busy and you are overwhelmed, do not worry about working on this book, except for small steps at a time on your Office Day (See chapter 20.). Put the components of your home management book together over time. Start *using* what you have built right away, but put it together slowly and deliberately. When we move carefully and methodically, one-step at a time, our new habits become stronger parts of our lives.

Once you get this in motion, you can print your papers out from the computer or just do some writing on the paper at first and then organize it better later. You need page protectors because PB&J-fingered children and coffee spills. You will use the sticky notes on the pages for adjustments as you go. Later, pull out these pages and redo them.

Take seven sheets of paper and, at the top of each, put the name of a day of the week. We are going to set up our household management like our grandmothers before us did. Monday is Laundry Day, for example.

There is beauty in order and rhythm. When we know what to do when, and our families know what to do when, it brings security, peace, and comfort. A secure and happy family is true beauty. If the order of days does not suit your family's life, then arrange your days according to your family situation.

Why set up days of the week? Can't I just see the work and do it? Sure! However, there are many overwhelming days when we don't know where to start. We get distracted, starting one task, and halfway through, move to another and then another. When the day ends, we look around and see several things started and not finished.

A Home Management Book builds efficiency into the work. The more efficient home management systems are, the more smoothly life flows. Planning ahead keeps things simple.

You know those embroidered towels that you see on estate sales and in antique stores? Our grandmothers and the mothers before them knew the value of ordering their work, and though they had fewer tools at their disposal than we do now, they accomplished more than most women do today. What has happened in the last couple of generations? In the industrial revolution women began to be blessed with an array of tools to free their time to be more efficient. One of the results was that the majority of women lost the home and family skills that were once commonplace among homemakers. The accumulated homekeeping knowledge of many generations didn't get passed on because there was less physical work and children were in school for longer days and for more years.

Significantly, God did not create everything in the universe in one day. He took six days to do it in an orderly manner. He divided the creative work among the first six days of the week, focusing on creating specific parts of the universe and specific animal kinds on specific days. Then God rested on the seventh day. He didn't have to do it like this, but he did, and it sets a pattern for us to do the same. Focusing on one area of the home on a weekly basis keeps it under control. We are not so tempted to postpone certain housekeeping tasks forever when we have a day set aside to tackle them specifically.

Your days will not always go according to your schedule. Learn to see interruptions as a blessing from God. Roll with it, smile, and look for the silver lining in the black cloud. When you have an interruption, your Home Management Book gives you a reference point to return to in managing your home. When you are done with the interruption, go back to your reference point and do the next thing. With a plan in hand, you work with direction and manage your home in an orderly manner.

MONDAY IS LAUNDRY DAY

Commit this day to your laundry equipment. Start the day as soon as you can—even get up earlier than normal—and set the timer for switching your loads. Fold as soon as you pull the clothes out of the dryer. Between loads devote some time to mending and ironing, chores that can be done near your children so that you are available to them.

TUESDAY IS KITCHEN DAY

Commit this day to your kitchen. Use this day for extra baking, making yogurt, starting sprouts, fixing freezer meals. Also, spend some time cleaning in the kitchen. Remove the clutter and wipe the counters. Clean out the refrigerator. If you do this every week, it is a ten-minute job and never gets disgusting. Organize your cupboard of plastic containers. Clean and organize one drawer, one cupboard, and one pantry shelf, working through your kitchen as the weeks go by. This might sound like a lot of work that will take enormous amounts of time, but actually, it is not so bad. Use your timer and see how long it really takes! If you have big kids, give each one a task and have them race each other or the clock. You don't need to deep clean your entire kitchen every week, just a small area every week will keep it up.

WEDNESDAY IS OFFICE DAY

On this day, work on fine tuning your Home Management Book, plan menus and grocery lists, balance the checkbook, pay bills, file papers, and plan vacation. If you need to make phone calls, do it on Office Day. Schedule an appointment with each child to review schoolwork and chores, and to do some extra connecting. Clean and organize one drawer, cupboard, or shelf in your office area.

THURSDAY IS TOWN DAY

Schedule appointments and music lessons as much as possible to all occur on one day. Do your shopping on this day. Plan your driving route and the route in each store ahead of time. Work on speed and efficiency. If you have little children, try to do all of your errands right after breakfast when they are freshest, and get home before lunch and naptime.

FRIDAY IS CLEANING DAY

During your daily Afternoon Chore Time, add vacuuming, dusting, and some Deep Cleaning work. When Afternoon Chore Time happens every day, the house stays picked up. Minimize the clutter, and the house is much easier to dust and vacuum. After the whole house is dusted and vacuumed, then do Deep Cleaning in one area. By rotating the Deep Cleaning areas through the month, each area gets a regular deep cleaning.

SATURDAY IS GARDENING DAY

Work in your flower and vegetable beds, mow, pick up the yard, and sweep the deck on Gardening Day. In winter, clean the walks, plan your gardens, and order seeds. Clean your vehicles and the garage. Once again, if your family does these jobs weekly, they never become huge ugly monsters. Dedicate time in the day to prepare for the Lord's Day so that Sunday is restful. Lay out clothes and shoes. Pack the diaper bag. Put food into slow cookers and then the slow cookers into the refrigerator overnight. Make the salad.

SUNDAY IS THE LORD'S DAY

Rest in the Lord. Enjoy your family and friends. Relax.

YOUR MORNING ROUTINE

Write at the top of each page your Morning Routine, every little bit of it. If you are using your computer, copy and paste it on the top of each page. You will do this routine every morning for the rest of your life; it will become an ingrained habit, much like brushing your teeth. Of course, at some point, you might decide you need to drop a habit, or add a new one, but for the most part, you need to focus on the same routine every day.

YOUR EVENING ROUTINE

At the bottom of each page, put your Evening Routine: every little thing that you need to do before going to sleep. Writing down the details of your Evening Routine helps establish them and aids tremendously in having a good morning.

MEAL TIME ROUTINES

In the middle of each page, put the Noon Hour and towards the bottom, the Dinner Hour. Your routine in these hours include Table Chores.

Establish habits that go with meals. Write Meal Routines and Table Chores big and bold on a poster in your kitchen to help your family master the new habits you have established. If they don't remember what a chore involves, you can direct them to the poster.

THE REST OF YOUR DAY

Write down the order of activities you want your family to do during the day. This will be determined by the age of your children. A family of children under the age of eight will have a very different day than a family of elementary and young adults or a single person. A family that includes all three age groups and a baby will have another schedule. I use the term schedule lightly; we need to be flexible and roll with whatever the day throws at us. An Order of Events to follow is a better description. Put the least important things at the end of the schedule so that it is not a crisis if you drop it.

A few things you will want to include are:

Table time for homeschool families

Do this after the breakfast table chores are done and before everyone starts going their own direction. Include Bible Study, reciting memory work and catechism, practicing reading, learning manners, and other group activities that need to be done at the table.

Work on phonics with your nonreader

Spending fifteen minutes a day with a preschooler and/or early elementary age child goes a long way toward the goal of reading.

Make it fun and break it up with reading an easy-reader on alternate days.

One hour of Quiet Time

You need a break to nap, read, write, and think, and the children need to learn to be quiet and do something alone for a while. The children will learn self-discipline and respect for others during Quiet Time. The little children will get their well-earned nap.

Read-aloud Time

At our house, this is everyone's favorite part of the day. I find it best to do it after Quiet Time so that I don't fall asleep reading! We have had seasons when it is done right before lunch or in the evening. Do what works for your family.

Afternoon Chore Time

Your family may choose to do chores at a different time of day or break it into two separate times. It's important for our family to do a serious house pickup time before Dad comes home from work. Those who are gone during the day like to come home to a haven of peace and harmony and to the smell of supper in the air. When you are at home, you might not notice the disarray and clutter that accumulate during the day's activities. However, it can look like a picture of chaos to fresh eyes! Create a respite from the world for the family and set the stage for a pleasant evening.

LAUNDRY DAY

Do you have a Laundry Monster living in your home? Do dirty clothes grow mold and mildew in your hampers? Do your children have dirty clothes mixed with clean clothes on the floor of their bedrooms? Are there huge heaps piled around your washer and dryer? Believe me—I've been in that spot in the past and still have the battle with the monster when the rest of life crowds out the regular duties of home. Yet one sure thing will keep the Laundry Monster from growing any larger than a yipping dog. Assign a day of the week to laundry. In our house, it is Monday.

MANAGE THE MONSTER

Add a daily plan of Laundry Day to your Home Management Book. Doing this helps to focus effort and put a big dent in the never-ending job of laundry.

When I had only a few small children, laundry had the potential to depress me. Yet those days were nothing compared to the amount that can pile up in a heartbeat in the days I had with nine children and one farmer husband, including three adult-sized people who seem to delight in seeing how much manure they could cake on their clothes. Yuck. If it's not manure, then it's grease and oil from the shop. The next day it might be dried-on cement. Add to that a passel of girls who like to change clothes as the mood strikes throughout the day (we're working on that), young children who seem to *wear* food rather than *eat* it, and a peanut-butter-and-honey-smeared toddler. And don't forget the baby with regular dirty diapers and banana gunk!

I have seen the heap under our clothes chute nearly as tall as I am and I say aloud, "How can this be? We *just* did laundry?!" I think "Laundry Monster" is a mild term in this situation—"Monumental Massive Mega Mammoth Monster" seems more appropriate. I'm not exaggerating. I laugh at my old self who used to get so despondent over five measly loads waiting to be done. Perspective is everything.

You tame the beast and your beastly attitude by making a commitment to your laundry. Act as if you are joined with the washer and dryer. They are your new best friends. You will not leave them nor forsake them all the day long. This is an important point that I believe is the key to managing your family's laundry. It changed my life.

You tame the beast and your beastly attitude by making a commitment to your laundry.

Early in the morning—first thing, before coffee!—meet with the washer and dryer. Feed them their first loads. Set the timer and clip it to yourself; tie it with a ribbon or a shoelace around your neck, stick it in your pocket, or duct-tape it to your wrist! Time your loads, as some will dry faster than others, and adjust your timer accordingly. The point here is that as soon as your timer goes off, you run—yes, you are also exercising—to the washer and dryer and take care of the laundry. You will switch loads and fold clothes each time the timer beeps.

When you are done folding a load, look around and ask, "What can I do to make this area look nicer?" Wipe the laundry equipment, sweep the floor, catch the cobwebs—these are three good ways to improve the cleanliness of your washroom. Is there clutter collecting on top of the washer and dryer? Put it in its proper place. What can you do to keep clutter from collecting there? How about a little basket for all the things that people leave in their pockets? If you do one little clean-up chore after each load, the room will stay clean. Between loads, work on mending and ironing. Take these two tasks to the same room the children are working in.

How do you hold a Laundry Day and homeschool? When you leave the room where the children are working, instruct them to keep working and try to figure things out for themselves. When you return, praise them for their diligent work, help them with their questions, and if misbehaviors occur, hand out consequences. Use Laundry Day to wean your children from needing your constant instruction and handholding. They need to be able to focus and learn how to learn something for themselves, for they will not have you teaching them their whole lives. Teach them to be independent learners.

The discipline to be self-teaching is an important skill they need to have for successful adult life. Laundry Day helps facilitate this. There have been times when I have had to attach a child to me because he couldn't behave without me for even a second. I take a long soft strip of knit material and tie it to the little child's wrist and to my own. When a child is attached to me, I give him work to do with me. The attached child also gets lots of love and instruction.

When the children are old enough to help more, have them take turns switching loads, folding, and doing a clean-up chore. Start with the oldest and run down the line of children. When it comes time for the little children's turn, go with them and teach them how to run the equipment. Use a permanent marker to mark the most commonly-used settings on the equipment. For the older children who are able to do laundry alone, make a big poster explaining how much soap, water, specific temperatures for certain loads, clean-up chores to do, and whatever else your particular laundry situation calls for. Make a stain treatment book available for them in the laundry area.

How old are your laundry helpers? This will depend on your unique family, house, and laundry equipment. Some of my children were very helpful in using the equipment at ages seven to ten. Little children who know colors can sort and switch loads. When each member contributes to the good of the family, he or she builds self-worth and confidence while learning a lifelong chore. This is education.

Anything less than a full load is not acceptable in my house! A large family makes a lot of laundry, and many hands make light work. Fill the machine up for the good of all. Additionally, it is a better use of resources.

Inspect what you expect.

Part the regular Laundry Day includes the chore of putting things where they belong. Every morning of the week, dirty laundry goes to the laundry room or is sorted into hampers. Learning this habit early and carrying it through life is for their good.

This means self-discipline on your part in checking up on them regularly: inspect what you expect. Make it a habit of yours to take a house tour with the little children every morning. You have to keep doing this, or things will slide into mess, and then you'll have the Laundry Monster taking up residence again.

Make a five-minute bedroom pickup part of their morning routine to keep the laundry off the floor. Clean laundry needs to be in drawers, on shelves, or hung up. When all you have is Littles, you will need to do this with them. Talk to them about what you are doing and why you are doing it. Hand them the laundry to put in the basket or throw down the laundry chute. Make laundry a fun game as you identify colors, count items, and so on. Help your children to lay the clean clothes on the shelves or hang them up. This teaches them order and organization. Of course, it would be faster to do it yourself at first, but your end goal is self-sufficient, self-disciplined adults, and it starts with these baby steps. It can be hard, but the payoff will be great.

When these things are not done, the result will be a huge laundry monster that seems to have the ability to eat the house alive. The other result: You will not be blessing your children with the ability to care for themselves if you don't teach them responsibility when they're young, and they will grow up to be slovenly adults.

On Laundry Day, your goal is to do as many loads of laundry as possible until it is time for your Late Afternoon Chore Routine. Part of that routine on Laundry Day is collecting full baskets of folded clothing, putting clothes away, *and* bringing the basket back to the laundry area. If you have older children, they can do these things either instead of you or with you. If you have all little children, then make an effort to find little baskets or plastic dishpans they can use to carry their own clothes.

If you are a morning person and love to see clothes waving on the line, then make it a goal to have all of your loads of wash flying in the breeze by noon. We save a step and fold our clothes directly off the line into baskets. Doing this outside gives you exercise in bending and stretching, gets fresh air into your lungs, and a bit of sunshine for Vitamin D. It is also a beautiful thing to hear the birds singing and the children playing nearby. If you have a baby, take him out with you on a blanket while you take down the laundry.

It is easier and more enjoyable to do laundry when the whole setup—from clothing storage to cleaning and folding—is efficient. Efficiency saves you time, and we all appreciate more time. The specific steps to make your laundry and clothing system reach maximum efficiency will vary, depending on the house you live in. What works for one will not necessarily work for another. Ask for ideas from others. Browse through the laundry, shelving, and storage aisles of home stores to look for solutions to improve your laundry workflow.

At one time our laundry set-up was in the unfinished part of our basement. Across one side of the room, we hung a one-inch pipe for hanging shirts, drip-dry clothes, and out-of-season coats, jackets, and snow pants. We put a laundry chute from the second story, through the first floor mudroom, that emptied beside the laundry equipment in the basement. The laundry chute was an 8-inch PVC pipe. The laundry chute really helped keep dirty laundry from lying around the main floor and the second story (yes, I have people who take off socks and leave them lying about).

In this Laundry Room, we had big shelves with large clear plastic containers of out-of-season clothing and sizes that weren't currently being worn. I save only the best clothes from one season or child to the next. I have discovered that my perception at the end of a season is not that great. I think something is nice just because it was at the beginning of the season. I have to be very strict with myself when putting clothes into storage. There's not room to keep everything and keep track of it. Keeping only the nicest things saves time, effort, and prevents children from wearing bedraggled clothes.

When you begin ironing and mending on Laundry Day, you won't likely knock out the whole stack at once, yet consistency is the key to success. On Monday, iron for a certain amount of time (I love the timer!), then mend for a certain amount of time. After a few weeks of this, you will be caught up on your ironing and mending. If you stay disciplined to committing Monday as Laundry Day, you will stay caught up.

It is helpful to have the members of your family learn to take their clothes off right side out, to unball socks, and to remove layers of clothing from each other. Sometimes gentle reminders are all it takes, but there are times when the consistently-guilty culprit needs to be brought to the scene of the crime and instructed to undo their dirty laundry themselves. Explain to the family that laundry in this state does not come clean, and show them an example of the balled-up sock that is still filthy after being washed and dried. Showing the "why" of certain things we do helps to reinforce the "what" and "how."

Start this when they are little so that it will carry on when they are older. Explain to them that keeping their laundry right side out is being considerate to others and simply good manners. Teach them this when they are little when you are undressing them for their bath. You'll be glad you did later in life!

FOUR BY FOUR

Having a regular Laundry Day will be a big help in keeping the laundry under control but, of course, laundry occurs all the time. As soon as eleven people change clothes at the end of each day, there are three new loads. Add in baby laundry, towels, and sheets, and the laundry will about bring you to tears. But don't let the Laundry Monster win! Keep the upper hand by having a daily goal for laundry in addition to keeping a Laundry Day.

Our goal is Four Loads by Four. In the summer when we get up with the sun and hang out laundry, the goal is Four Loads by Noon. I love it when I have a load on the line before breakfast. Some weeks we do well to keep loads going each day, and because of our daily goal of four by four, we get a light day for Laundry Day! Some weeks we are especially busy, and our daily goals aren't reached, which makes Laundry Day another battle to be won with the Laundry Monster.

I LOVE TO DO LAUNDRY

This might be a very strange and foreign thought, but *learn to love doing laundry*. Replace all the bad feelings and ugly thoughts with Scripture and God-pleasing thoughts. Do the laundry *as unto the Lord*. You wouldn't complain about doing God's laundry, would you?!

Less than a hundred years ago, women were still standing over a fire, stirring their boiling clothes. I once heard a story of a mother who died from the burns sustained when her dress caught fire on

Wash Day. Even today there are more women around the world who do their wash by hand than have a machine. Live gratefully. We have it easy by comparison—we throw the wash in a machine and walk away. In addition, we have easy access to so many beautiful and comfortable clothes compared to those who came before us.

Take care of the blessing God has given your family! Thank him for each person whose laundry passes through your hands. Thank him for the sun and breeze. Thank him for the clouds that bring rain. Thank him for soap and clear water. Thank him for the day he made and blessed you with. Thank him for strength for the tasks ahead.

LAUNDRY TIPS

- ☐ Time how long it takes to fold a load. You will be pleasantly surprised!

- ☐ Buy some kind of laundry stain treatment that can be applied up to a week before washing. Keep it handy and use it on clothes before they land in the dirty basket. Keep it in each bathroom to be used when the clothes are taken off. Teach your family to use it.

- ☐ Put bibs on little children while they eat.

- ☐ Never buy white shirts, pants, or dresses for your children. If you do, do not let them eat and play while wearing them!

- ☐ Always read labels and follow instructions. Teach your helpers to do this also.

- ☐ Read labels before you buy a garment. Save yourself effort and don't buy high-care fabrics.

- ☐ Use vinegar for your fabric softener—it rinses the soap out, softens, is inexpensive, and is better for those sensitive to scents.

☐ Hang up towels immediately to keep them from smelling musty. Wash them in hot water and put vinegar in the wash and rinse to help keep towels smelling fresh. Hanging them out in the sunshine will also help, but it makes for stiff towels. When worse comes to worst, use bleach, but be aware that it will ruin the color.

☐ Remove clothes immediately from the dryer when the timer buzzes to eliminate wrinkles. If you miss the buzzer, throw a damp towel in to help unset wrinkles. There are also spray-on products that will release wrinkles.

☐ Fold the laundry all together as a family and listen to audio stories or watch a show.

☐ Use small baskets or dishpans for little people to put their clothes into for carrying to their closets.

☐ Iron when clothes still have a hint of dampness in them or sprinkle with warm water to aid in ironing.

☐ Label your linen closet shelves to assist the people who put away or remove linens.

☐ Sunshine brightens whites, fades stains, removes smells, and kills germs.

☐ Wipe your clothesline with a damp rag before hanging out to prevent black marks on the laundry.

☐ Be efficient when hanging out your laundry by pinning side-by-side garments with the same clothespin.

☐ Before you hang up clothes or move from washer to dryer, give them a good snap or two to remove wrinkles.

☐ When hanging up wet button-up shirts, stretch the wrinkles out by pulling with your hands from the top and bottom and the sleeves from the body of the shirt.

☐ Do not overload the washing machine, and teach your family this. The clothes will not come clean because the soap and water cannot circulate around and through the clothes.

☐ Sort your clothes by color and weight to get longer life out of them.

☐ Mend tears before washing to eliminate the fabric from unraveling in the wash.

☐ Wash lightly-soiled colored clothes in cold water to keep them bright.

☐ Blue jeans bleed for their whole lifespan; do not wash them with other clothes.

☐ Wash whites and very dirty clothes in hot water to remove soil and kill germs.

☐ Wear old clothes or aprons for dirty jobs that will stain clothes, such as when pitting cherries, cutting peaches, gardening, and painting.

☐ Fresh blood will come out if immediately rinsed in cold water. Heat will set the stain. Hydrogen peroxide removes blood stains.

☐ Grass stains come out with a vinegar pre-treat or when allowed to soak in a bucket of water with an enzyme cleaner.

☐ Grease stains come out with a citrus-based pre-treat.

☐ Bodily fluids come out after pre-treating with a bacterial enzyme based "pet stain remover." This also works great for carpet, furniture, and car upholstery.

☐ Keep softener salt in your water softener.

MAKE A LAUNDRY PROTOCOL POSTER

Making a Laundry Protocol poster will aid your family in knowing how to use the equipment and will help them know how to wash certain loads.

At the top, in large letters, write, "Laundry Protocol." Under this heading, write specific instructions for detergent use in your machine. Check your owner's manual and the detergent box for specifics.

Explain sorting categories. Then make a column for the days of the week. The second column is to correspond with the days and will explain which laundry to do on each day, including a couple of days off. Keep things simple and don't try to do laundry on your Town Day or the Lord's Day.

In the third column, write how to wash each particular load and which cleaners and settings that you want used on a particular load. Some things that are obvious to us are not so obvious to the uninitiated. Help your young apprentices with specific instructions on how to do the job well. For example: Friday: Towels and Sheets. Use hot water.

Hang the poster near your equipment. Then take your helpers to the poster and read through it with them. Ask them if they have questions. If, while doing laundry, they ask you how to do something, refer them to the poster. Teach them to think. Maybe something is not clear on your part and needs to be modified. The poster is your teacher's aid in helping get everything done that needs done and done well.

VICTORY IS YOURS

Each home is different, each laundry set up is different, and each household's laundry is different due to the family members' activities. One house might have toddler food, the next grass stains, the next red clay, and the next chicken manure. One house might have the laundry room in the garage, the next on a back porch, the next in the kitchen, and so on.

Take the ideas here and use them to get your creative juices flowing. Make a system that works for your family in your home. The bottom line is to do the laundry and keep on top of it; it's that simple. Between each activity that you schedule in your day, switch loads and fold. Work at it daily—early morning, late morning, noon, and early afternoon—then stop and put it away.

Learn to love laundry, study how to do it correctly, and make it an art! This is how you gain victory over the Laundry Monster.

KITCHEN DAY

When you walk into your kitchen, what's the first thing that catches your eye? The counters can quickly be a catch-all clutter collecting point. Even if all the dirty and clean dishes are taken care of, the food put away, and the papers stashed, the counters can still be cluttered with decorations and appliances that we think we need to have out.

KITCHEN ORGANIZATION: COUNTERTOPS AND ISLAND

How do we keep these areas clean and clear of clutter? Just like everything else in home management, we need to be diligent ourselves, and we need to train our children to put things where they belong: "Don't lay it down, put it away!" Remind yourself and your family that this habit keeps the kitchen neat and tidy and easier to clean. If you have severe offenders, then institute appropriate consequences and rewards for successfully overcoming a bad habit. Perhaps place a new object such as a potted plant in the location where people are tempted to lay things down and walk away, this may throw them off from the habit.

During Afternoon Chore Time, one of the chores for the Kitchen is to clear the table and counters of all clutter. It's not a bad job when we are all practicing, "Don't lay it down, put it away!" When we are lazy and let things pile up, it can be a real drag to put all that stuff away. When these clutter areas are dealt with daily, then the room doesn't become an eyesore.

Everything has a place, and everything in its place.

—Benjamin Franklin

When my husband comes in the back door at the end of the day, the first thing he sees is our kitchen island, dining room table, and the floors. If all went well with our Afternoon Chore Time, what he sees is pleasing to the eye: the table set for supper, the counter clean, supper smells in the air, and projects and toys put away. But there are evenings when he walks in to find schoolwork, food prep spread all over the kitchen, and a floor of crumbs, papers, and toys. This is not relaxing for him at the end of his work day. He feels like he's coming home to more work and frankly, on those days I do need him to pitch in! Our evenings are so much better when the work has been done in a timely fashion in the late afternoon.

The next time that your kitchen is completely clean and your countertops cleared to what is your normal standard, leave the room and then come back in, pretending that you are seeing things through a visitor's eyes. You might find that you can make things look a bit tidier by doing this trick. Is there still unnecessary clutter? Do you really *need* to have that appliance out? How often do you really use it? Is there room for it elsewhere? We grow accustomed to things and stop seeing them. Pretending that you are someone else and seeing something for the first time gives things a different perspective in your mind's eye.

Look for your kitchen's natural focal point, and do what you can to enhance the beauty of it. It might be the light, it might be a window, it might be a countertop, or it might be the cupboards. Something that might not catch the eye at all in one kitchen can become the focal point of another. Each kitchen design is unique and has its strong points of beauty and eyesores that should be minimized. Find what it is in your kitchen and enhance that area. It might be as simple as keeping it clean and shiny.

How do you avoid paper piles in your kitchen? Start with identifying what the paper is and where it came from. Sort mail over the trash can, and immediately dispose of junk. Put bills in a place just for them. Put magazines and newspapers at the place where they are read. When they are finished being read, recycle them. Have a place for mail for specific family members. Keep schoolwork and books in a specific place. Put an end to the habit of stacking stuff on the kitchen counters.

Do you have family who come in and empty their pockets of tools on the closest flat surface? In our house, I emptied the drawer nearest to where the "dumping ground" was. In that drawer, I placed baskets: one basket is for pliers, screwdrivers and other tools; one basket is for money; another basket is for the small things like nuts and bolts, golf tees, and pencils. Also in this drawer are the flashlights which seemed to lie around in odd places by the back door. By keeping a drawer for this stuff, things are out of sight, and family members know where to find the things that they dumped the day before. They are actually learning to empty their pockets into the drawer and sort it into the baskets and they know where to look for a specific item. At some point, clean this junk drawer too. Assign better spots for things, put things away, replace broken baskets, and dispose of the true junk.

By keeping your counters and island free and clear, it is more pleasing to the eye and makes a nicer workspace for you to be in. Clearing the clutter from the kitchen is not a once-and-forever job; it's something that needs to be evaluated every few months. Clutter creeps up on us, and we need to keep our eye on it so that it doesn't take over. Clutter makes our daily work harder to do because we have to fumble around it. Living clutter-free makes life more simple.

KITCHEN ORGANIZATION: A START

I once read an article about a woman who, with her husband and six-year-old daughter, moved for various reasons from a 1,500-square-foot apartment into 150 square feet of living space on a sailboat. Yes, they were going to live in the sailboat. The crux of the article was about making choices and simplifying life. They had to pare down their stuff tremendously, and this alone helped to simplify their life.

This woman's new kitchen was the size of a shower stall. She had one gas burner, a toaster oven, and a tiny refrigerator/freezer. The thing that struck me at the time, and motivated me to do a big clean out in my kitchen, was that she had only two knives; a chopping knife and a paring knife. Even though she loved to cook, she found that with the barest minimum of utensils she could still make great gourmet meals because she was focusing more on the *ingredients* rather than the process of using all the gadgets that a person thinks she needs.

After reading this article, I immediately got a box and went to my kitchen and starting pitching in all the things that were overflowing my drawers and cupboards that I never used—especially the knife drawer. While reading the article, I realized that I only use maybe three knives on a regular basis. I do have favorite knives for certain things, but I rarely use them.

I quickly realized that my kitchen held a plethora of unused items that were simply taking up space and making my life more complicated. I did not need to risk my fingers scrambling in the knife drawer or waste minutes digging in the gadget drawer for the few things that I actually used. I quickly filled a box with stuff to give away. I kept the box on my counter for a month or so *just in case* I had acted hastily. As I came across other things in the drawers and cupboards, I added to the box. I don't think I pulled a single thing back out. This box went to the thrift store and then, throughout the year, I kept on purging the kitchen and adding to the give-away box I keep at the backdoor.

If you're not ready for a complete organizational overhaul of the kitchen, or if you're short on time, just setting a give-away box at the back door is a good start.

CREATING EFFICIENCY

When I started paying attention to how many steps and movements I was making in the kitchen, it caused me to think of better ways to arrange things. In my kitchen, the refrigerator is at one end and the knife drawer at the opposite, yet I do most of the cutting in the middle. By simply moving the knife drawer directly under the cutting area, I have saved many steps. A change like this may not seem significant, but multiply this several times around your kitchen, and you will find yourself enjoying your time there more and being faster with your work.

When things are simplified and set up efficiently, creativity has a place to bloom.

We eat three meals a day, 365 days a year in the kitchen. That's a lot of time and energy spent in the kitchen prepping meals! Given this fact, creating an efficient kitchen is one of the biggest ways to save precious time in your life. When things are simplified and set up efficiently, creativity has a place to bloom. Your family will appreciate your more cheerful attitude and want to join you. By creating an efficient workspace in the kitchen, you will make it easier to teach and train your children in cooking, cleaning, and managing. Make your kitchen a place you want to be.

Caring for the kitchen and meals is one of the biggest tasks in home management. It is easy to become overwhelmed by this due to inexperience or lack of teaching, but just because you were not taught how to manage a kitchen is no excuse for throwing up your hands in defeat.

Think of all the other things you have had to teach yourself. Learning never stops in life unless you stop seeking to educate yourself. I have seen people not try and heard them say things that indicate they think they *can't learn anymore* or that they *can't be good at something.* It's simply not true. We can always try new things and learn new skills with God's help and a bit of determination. He is Jehovah-Jireh, God the Provider.

So how do you start making your kitchen more efficient? It comes by observing and thinking while you are working in the kitchen—how many steps am I taking, how many times am I bending over, reaching up, digging through a drawer, scrounging in the back of a cupboard? Then make informed adjustments to make the kitchen and food prep simple.

Observe yourself for a week as you work in the kitchen. Keep a paper on the frig, and write down ideas for improving organization and workflow as they come to you. Then begin to implement these improvements. You'll be glad that you did!

KITCHEN CENTERS TO IMPROVE EFFICIENCY

Think about dishes that you make often, and create centers or locations in the kitchen so that the work can be done quickly. Place like with like; organize to minimize steps.

1. Cutting and Sink Center: knives and cutting boards, coffee and coffee maker, dishwashing tools, colander, drinking glasses, pitchers, juicer, liquid measuring glass, plant watering can.

2. Cooking Center: pots and pans, cooking oil, rice, pasta, cooked cereals, serving dishes, platters, trays, timer, teakettle, tea.

3. Mixing Center: mixer, bowls, bread pans, baking ingredients.

4. Serving Center: dinnerware, flatware.

5. Refrigerator Center: Plastic bags and containers for leftovers, marking pen, sack lunch items.

If you do a lot of juicing, then create a Juice Center. If you make salads every meal, then create a Salad Center. Personalize your kitchen centers to suit you and the way that your family eats.

Put the items that you use daily between your eye level and your hip level. If you have children that do a lot of cooking, then take that into consideration. I recently moved my mixing bowls to a low spot to stop my children from climbing the counters every day.

If you have cake pans that you use every year or two and don't want to give them away, store them in a high cupboard or a back corner cupboard. I cleaned and organized a shelf in my basement's unfinished area for my infrequently used items.

There is no perfect kitchen anywhere; there will always be a spot or an area that irritates you. Some of these centers will overlap in your kitchens, and that's okay. You might want to keep two of the same tools or knives in your kitchen—one for each center—to save you some steps. I like to have several sets of measuring spoons in my kitchen. Some of you might have a kitchen that is so tiny that centers are nearly impossible, but at the same time, it's so tiny that you aren't taking any steps but simply turning around and around. The bottom line is to arrange things for the greatest efficiency possible.

As the years go by and your cooking changes, you will find that your kitchen needs to be rearranged again. I discovered that, as I started making double and triple batches of things, I needed to bring my biggest pots, pans, and baking dishes to the front and center and move the smaller things to the back.

Do *not* walk into your kitchen and start tearing it apart right away. Take a few days to observe yourself and think about things. It could be that you already have things set up in an efficient way in your kitchen, and it only needs a little bit of tweaking. If it's not broke, don't fix it.

KITCHEN DAY

Add a page to your Home Management Book for your Kitchen Day. This is the day when you do the big tasks and clean in your kitchen. Set aside a day of kitchen work for the sake of efficiency. If you keep your focus in the kitchen for a day, it will help out your family's health, grocery budget, cleanliness, and general well-being.

To start with, write out the weekly cleaning chores for the kitchen. This is the day that you and the children do those chores. If everyone does one or two tasks from the list every week, the kitchen stays clean with little effort. Each task can be done in *just a few minutes* if it's done weekly. But if tasks are left undone for weeks on end, it will take much more time to get things back into shape.

Weekly Kitchen Cleaning Chores

- ☐ Wipe appliances

- ☐ Clean stove hood

- ☐ Clean top of stove

- ☐ Organize and clean one drawer

- ☐ Organize and clean one cupboard

- ☐ Organize cupboard of plastic containers

☐ Organize and clean one pantry shelf

☐ Remove counter clutter and wipe counter

☐ Wipe appliances that sit on counter

☐ Clean out refrigerator

☐ Clean top of refrigerator

☐ Clean kitchen window

☐ Scrub kitchen sink and faucet crevices

☐ Scrub dish drainer

☐ Mop floor

☐ Dust

☐ Remove cobwebs

Kitchen Day Examples

The night before Kitchen Day, soak dry beans. In the morning, before breakfast or during breakfast table chores, drain the water. Put the beans in the slow cooker, cover them with water, and cook on low all day. During Afternoon Chore Time, turn it off and cool, then put the beans in freezer boxes or bags and freeze. This is an easy and inexpensive way to build a healthy freezer pantry.

Early in the morning, put chickens and vegetables in a big pot to simmer all day. In the late morning, when you're making lunch, pull the chickens out to cool and, after lunch, debone the chickens. Then freeze the meat in plastic bags and put the bones back in the pot. Simmer the bones all day. During Afternoon Chore Time, cool the broth, strain, and put the broth in freezer containers. Chicken broth is handy in many recipes and one of the healthiest and tastiest things for your family when made from scratch.

In the morning, set out ground meat to thaw. During Afternoon Chore Time, make meat loaves, meatballs, and/or brown and freeze.

In the morning, while the children are doing their independent schoolwork, start bread dough and let it rise. While the children are doing Table Chores after lunch, shape the loaves and let rise. During mid-afternoon, put the loaves in the oven.

During your family's Read-aloud hour, you read while the children mop. You can also listen to audio stories while you do the kitchen cleaning chores. My children tend to work faster when they are listening to a story and not talking to each other.

Do not feel that you have to do everything every single week. Take inventory of your freezer to see if you need to restock your browned meat or chicken broth.

Do not think that your little children can't be helpful in the kitchen. They can mop and wipe appliances and cupboard doors. They can debone a chicken. Little children think work is fun! Don't send them off; put them to work with a smile!

FLOOR MOPPING

This might sound a bit crazy to you, but I like to mop the floor.

In the past, I had a Swiffer. I think they are made for mopping floors that don't get dirty. At my house, the pads just seemed to make mud (a big problem for any farm). When I ran out of pads, I used a microfiber rag on the Swiffer, and that was a little better. But the Swiffer was eventually gotten rid of. I have used sponge mops too, and I rate them as okay but they also have a tendency to make mud.

The best mop I have owned is from Don Aslett's Cleaning Center catalog. It has different kinds of heads for specific uses and it swivels nicely, but you have to bend down and wring it out. If you're bending down, you might as well bend all the way down and just mop the floor with your hand. With the Aslett mop, you still have the problem of the dried-on food spots or stickers someone stuck onto the floor. One solution is to let them soak and come back later, but I have a lot of those spots on the floor. Am I supposed to flood the whole floor and come back in ten minutes to mop it?

Naptime is the most logical time of day to mop. Those children who are not napping when you mop can gather their things, visit the toilet, go to their Quiet Time spot, and stay parked for the mopping and drying time.

When I do the mopping, I put on some relaxing classical music and fill a bucket with soapy water. I use a terry rag or micro-fiber cloth, and a dish scraper for the stickers and other things that need scraped off. I get down on my hands and knees and start mopping at one end and finish by the toilet in the mudroom. Then I dump the dirty water down the toilet. It takes me twenty minutes when working alone. If three or four of us mop together, it takes less than ten minutes. Time the task so that you can plan for it and get over the thought of beginning. Mopping can be one of those things that we put off because it takes effort to get set up. To make the startup easy, keep a mop bucket under a sink and store supplies inside the bucket.

When the floor is very dirty, I use the two-bucket method, one for soapy water and one for rinsing the wash rag. Sometimes I even need to change the rinse water because it turns black so quickly. That happens more often in the summer during canning season. Plus, I live on a farm and have a mudroom that is called a mudroom for a reason. The two-bucket system is good for a muddy mudroom.

I find mopping to be relaxing because the house is quiet with everyone doing an activity elsewhere or sleeping; the music is relaxing; and I can just mop and think. I like to have that quiet time, though the mopping is over before I know it. Then I find a quiet spot to read with the children until the floor has dried.

Now, in my quest to multitask, be efficient, and teach my children how to work, my method the last few years has been to have the big kids mop while I read aloud. With four of them mopping, it gets done in a flash. They start at one end and race each other to the middle. They also point out to each other when they miss a spot. The mop bucket is behind them, and they go from it to their mopping spot on the floor, moving backwards towards the bucket. I sit on a nearby chair and read to them. This system has been working great and is a happy time.

The Spot Mop Method: When someone spills something (which happens at least once a day at our house), we mop not only the spill area, but also everything that can be reached within an arm's length. Using this method, the floor can be kept decently clean for a while. Another version of this method is to walk around with a spray bottle of soapy water and a wet rag, looking for the dirty spots. This is a good method to have a child do when you are getting surprise visitors! It's also a good task for a preschool age child during Afternoon Chore Time. Keep this squirt bottle and rags handy under the kitchen sink.

BUILDING UP HELP IN THE KITCHEN

Assign a day of the week to each child. The 'special' child for the day gets extra privileges and is your right hand in the kitchen. By assigning each child a day in the kitchen, they learn how to cook. My children love to cook and try to cook on days that aren't their day, and this often turns into a squabble. They often get excited about a recipe and are told to save it for their special day. Ingredients that they need are added to the grocery list.

The child assigned for the day is required to be in the kitchen during meal preparation. Involve the child in the recipe making and, if they can, let them do it alone! Start this when they are little, and by the time they are eight, ten, and definitely by age twelve, they will be able to make meals alone.

Show no fear. When your children want to make cream puffs, and you think the recipe sounds too complicated, let them do it. Tell them to follow the directions of their recipes exactly. I tend to be a dump cook, which is good and bad. The good is that a dump cook can make something out of nothing and with no recipe. The bad is that a dump cook tends to rewrite the directions to a recipe (to simplify, substitute ingredients, or speed it up) and can end up wrecking it. I have learned the hard way that when the kids want to make something that requires exaction—baked goods, for example—and they have a reliable recipe, I should get out of the way. If they see a recipe made on a TV cooking show, let them get the recipe off the Internet and make it. Help them out with collecting the ingredients and being their dishwasher and supporter in the production. Then sit down and enjoy the food.

LITTLE CHILDREN IN THE KITCHEN

Little children are fun to have in the kitchen. They are so delighted and curious about everything. Of course, sometimes they can be in the way, especially when you are hurrying, but try not to squish them. Give them something to do:

- ☐ A container of beans or rice and various measuring cups and spoons. Have them transfer the beans from one bowl to another. This increases coordination and teaches fractions. A funnel is also fun.

- ☐ A cheese shaker full of toothpicks. Put the toothpicks on a plate and have the child put toothpicks in the holes of the shaker. This activity increases finger dexterity and concentration.

- ☐ Securely stand a child at the sink, perhaps while you are washing dishes, and let him play in the water with a funnel and slotted spoons.

☐ An older preschooler can play with little cups and pitchers and learn to carefully pour from one thing to the next. When she is done, hand her a rag, and she can wipe the cupboards and mop the floor.

☐ Stacking plastic cups is fun for a toddler.

☐ An older child can layer different color beans in a jar. After everyone has admired his art project, soak the beans in water, and cook them for soup.

OFFICE DAY

Assign a day of the week to your Home Office and add a page for it to your Home Management Book. The goal is a Home Office where you tend to the business side of home life. This may include everything from menu plans to financial investments—anything to do with paper, pencils, numbers, money, and planning. Take this work seriously and respectfully and in an orderly manner keep the desks in order, file papers, make phone calls, and pay bills. My husband has traveled with his off-farm work for nearly all of our married life, so a lot of the business tasks have been my duty. Once again, untrained for this job, I made many mistakes along the way, learned too many things the hard way, and created personal coping strategies that I will now share with you.

We live in a paper age. Paper, paper, everywhere. When we don't take time to deal with all the paper in our lives, it turns into a monster—the paper monster. While whole books have been written about this pesky creature, I'm going to share with you the simple way I've found to handle paper.

Take one day of the week and spend it at your desk, not surfing the net or reading e-mail newsletters, but use the time to get the finances and paper under control. Call it Office Day. At first you might spend hours putting things in order, but eventually you will come to the place where you will spend only half an hour a week paying bills and taking care of the paperwork.

If the thought of a whole day fighting this monster is overwhelming, then break it up into chunks. Spend ten minutes tackling one paper pile. Then go read a story to your children. Come back to the desk and spend ten minutes straightening a drawer. Then go get a drink of water and look out your kitchen window for a bit. Then tackle another paper pile.

Just work slow and steady. You're coming back next week—same day, same place—and sooner or later, you will be the victor. You will be a Home Office Manager, and you will be great at your job, ten minutes at a time, one day a week, for the rest of your life.

Every time you clear an area or clean out a drawer, claim it as yours—it no longer belongs to the paper piles. Do not let anything be placed there to clutter it up again. Put a vase of flowers, framed art, or a picture of your children there to claim the spot. You will not lay paper there again. The paper has its place and that's where you will keep it, whether it is the trash can, a lovely basket, or a file cabinet.

You will be a Home Office Manager, and you will be great at your job, ten minutes at a time, one day a week, for the rest of your life.

Once you have the paper under control, clean out the desk drawers, cupboards, shelves, and other areas that are part of your Home Office. Do not get overwhelmed—do this slowly, one place at a time, ten minutes at a time, taking frequent breaks. It may take weeks to gain victory over the mounds of paper lurking here and there in your house, but you can get the Home Office up and running.

Some of the paper deluge we need, some of it we want, and some of it we don't know what to do with. There are auto, legal, receipts, taxes, and so on. I have travel information about that area we took a vacation to a few years ago, just in case we want to go back to the same place. I have information on all the paint colors and brands that I used the last time the house was painted; they are set aside for the next time I repaint. It seems we can file things forever. Thanks to the online age, we no longer need to keep files for every single last iota of something. It can easily be found online. Keep files for only the most crucial things and this will save you a lot of space.

QUICK FAST PAPER RECOVERY

Looking at paper piles can be depressing, but do not fear. Most of it can be tossed into the trash or recycling. When you're climbing one of those mountains, grab a trash can and two boxes. Throw into the trash all junk mail, catalogs, newspapers—anything that doesn't have to do with money or important papers to file. Put all the bills into one box labeled "Bills" and all the rest into the other box labeled "File." Pay all of the bills that you can and put the invoices into the File box. As you pay the bills, sign up for autopay and paperless billing. These two things will save you time and effort.

File the important papers, the ones you think you ought to keep, into gallon-sized zip bags that you have labeled with the pertinent year. I suggest zip bags because you probably have some handy in your kitchen. Each day, keep putting your papers to be filed into these bags. This is a temporary situation. You need files to properly control your paper by topic. When you get the mail each day, sort it, and put your important papers in a zip bag labeled with the current year. Again, this is a temporary situation. We're just trying to get through the accumulation.

Put your bills that are waiting to be paid in a gallon-sized zip labeled "Bills" until you get a bill paying system in place. Remember, the zip bag filing is temporary. Do not grow accustomed to it. It is a stepping-stone to your new life of regular paper management.

To take dominion of this area, you will need to invest in a filing system. At office supply stores, there are desk top files and file boxes with hinged lids and handles that you can purchase. There are file boxes that are also fireproof for your most important papers. These are a very inexpensive alternative to the cabinet type file drawers. You will also need to buy hanging files and manila folders to slip inside the hanging files.

For paper from last year and beyond, keep only the most important documents—the ones that might draw attention from the IRS. Sort the papers only by year, not by topic. You have too much else to do to file more specifically now. It will only matter if you need to go back into time for some reason. Put the zip bags, labeled by year, into a box. Label the box with the years included, and put it in storage. If you ever need information from those years (not likely), then you can sort the papers further at that point. Your most important goal at this early stage is to get your current papers under control.

WHAT ORDER LOOKS LIKE

Now that everything is clean and neat, work on getting your plans in place. A three-ring binder with pockets for each of the following topics will be helpful. I prefer binders to files because the binder can store on a shelf and be flipped through for easier access to information.

- ☐ Appliance books/warrantees, paint colors, anything to do with the house

- ☐ A menu plan of 31 meals that you can reference for meals

- ☐ A home book for writing down decorating ideas and pasting in pictures, unless you're on Pinterest and have boards there where you collect ideas

- ☐ If you homeschool: your own family's homeschool scope and sequence plan

- ☐ Educational information for each person

- ☐ Financial goals and the plans to reach those goals

- ☐ Garden and landscape information and plans

- ☐ Vacation plans

As Home Office Manager, you will now be more calm and relaxed because you have an orderly place to plan your work and reference your plans. The Home Office will be a rock in your house—the hub from which you run your daily operations. It will be a well-ordered reference point from which you plan and set forth orders.

Little by little, you will continue to gain control of this area of life. Once you have your base operations established, you won't know how you got along without it. With structure and routine, you will know what to expect. You can anticipate surprises and plan for them. Based on my experience, it is well worth it to dedicate one day a week to the Home Office.

OFFICE DAY TASKS

Do each one of these things every Office Day:

- ☐ Balance the checkbook

- ☐ Pay bills

- ☐ File papers

- ☐ Plan menus

- ☐ Plan the stops and the route for Town Day

- ☐ Plan lessons and add supplies or library books to the Town Day list

- ☐ Schedule an appointment with each child to review schoolwork and chores

- ☐ Save your Internet research and shopping for Office Day. Keep a running To Do list for the things you will research on Office Day

- ☐ Write a letter to a friend

- ☐ Write your nonessential e-mails today, for example, contact customer service regarding broken tent poles

- ☐ Clean out one desk drawer or cupboard

- ☐ Clean the desktop

- ☐ Restore books to shelves

- ☐ Gather library books and put in the vehicle

SETTING UP YOUR DESK

Because a desk is a level surface, it can quite easily become a collective dropping ground. When people see a pile of papers there, it can become a magnet to place another paper on the pile rather than going the extra step to put that paper where it belongs.

Make a daily effort when you sort the mail to not allow paper piles on your desk. Keep a basket or stacking files for papers that you need to file. Do not put junk mail or bills in this basket. Make space on your desk for you to spread out your work. Get a container to hold your pens, pencils, and a letter opener conveniently located on your desk. Put a pretty coaster on your desk for you to set a water glass or cup of tea when you sit down to work. A small vase for a garden flower is also a nice touch. The point is to keep it cleared and make it look nice so that it will invite and inspire you rather than look like a big pile of paper drudgery.

Stacking horizontal files make a handy paper system. You can slip papers into the appropriate file when you sort the mail. Use three files, and label them "Action," "Pending," and "File." If you don't like the names for those categories, then name them something that makes sense to you. This is a personalized system and you are unique.

The Action file is for things you need to take care of within a week. Schedule time on Office Day to go through this, and leave it clean for the next weeks' worth of paper.

The Pending file is for tasks that require action, such as invitations to respond to, mail order receipts for things that haven't arrived yet, tickets to purchase, and other tasks. Go through this file on Office Day, take action on the items, and throw out the unnecessary.

The File folder is where you put things to file. Every Office Day, file the papers that you've placed in the "File" folder during the week.

This same system can also be used for a home business.

MANAGING YOUR DESK

Holding a weekly Office Day will keep things under control. If you sit there every day to check e-mail or if you keep your calendar on the computer, be sure to not leave a pile of debris behind you. Make it a habit when you stand up to take your glass back to the sink, have a child put away the toys he brought you, put the burp cloth in the laundry, hang your purse on its hook, straighten papers, throw away the junk mail. In short, clean up behind yourself.

Give yourself a rule of only a certain amount of objects to clutter the desk. These are the four things that I limit mine to:

1. A glass of water

2. A pencil holder (Dejunk this regularly.)

3. Stacking files

4. Computer and mouse

MANAGING YOUR CALENDAR

Check your calendar twice daily: when you wake up and before you go to bed. It is wise to have a calendar on the wall so that everyone can reference it and know when and what things are going to happen. You will have a happier family when they know what to expect. Require that everyone put their events on the wall calendar. Some moms do well with a calendar on their computer and/or smart phone; some are paper people and like to have a date book they carry with them. Everyone is unique; the important thing is that you have a system that works for you and your family.

In one exceptionally busy season in life I had one calendar on the wall for events and a second calendar beside it with work projects that had to be done by certain dates. Doing this informs the family of the work expectations for each week.

MANAGING YOUR INTERNET TIME

Ha! Are you laughing at that title? Those rabbit trails can be pretty long sometimes, can't they?

It is wonderful for the mom immersed in a world of children to have that brain stimulation, learn new skills, research curriculum, and meet great people from all over. When you're in the middle of a project, it is such a cinch to punch in the right words and get just the right information. The Internet is a great thing, but it can be a time stealer.

Here are a few practices that have helped me manage my time online more efficiently:

1. Do your work first: kitchen, bathrooms, floors, meals, school. "We work before we play."

2. Multitask by nursing the baby at the computer. Do not burp your baby for an excessively long period of time; you would call that malingering if your children pulled that.

3. Use a timer, and give yourself a certain amount of time for each day.

4. Take one day (Office Day) to do any research and to allow time for the inadvertent rabbit trails. Then go for that rabbit trail and see where it takes you.

5. Categorize your browser bookmarks by person who uses the computer and subject.

6. While you're categorizing bookmarks, make one for Daily and one for Weekly. In the Daily folder, put those bookmarks that you like to read daily. In the Weekly folder, put the occasional reads.

7. Subscribe to favorite sites and groups for specific information so that you don't waste time scrolling through unnecessary information.

8. When doing a web search, don't read only the heading and click or scan the blurb and click. Look first at the address where it came from. This will save you time from visiting sites you've already been to, give you an idea of what kind of site is passing out the information, or let you know if the blurb is a distraction to get you somewhere where you really don't want to go.

9. Handle the e-mail just like you do the snail mail. Sort through it over the trash can. File what needs to be filed immediately (such as invoices from online purchases), answer what needs answered, and immediately dispose of the spam and mark "block sender" immediately. If you're in e-mail groups, and they start to pile up unread, hit Select All and Delete. The topics of discussion that you missed will come around again someday. Keep your e-mail box clean and tidy.

10. Put your computer near the main part of your house so that it's another workstation for you and your kids. My computer is just off the kitchen, ten steps from my stove. I can hear everything that is going on in the main part of the house, and I am able to monitor the children's activities.

11. When you sit down at the computer, prioritize your time. Check your bank balance and balance your checkbook first. Sort your e-mail and do the most important items first. *Then* visit your favorite sites in order of importance to you. Do your important research tasks before fun time. If the research to be done is not very important, save it for Office Day and schedule time for it.

12. Before getting up from your chair, straighten your computer area. Put your pens and papers away. Push your chair in. If it's Office Day, allow extra time for tidying, then dust your computer, peripherals, and desk. Pick up things that have fallen on the floor. Call your children to pick up things that they dropped while visiting you. Put your glass in the sink or dishwasher. Empty the trash basket.

Take these ideas, make a list of your own, and then tape it above your computer. Start implementing them into your daily life. Make your computer time one more routine in your life to improve efficiency, productivity, and simplicity rather than a distraction that takes you away from more important priorities.

PLANNING MENUS

Every week on Office Day, look at your menu plan and write changes. Look at your recipe books and add new recipes to your menu plan. Write your grocery list in an organized way so that you can move through the store faster. If a holiday or hospitality event is coming up, plan your menu, the grocery lists, and the order of events that need to happen for the recipes you are going to use.

PLANNING CHORES

Take the time on Office Day to adjust your chore charts. If the seasons are changing and there is new outdoor work, then make a plan for it. If you are having a hospitality event, plan the work to be done for it.

Create chore lists on your Office Day. Each room has particular work that needs to be done in order to make it look neat and clean. Make a Daily Chore List, Weekly Chore List, and Quarterly Chore List for each room. Start the list with the obvious, such as straightening the room. If it's a playroom or bedroom that can have a lot of clutter on the floor, divide the clutter up into categories. Number the chores so that the cleaning moves from top to bottom and left to right. Take a picture of what the clean room looks like and attach that to the chore list. Put it in a page protector, and place it in each room. When it comes time to train a child to clean a room, the chore list and picture for the room is the guide.

HOMESCHOOL PLANNING

If you are a homeschool family, use Office Day to plan for what you want each child to learn over the next school year.

A few years ago, after being pulled this way and that by every homeschool catalog, great website, book I read, magazine review, and the praise of other moms of certain curriculum, I decided to make my own Scope and Sequence.

A Scope and Sequence is a chart of what subjects are studied each year. Many textbook providers offer a Scope and Sequence as a guide to their curriculum. I took this idea and made it my own for our family. My goal was to chart out a direction for my family's education rather than being blown about by the wind. The purpose of the Scope and Sequence is to serve as a guide for your family's homeschooling vision. Whether you call it a "Scope and Sequence" or something else, it is important that you establish goals for teaching your children, both academically and otherwise.

Gather all of your favorite homeschooling how-to books, catalogs, booklists, a three-ring binder, page protectors, a pencil, and sticky notes. Put it all in a tote that you can grab whenever you work on this project. You could:

- ☐ Work on this a bit each day while the children do schoolwork.

- ☐ Work on this once a week on Office Day.

- ☐ Set aside a day and tackle it all at once.

- ☐ Work on it in the evening with your husband after your children go to bed.

Start by figuring out how old each child will be in each year of the future. This helps to see things in a different way and gives you a big picture idea of how many children you will have of "school age" each year. This can be an intimidating look into the future, and you must remember that God will bless you with strength and wisdom for each year.

List the upcoming years in a column on the left. Make a column for each child, listing each name at the top. In each box of the chart, write down the child's grade for each year. Along the way, things will be more flexible in regards to what grade a child is in his subjects. This exercise is simply to give you a picture of the future and help you plan for it.

Once this exercise is done, take twelve sheets of paper and write a grade level at the top of each. This is not to lock your children in at certain grades; it is simply a guide in planning what to study when. If you prefer to put an age instead of grade at the top of your papers, then do so. Each child is different and will develop at a different pace.

Starting with your preschool page, write down what subjects you would like the children to do. How much time do you want them to spend doing certain activities during the day? If you or an older sibling is going to sit down with them and teach the alphabet, write down how much time per day to devote to this. If you want them to have a music time, what specifically do you want them to listen to and for what period of time? What will they do with their hands while they listen—play dough, blocks, puzzles, or coloring? What literature do you want read to your preschooler? Do you want a boxed curriculum for your preschooler? Will you implement a Montessori approach? These are just idea starters, do what is personal for your family.

Now do this for each grade, using your favorite books and catalogs to help you choose curriculum. As the years go by, the lists of subjects to study will grow, and once you have readers, you will want to add a booklist of literature that you want a particular aged child to read. My Scope and Sequence has a list of subjects and curriculum on the left page with a book list on the right.

Once things are completed, and you have things the way you think they should be, enter your Scope and Sequence into your word processor, save it, print it out, and put it in page protectors and into a folder. You now have a Scope and Sequence to use over the next several years.

This is a huge project, and it will take time. I did most of it at the end of my fifth child's pregnancy when I was sitting around a lot anyway. It may be a summer project for you or something you just peck away at over time, even year by year.

Keep in mind that all children are different. Some children will take off reading and will read the book list for a year in two months' time. Never fear: There are plenty of good books out there! Another child might not read well until age ten. You will have to work with various learning styles and learn each child's bent. Making your own personal family Scope and Sequence helps tailor education to your particular family. Ask what are your family's strengths, weaknesses, ministries, gifts, setting, goals, and so on. The Scope and Sequence helps plan the how and why of these particular variances.

Keep in mind that all children are different.

A Scope and Sequence is a guide to assist you, not a book of curriculum commandments. Do not be legalistic with it. Its purpose is to give direction to your school plans, not to tie your down. It is a tool.

Using a Scope and Sequence also helps in planning what to order when and in budgeting for future expenses. It will save you money. It will help hold back impulse buys, and when you see something that you know is on your list and the price is right, you can buy it with confidence.

The biggest advantage for doing this is that it keeps you from waffling and wavering between curricula. When you hear about a new curriculum, you can look back to your Scope and Sequence and evaluate: "Is this better than what I already planned? How much better? Is this a good second choice?" Keep sticky notes and a pen in the binder pocket for this very reason. Use them to jot down notes and ideas.

When another successful homeschool family nearly convinces you and your husband into switching to a video curriculum because you just had a baby, you can go back to your Scope and Sequence and think about it. Is this really necessary? Is the Scope and Sequence working? Would it cause more disruption to switch (children get accustomed to a curriculum)?

When you read about the newest math curriculum and are tempted to switch to it, you can look at the Scope and Sequence and say, "What I'm using is fine. We have no problems with it. It costs less. One child completed the series successfully, and the other children have no problems with it."

Take a deep breath and let the temptation go. When a new curriculum comes out that is much more thorough and easier to implement than what you had originally planned for high school, then you can put sticky notes for a new plan on your high school pages.

Years down the road, you might have so many sticky notes of changes stuck to your pages that it is time to rewrite the Scope and Sequence. That's okay; it's a guide for your personal family's education. As you and your family grow and change and better curriculum becomes available, your guide will change. But having this guide is a reference point for evaluating and making changes. It will help keep you from being a curriculum junkie.

CHILDREN'S MEETINGS

Make an appointment with each child to review his or her schoolwork. This idea is for all parents, not just homeschool families. When life is busy, it is pretty easy for one or more of the children to fly under the radar and get away with things. It is also easy for someone to look like they are getting along fine in a subject when they really don't understand the concept and are doing things wrong. It is wise to keep on top of this day-to-day while our children are working, but let's be realistic, the days are busy. By taking one day a week to have a meeting with each child about schoolwork, you can avoid long-term problems going unnoticed.

An appointment won't take very long for the small children. Give them lots of praise, stickers, hugs, kisses, and promise to tell the family about the great job they are doing. Explain what needs to be explained, and be sure to keep an eye on problem areas daily until they are resolved.

Meeting with an older child will take longer, and if there is a problem to rectify, it might take a lot longer to explain the concept and work through the problems. You might need to stop and continue the meeting later during free time or in the evening with both parents.

Use part of the time when you meet for prayer. Keep a notebook for these meetings with your children and record their progress, along with prayers you prayed with them.

THE BILL PAYING SYSTEM

An easy way to add time to your life is to simplify your bill paying system. Online banking is a great way to streamline your finances and keep track of your balance. Next Town Day, stop at your bank and set up your account so that you can access it online. Get an app for your phone. Every Office Day, look at your account online, reconcile it with your checkbook, look ahead at upcoming expenses, and know where your money is and where it is going. Put everything that you can on autopay and paperless billing.

MANAGING YOUR FAMILY'S FIXED EXPENSES

Take a notebook page and write down "Fixed Expenses" at the top. These are all of your monthly expenses that don't vary much from month to month.

Collect your bill statements and take a good look at them. Put the Fixed Expenses in the order of when they are due in a column on the left side. For instance, if your mortgage is due the first of every month, that goes at the top; the phone bill is due the 15th, so it goes in the middle; the electric bill is due around the 22nd, so put that towards the bottom of the page; and the bank service fee comes out at the end of the month, so put that at the bottom. Don't forget monthly expenses for things such as piano lessons.

Write what the bills are, the date they are due, and the amount. This will help you know where and when the money is going. It will also help you look at ways you can reduce expenses. One very handy thing that you can do for Fixed Expenses is to have them electronically withdrawn or put on autopay. Set this up to save you time and stamps. Mark on your Fixed Expense paper the bills that you have set up for electronic withdrawal so that you don't send off a payment for something on top of an electronic withdrawal. Yes, I have done that!

Next, check to see if your bank does automatic payments. Use this for those businesses that do not offer electronic withdrawals. The bank prints the check and mails it on the date that you specify. This can be changed at your discretion with online banking. One important tip: check your bill statements to confirm that they are truly being paid when you scheduled them.

If illness strikes and puts you out of commission, the major bills that keep the lights on will continue being paid.

HOW TO PLAN FOR VARIABLE EXPENSES

Variables Expenses are those that change from month to month, such as gas, food, clothing, cleaning and paper products, and entertainment.

How much do you spend per month on Variable Expenses? Look at past banking statements and your checkbook register to learn where this money goes and how much you spend in each category. These numbers must be kept within what is in your checking account, or you will overdraw.

Make it a habit to look ahead for anything that you need to save money for.

Write the categories for Variable Expenses and the average money needed for them on your notebook page. On Town Day, you will know that you have x amount of dollars to fill the vehicle with gas, x amount of dollars to spend at the grocery store, x amount of dollars to spend at the superstore. Some people find it helpful to carry this amount in cash to help control their spending.

Make it a habit to look ahead for anything that you need to save money for. For instance, next week you have plans to go out to eat at a new restaurant with friends. If you don't look ahead and plan to save money for the dinner date, you might accidentally blow it all when you're at the superstore on Town Day. By looking ahead, you can buy exactly what you need at the superstore, thus saving money for your special dinner date.

How often does your family receive income? If it happens on fixed days, then write this in the column of your notebook paper on the day of the month that it happens. This will help you see how the paychecks are weighted. It might be that most of your bills come due towards the end of the month, which is why you seem to go through the second paycheck so fast compared to the first. If this is the case, then you are going to have to be more careful with not spending so much the first part of the month and saving it for the Variable Expenses that occur in the second half.

If you are paid biweekly, then the pay date is constantly moving, and you will have to gauge your spending accordingly. In the biweekly scenario, you will find it helpful to take another paper and write down the date of every paycheck for the next year. Then, figure out how much cash flow you will have for each pay period. Subtract all the Fixed Expenses from each pay period. There will be two months of the year that there are three paycheck months that look like a bonus. However, there are also two pay periods that have very small cash flows compared to the rest, leaving little for the Variable Expenses. When you write it all down, it becomes much more obvious how the money comes and goes and why you need to be very careful about spending.

Keep this list of Fixed Expenses and Variable Expenses in your Bill Drawer, and look at it every Office Day when you pay bills and plan spending.

To give you breathing room in your checking account, keep an extra month's pay there and, in the current month, spend what was deposited the previous month. When you follow this approach, the money coming this month will be for next month's expenses.

THE BILL DRAWER

Bills should have a place for safe keeping until they are paid or filed. To achieve this goal, first choose a desk drawer and empty it. Nothing in this drawer is as important as keeping your bills in one place. A paper pile or more than one paper pile sitting around the house is how payments are missed or late, and important papers are lost.

Be very disciplined about the bill drawer. You cannot allow junk mail to accumulate there. The only things that belong in the bill drawer are the bills and the tools used to pay them. Every day when you sort through the mail, take the bills straight to this drawer.

The tools you will want in your Bill Drawer are envelopes, stamps, address labels, and calculator. Two other tools you will keep there are your list of Fixed Expenses, your plan for Variable Expenses, and your Short-term Savings Plan.

Do not let your children meddle in the Bill Drawer. Do not keep in it anything they would want or need. Make it clear to them that it is full of mom and dad's very important papers. You might consider keeping stamps in your purse or in a high place because, in your four-year-old's eyes, stamps can be very pretty when stuck all over an art project or on the wall.

An alternative to the Bill Drawer is the Bill Bag. In the past, I have kept a tote bag with all of the Bill Drawer items and a manila folder for the bills. Instead of putting all of the bills into the Bill Drawer, I put them into the Bill Bag. I would grab this bag on our way out the door to piano lessons. While the children were at lessons, the rest of us shopped at the grocery store, visited the library or park, and then we waited in the van until the piano kids were done. While we waited, the children listened to an audio story or looked at library books, and I paid bills using my Bill Bag. This worked fine for a couple of years.

When the mail comes, sort it immediately. Do this over the trash can and pitch the junk mail.

If there are important papers that need to be filed, put these in a file basket on your desk. Ideally, you would file these papers in their proper place right away (try to do this!), but filing can take some time. The reality often is that while you are sorting the mail, some sort of crisis erupts. Children and life can be quite unpredictable. Put your important mail in the file basket, and on Office Day, file these papers away. Do not let this file grow into a huge disastrous mess. Write down on your Office Day routine to file, it is a task to be completed. It will be so helpful for you to have everything in its proper place.

Put newspapers, magazines, and catalogs in a basket or on a table beside the chair where they will be read. It should be the weekly chore of the person who cleans that particular room to clean out the old newspapers and magazines. Write this down on the chore list for the room.

Paper management is just another area of life where we deliberately keep things in their place. It's a habit to work on. You already have habits with your paper system; you just need to replace the bad habits with good ones. It might even help you to write down what your current paper habits are. This will help you see what needs to change. Remember, creating new habits requires thought, but soon it will become ingrained, and you won't have to do the extra mental work. Your bill system and paper management will just happen automatically

HOW TO PLAN SHORT-TERM SAVINGS GOALS

Take a fresh notebook page and write Savings Plan at the top. Next, get your family calendar from last year and look at all the activities that your family did that cost money. Make a list of the months of the year in a column on the left-hand side. Using your old calendar to help jog your memory, write down the yearly recurring activities beside each month in the column and the expected cost associated with each.

For example, the local homeschool convention is in June, but there is an early payment discount plus hotel booking, so I write beside April, "Homeschool Convention." This is a reminder for me to save up for this event. When I look back over the years, I can identify certain expenses that come with certain seasons or months that our family needs to be financially prepared for.

Look ahead and plan for when you will need to hold back money for these events. Otherwise you will be surprised with the extra financial demands the week they occur and may run into a money pinch.

This is also helpful practice to follow in order to have money set aside for future good deals that can be reasonably anticipated. Some businesses run various specials on things throughout the year. By anticipating this, you will have money when these specials occur.

If you have months where you have no big expenses due, plan to use these times to buy those things that aren't on a time frame, such as books and curriculum, home projects, magazine subscriptions, or clothes shopping (even for the next season). Write relevant items that fit this category down on your page so that you remember to save for and purchase them at the appropriate time.

Keep this Short-term Savings list in your Bill Drawer. Every Office Day, look at this list and think about how you can plan and save for these upcoming expenses. Home managing is about more than cooking and cleaning; it also involves managing savings and expenses.

PLANNING FOR VACATION

Many times, things you want to do that involve money never happen because you haven't given your finances the thought required to do them. Yet if we go through the brainstorming process, and we plan and save, we *can* often do things that we previously thought were financially out of reach.

Let's say that your family wants to take a trip to a specific event. In doing some research, you determine that it will cost your family $2,000 for the week at your destination. In addition, it will take you two days to get there and back, requiring $400 for gas. Add one hotel night, two rooms for your family: $250. Don't forget the hotel night when you come home: another $250.

Plus food: Eat breakfast at home the first day's travel, pack a lunch, healthy snack food and water for eating along the way, eat a decent supper out for $75 or eat off the $1 menu at Burger King for $25. Second day: Eat breakfast at the hotel's free continental buffet, lunch at McDonald's $1 menu, $25; and a decent supper somewhere, $75. On the way home, you have two $1 menu lunches for $50, and two decent suppers that total $150. Total food for the trip to and from the event: $375. If you don't eat off the dollar menu, then estimate the food costs for each person, each meal at typical fast food places on the road.

Your grand total for the trip is $3,275, plus or minus. You have six months until the vacation event, and you have no money in your vacation savings account, so you will have to save $546 a month for six months. If there's no way that you can save $546 a month this year, then maybe next year you can make it work.

Don't stop with the thought; do the math. Next year is 18 months away. Let's add 10 percent to the cost because you will probably have some children jump into the next age group that costs more. Your children might be hungrier next year, gas prices might go up. So let's plan on $3,600 divided by 18 months: that's $200 dollars a month to save.

Can you do it? Maybe you need to reevaluate things. How badly do you really want to go to this event? How badly do you just want a vacation, and you don't care where? Maybe your husband thinks that this event will be an extra, wonderful blessing for your family, and that other things that you normally spend money on will take a back seat, and you will go this year. Perhaps you can sell something and use the money for the trip. Is there a short-term or part-time job that can be picked up to pay for the vacation?

To plan for a vacation: pick a goal, do a bit of research and math, and then save the money back for it. Have it automatically transferred every pay date into a savings account. If you're doing online banking, this will take a minute or so to get that automatic transfer set up. If it automatically comes out, you won't miss it. You will mentally see it as another Fixed Expense coming out, just like all of your other bills.

Use this same system for anything you want to save up for: a home, your next vehicle, an emergency account, tiling the bathroom floor, or a patio, for example. Do your research, set a date, figure the monthly amount, and set up an automatic transfer to make it easier.

MAGAZINES, CRAFTS, AND RECIPES

Instead of filing articles and recipes, put them into three-ring binders. Articles that are filed are rarely seen again.

This is another project that doesn't need to be done all at once. Start now with anything you clip or print from this day forward. Use a binder for each season, and fill it with page protectors. The reason you want one for each season is that we live our lives seasonally. We make things with strawberries and rhubarb in June, decorate for Independence Day in June and July, make pumpkin pie in the fall, and paper snowflakes when the snow flies. Magazines have certain themes for each month that have to do with holidays, produce that is in season, and seasonal crafts and garden projects. Keep in mind that the articles and recipes will come around again in a year or two.

Start with seasonal binders, and if you would like to be more specific, then make one for each month. If you have time, make them pretty by using scrapbooking paper behind your cut articles and recipes. Do this regularly with your magazine subscriptions or projects printed from the Internet; save only the projects you want to do, and toss the rest of the magazine in the recycling. Plan the date or season for the project. When your binders get full, purge them. Do not keep making binders for the rest of your life. Keep only what you have real intentions of doing.

Put a certain theme of recipes in its own binder. Keep like with like. Get sticky tabs to sort sections.

DAILY TASKS FOR THE HOME OFFICE MANAGER

☐ Open the mail over the trash, immediately disposing of the junk mail. Handle paper once.

☐ Put bills into the Bill Drawer. Always open a bill in case it needs immediate attention.

☐ Place magazines and newspapers in predetermined spots—an end table or a special basket. Purge these spots on Cleaning Day.

☐ Take newsletters and invitations with dates of events straight to the calendar and write down their dates immediately. Then put the details into your Pending File.

☐ Place catalogs that you order from with your magazines and newspapers. Toss catalogs you don't use into the trash or recycling.

☐ File statements and important papers immediately or put them in the Action File and File them on Office Day.

☐ Schedule time daily for this chore—don't let it pile up!

TOWN DAY

The purpose of Town Day is to knock out your errands. Why establish a day for this? For some of us the answer is clear: We live so far from town, that to run in for every little thing would drive us into poverty.

For those who live conveniently close to all stores, I still strongly suggest that you establish a Town Day in your family life for the same reason we country folk do—efficiency. You will save time and money by disciplining yourself to doing your errands on one day. It helps keep life simple.

Keep track of the time you spend running here and there for this and that. It takes effort to dress, shoe, buckle in, grab the purse and diaper bag, just for a few things at the store. Work on being more efficient with your time, using the time and money you save for greater purposes. As much as possible, schedule appointments, lessons, and outside-the-house activities for Town Day.

It is very easy to get involved in lots of good activities; I know that all too well. But when we do that, we end up substituting the best with the good or even the mediocre. Sometimes we run around to various activities as a way of escaping responsibilities at home. For some, out-of-sight means out of mind. When we are busy going here and there, busy doing this and that, everyone tends to get tired and irritable, the laundry piles up, the quality of the food we eat goes down, and relationships suffer. Are events and activities worth it?

Little children thrive with routine in their days; if you have children, be mindful of their needs and how they are affected by your lifestyle.

Plan your errands carefully to make the most of your time. Following are my step-by-steps suggestions on how to do this effectively—starting with your routine the day before and continuing through the end of errand day itself.

THE DAY BEFORE

☐ Balance the checkbook.

☐ Make your menu plan and shopping lists. Put your lists in your purse.

☐ Pack the diaper bag.

☐ If you have items to take back to town, put them in the vehicle.

☐ If you have stops to make after the grocery store, then put an ice chest in for your cold items.

☐ Plan your route to be as efficient as possible. If you will need to eat in town, work that into your plan.

☐ If you have a lot of little children, you need to be extra diligent about how you plan your day. Miserable children make for a miserable day. Do not stress them more than they can handle. If they are even slightly ill, take that into account in how you plan your day.

THE NIGHT BEFORE

☐ Lay out town clothes and shoes for everyone. Put everyone to bed at a decent time, if not earlier than usual.

☐ Know what your supper plan is for Town Day, and do the prep work for it.

☐ Know your lunch plan, and either pack a lunch, get it ready to eat when you get home, or decide where you plan to eat out.

THE MORNING OF

Load the slow cooker so you do not have to worry about making supper that night. Leave immediately after breakfast chores are done so that you can be home as soon as possible for the little ones to get their naps. Require everyone to use the toilet before leaving.

Evaluate the conditions of the day, yourself, and your children. There are times when the Town Day must be called off due to health reasons, behavior, stress, anxiety, or the weather. Life with Littles can present challenges and sometimes it's just better to stay home.

HINTS FOR BEING EFFICIENT

☐ In scheduling your day, add in extra time for changing somebody's complete outfit at the last minute, for losing one of the toddler's shoes, and for hitting every red light.

☐ Plan your stops so that you do not have to backtrack. Do the most necessary stops first; if the little children begin to meltdown, you can head for home.

☐ Do not give the children anything except water to drink unless you *like* to go into the restroom of every store you visit. Take along water; my preference is for each person to have a personal water bottle, but it's also handy to have a case of water bottles along.

☐ Park your vehicle by a cart corral so that you can immediately put your little children in a cart and push them into the store.

☐ If you have a little baby, time your trip so that he won't be starving hungry halfway through the store. Keep an eye on the clock, and don't dawdle.

☐ Stores typically have low-volume traffic in the early mornings which makes the aisles much easier to move through. In the late afternoon and towards the end of the week, they tend to be very busy which can give an instantaneous headache. Do your best to plan the brunt of your shopping when the stores are more navigable.

STORE MANNERS FOR CHILDREN

Go over the Store Manners before you leave the vehicle, and review them again between each stop:

☐ Smile and enjoy the day; have fun.

☐ When you get out of the vehicle, do not rub your coat against the cars and get dirty.

☐ When you get out of the vehicle, be careful not to door ding the next car.

☐ In the parking lot, hold hands with your buddy (an assigned sibling) and stay together.

☐ Do not run around in the parking lot!

☐ Walk in age order behind Mom, with the oldest taking up the rear to make sure we do not lose anyone. Do not get out of line (A trouble maker or two might have to hold on to the cart.).

☐ No crawling on the floor.

☐ No wrestling in stores.

☐ No yelling or screaming.

- ☐ No asking for things.

- ☐ No hiding in the clothes.

- ☐ No hissy fits.

- ☐ Do not touch the price tabs in the grocery store. If you move price tabs, the next person will not know what the item costs.

- ☐ Do not touch items in the stores unless we are buying it. Would you like to buy something that smelled like a French fry?

- ☐ Do not touch each other unless you are holding hands.

- ☐ Don't go anywhere without mom!

I reward for good behavior. I think that we all need a treat to have on the way home. Going to town is an outing. We do our best to make it go well and have fun, and part of the fun is a treat on the way home.

Children who did not use their manners or were disrespectful are dealt with at home. I know that there are those that say to leave the store and go home with the unruly child. Let me say also that I am talking about children who don't have other issues going on, such as sensory disorders. We live too far from town to go home because of somebody's behavior. Having mannerly children starts at home. If they are respectful at home, they will be respectful in public. If I am concerned about a child's behavior, I have found that laying out clear expectations and their consequences and then following up with those consequences will usually prevent further infractions. If a child seems to want to test, I will discipline for the first infraction of the day while we are still at home. This prevents them from further testing. Sometimes I need to get down at eye level and have some words of instruction with a child in a store.

I have found that the way the shopping goes largely depends on my preparation for the day and my attitude. I try to make it fun, and we take time to smell the fresh strawberries in the produce section and even window-shop a bit. If you want your children to be pleasant in public, you need to take them out in public to learn how.

The children get accustomed to the stores and routines of your Town Day. They learn to help and anticipate your needs and the needs of their siblings. Children are a blessing. They will see things on the shelves that you need to buy and remind you of them. Believe it or not, you will come to rely on them and their memory jogs when you are shopping. They are like extra brains and right hands for you.

IN THE STORE

Put the baby into your baby carrier or the shopping cart's seat. Clean the cart first with a wipe. Put the toddlers into the back of the cart and require them to sit. It is nicer to sit on a coat or a package of toilet paper, paper towels, or diapers. If you need many items at the store, then have your biggest child push another cart. Or you can push one and pull the other. Some grocery stores have carts that are like a car in the front. Two children can fit in there. Fasten the seatbelt and teach them to keep their arms inside, and the toddler can ride in the seat while you have the littlest in the front carrier.

Some stores will shop for you, and you will only need to pick the items up when you're done shopping. Call around to your local stores to find out which ones offer this option. It may be the answer you need for a season.

EATING OUT OR NOT

Drive-through eating can add up to an unwanted expense in several ways; it often leaves the children still hungry and is extremely unhealthy—not to mention the fact that the smell of fast food in the vehicle can be nauseating! Given these facts, whenever possible, eat at home or pack sandwiches (Get them ready the night before.). It is a treat to stop at a park for a picnic and a playground.

WHEN YOU GET HOME

When you arrive home from running errands, put the little ones down for a nap first. Have the older children unload the bags and put away refrigerator items while you feed the baby. Then let everyone go to Quiet Time. They need a break from running around, and so do you. Take this into account when planning your day and keeping it a happy day. Sit down and have a glass of water with a lemon slice cut into it or a cup of tea.

Wash the salad vegetables. Cut up the dry vegetables and toss. This will keep for several days if you don't add tomatoes, mushrooms, cucumbers, and other moist items. Cut those at each meal. Put your older children in charge of cutting and putting items into the refrigerator. Many hands make light work.

During Afternoon Chore Time, have the family distribute the shopping items to their proper places.

RECOVERY

If it was a very rough day in town (and I know you know what I mean), thank the Lord you put food into the slow cooker. The bare minimum is to get the cold items put away, and then everyone can go to their Quiet Time place until supper is ready. The chores can wait until tomorrow. Rest and food restores the sanity as nothing else does.

The next day, balance the checkbook again. Staying on top of this small chore keeps the finances under control.

HOW TO DO TOWN DAY IF YOU ARE A HOMESCHOOL FAMILY

If your Town Day only involves a short trip, then you can do your daily school routine during the hours when you are at home. If you choose to do your Town Day in the morning, do your normal schedule after lunch. If you do your Town Day in the afternoon, then don't change your schedule until an hour before you leave, then stop your regular routine and have the family prep for leaving.

When you are out, listen to educational audios whenever appropriate. There are so many great audios available to learn from. Driving is the perfect time for them because the children are buckled in and are a captive audience. My children love it so much that they hate to stop the audios and go into a store.

If you are going to spend an extended time in a waiting room, pack schoolwork that can happen in the waiting room.

When the children get home from a big Town Day, they are often very tired. This is a good time to pull out an educational video and let them relax in front of it for a time. Then send them outside to run and play.

Do not forget that learning to be gracious to those around us is an important lesson to master. Set a good example and teach the children to be pleasant to other people, to smile, and to look others in the eye when speaking to them. When people ask us big family or homeschooling questions, smile and answer graciously, even if the question is rude. Love God; love others. If we see somebody that needs help, we help them. Hold the door for others. Town Day is an opportunity for ministry to our communities.

LARGE QUANTITY MEALS

In the early days of large family living, before you have to start doubling, tripling, quadrupling, and buying cookbooks with restaurant-size recipes, employ money-saving ideas like reading all the ads, shopping for the best deals at all the stores, keeping a price book, clipping coupons, and playing the coupon game.

At some point, however, if your family grows to be large, the effort it takes to do all those things will generally not be worth the time involved in the broader scheme of things.

There comes a time when you will simply want a pantry full of bulk goods that allows you to make virtually anything, and when you cross this threshold, your shopping habits will change dramatically. The convenience of bulk will outweigh the inconvenience of running out to get small things.

When you reach this point, learn to substitute food items creatively. For example: If you are out of cornstarch, use arrowroot powder instead. Out of arrowroot powder? Use flour as a substitute. Is minute tapioca a better choice? In other words, creativity becomes an important rule to get you by when it's impractical to make a trip to the store.

If you have a well-stocked pantry, you have lots of creative leeway. Buying in bulk is not always less expensive, but it saves time. The workload as mom to a lot of kids is huge, and looking at the big picture, it is better to spend precious time building relationships than itemizing a price book.

Stocking a pantry for a large family does not mean buying more boxes of Uncle Ben's rice; it means a 25-pound bag of brown basmati rice. Stick it in the deep freeze for a day to kill any bugs and it will be good for a long time.

You don't need to learn this method all at once. One step at a time, one food at a time is fine, just as with any other new thing you're seeking to master.

- ☐ Ask around your community to learn about food co-ops. If there aren't any, then start one. Create a group, contact wholesalers, divide the labor, and stock up your pantry.

- ☐ Buy in bulk from your local grocery store. Ask the management about ordering a case of an item for a discount. You both win with this scenario: you get a discount, and they are selling more products and might get a further discount from their supplier.

- ☐ Shop at a food service store. These supply restaurants and institutions.

- ☐ Shop at warehouse stores, especially for paper goods.

- ☐ Garden and buy produce from a farmer's market or a CSA (Community Supported Agriculture) farm.

- ☐ Shop at bulk food stores.

- ☐ Buy meat by the whole beef or pork. Get it cut the way you want it, and store it in a deep freeze.

Storing bulk food might necessitate creative solutions. Look around and reevaluate what is truly necessary. Look inside your cupboards and closets and think how you can group and arrange items more efficiently—like with like. Remove nonessential items and put them into storage. One thing we did to add more needed storage space was to put shelves in a coat closet near the kitchen. We also have shelves in the basement for extra food. Five-gallon food grade buckets are the most common way to store large quantities. Also be sure that your storage containers are mouse-proof.

CLEANING DAY

Cleaning is a task that is easy to do if all the stuff that your family leaves lying around is picked up. Those of you who have had a housecleaner know what I mean. A housecleaner comes and whips through the house, and its spic-and-span. She's like a magic fairy. How does she do it? I'll tell you how: she has the *easy* part, the actual cleaning. You did the hard part of putting away everything that you left lying around since the last time she came. The actual cleaning part is not that hard. It is everything that has to happen in order *to* clean that is hard. Put simply: your stuff is in the way.

PICK UP THE MESS

Flat surfaces are magnets for people to put stuff on. Catch people at it, catch yourself at it, and stop the bad habit. Instead, put things where they belong. "A place for everything, and everything in its place." Say it over and over and over to yourself and to your family. Make fold-up signs in bright neon colors on every level surface for three weeks to train them to stop laying things down where they don't belong. When things are constantly put in their proper place, then the house is not messy.

This is another reason why Afternoon Chore Time is so important. Do a daily pick up of every room and clear all flat surfaces. Do it to catch everything that those still in training (toddlers) leave lying around. If everyone works on a room, the load is shared, and the pickup time will be finished much more quickly.

If you don't have enough big kids to help, then it is essential to your peace of mind to *limit* the stuff that can be carried about. Here are some practical ideas to help you control needless clutter:

- ☐ Lock the cupboard of games, puzzles, and art supplies. Keep the key out of reach, and get activities out only at designated times of the day. When the children are done, help them put the activity away.

- ☐ Limit the number of toys your children have. Do a massive declutter. Focus on quality and imaginative toys.

- ☐ Rotate toys by the week, month, season. Keep the rest boxed and stored, out of sight and mind.

- ☐ Designate specific places for things. Make sure everyone knows where certain things belong and what rooms/cupboards/shelves should look like when they are clean and straightened. Take a picture of the spot so the cleaner knows what it should look like.

HELP ME, PLEASE!

If you're a mom with a lot of littles and no big kids, or you are having a difficult time keeping up with the cleaning for some other reason, then, by all means, get some cleaning help. There are seasons in life where you just need some help. Trading services for goods or bartering is a wonderful way to meet needs without using money. Some professional services will let you pick and choose what you want help with. Maybe you want two hours of help, or perhaps you just need the kitchen and bathrooms really scrubbed once a month.

CREATING A CLEANING DAY ROUTINE

In the Morning

Instead of making the beds, strip them and take the sheets straight to the washer. Wash the nappers' bedding first, and remake those beds before lunch. That way, as soon as lunch is over and the Littles are clean, they can go straight to their naptimes.

Afternoon Chore Time

First, put the baby/toddler in the playpen, and get the preschoolers involved in an activity that will occupy them for one hour, or send them with their buddy to help and learn how to clean. Which one you do will definitely depend on the preschooler and the older buddy's unique personality and personal work ethic. Matching him up with a buddy can be a great thing or not, depending on the children involved.

After the youngest children are settled, you and the older children do your regular room chores just like you always do during Afternoon Chore Time, but today add dusting and vacuuming for each room. Vacuuming and dusting will not add much time to each room's regular daily chores. Work around a room top to bottom, left to right.

Another way to do it, depending on each family's dynamics, is for the children to team up and straighten rooms as a group, with one child the Duster, one catching cobwebs, and another child the Vacuumer. Think about your family dynamics and what will work best in your situation. When the children are very little it will all fall onto the adults, choose a room and go through it methodically and be gracious with the interruptions that little children bring. This is when a cleaning list in your Home Management Book is so handy, just take a glance to recall what you have done and what to do next.

Remake the beds with the clean sheets. Get it done as early as you can so that when bedtime comes you can just fall in and relax.

Reward the children with a break and a treat. Then do the Deep Cleaning work.

KEEPING UP WITH THE WORK

Beat the clock is a fun game for the children. We love challenges, and it is fun to beat old records. What speed-cleaning does is teach the children to not procrastinate. When they know that a certain task takes a certain amount of time, they will do it and move on. Eyeballing a task for a long period, dragging our feet, and grumbling through it allows a poor work ethic to develop. Teach your family to stay on top of work by doing it thoroughly and quickly.

By contrast, without a system, a plan, or a simple chore chart, nobody gets much done because they don't know what they are supposed to be doing.

The good thing about systems is that they don't require a lot of thought once you understand and master them. You and your team can just go to work and do what needs to be done without a lot of deliberation. The tasks and methods are in place; the workers just need to show up and do the job.

By contrast, without a system, a plan, or a simple chore chart, nobody gets much done because they don't know what they are supposed to be doing. If the team is told to do something, but does not know how to do it, they will be frustrated! Without systems, without knowing how to do a task, the cleaning *will* be hard. It will lose its joy and be depressing.

A good system and willing workers promote a good attitude in everyone. It's a good feeling to look at a mess and know that it will all be put back together with a little time and elbow grease.

Make it enjoyable for you and your cleaning crew by having the right tools on hand and keep them stored in accessible places.

- ☐ Dustcloths. Keep plenty on hand for passing out to little children.

- ☐ Feather dusters are great for everyday dusting. Little children love to use them.

- ☐ An extending cobweb duster.

- ☐ Broom and dustpan for hard floors (necessary when you don't want a vacuum to wake a light sleeper).

- ☐ Vacuum.

- ☐ Glass cleaner.

- ☐ Cleaning rags or paper towels, especially for little children to wipe doors, light switches, or appliances.

- ☐ Fast-paced music.

- ☐ Timer to find out and show to the cleaning crew how long it actually takes to do a task.

DEEP CLEANING

In times past, people did spring cleaning and fall cleaning. We no longer have to clean the grime that our foremothers did, but we still need to dig in deep on a regular basis in order to keep things clean that are in, under, and behind the furnishings of our homes. Deep cleaning can be done regularly so that we don't have to upset our home for a week. A little bit here and a little bit there goes a long way in getting deep cleaning work done so that it won't become an overwhelming job.

RECOMMENDED COURSE OF ACTION

Divide your home into key areas. I call them "Focus Areas" because we are good at what we focus on, and I want to focus on an extra-good cleaning on a regular basis. Each home will have a different arrangement of Focus Areas, depending on the structure of the home and the lifestyle of the family.

In my home, I have each Focus Area written on a specific week of each month on our wall calendar. I also keep a list of the Focus Areas by week in my Home Management Book. We do deep cleaning work for each Focus Area and then extra things that are situation-specific to that area.

Week 1

Dining room/schoolroom/bookshelves

Devote time this week to going on a book hunt throughout the house and returning all books to their proper place. Pull out a shelf or two of books and thoroughly dust the books and shelf. Thoroughly dust dining room and schoolroom. Vacuum edges.

Week 2

Bathrooms

It doesn't take long for a large family to make a bathroom gross. If you keep the bathroom work assigned to certain children to clean daily, then the rooms shouldn't be too bad. However, once a month, clean all the corners, cracks, and crevices. Declutter the cabinets and drawers, and organize all the ponytails, barrettes, headbands, bows, ribbons.

Mudroom/backdoor entry

The entries that you use most frequently need special focus. They can get cluttered and dirty quickly. Assign a family member to do daily maintenance on this area during Afternoon Chore Time.

Scrub the walls once a month. If everyone takes a wet rag for fifteen minutes, the work will be done in no time. If you involve the kids in the cleaning, they will be more apt to catch themselves and notice when a sibling puts their grubby mitts on the wall. During a Project Week, paint this area with a high gloss paint. This will make cleaning the walls much easier.

Week 3

Bedrooms

This should be an easy week if you have your children work on cleaning bedroom areas as part of their chores throughout the month. Have them spend a few minutes each day picking up as part of their Morning and Evening Routine. Then have them spend one 15-minute period per week working on a Bedroom Management Focus Area. If you follow this approach, keeping the bedrooms clean will be a cinch.

Week 4

Living room and family room

Vacuum the dust out of the furniture. Clean in couches and chairs, under tables, behind furniture, and under curtains where cobwebs hide.

Week 5

Playroom/toys/games/crafts

This week is devoted to decluttering and organizing efficient systems in playrooms and other places where games and crafts are stored and used.

WHEN DO I DO THE WORK IN THESE FOCUS AREAS?

There are two ways to go about Deep Cleaning in your week. You and your children can do a small part each day which you write into your daily routine. You can devote a larger segment of time on Cleaning Day; write out the tasks for that day. Or you can do both.

Give it thought and do what will work best for your home and family situation. You might try one thing and then find that you need to adjust to fit your family's schedule. As the weeks go by and the house becomes better managed and more consistently clean, Deep Cleaning will become easier and easier, which means that it will take less time to do.

The following is a listing of how we have Deep Cleaning chores divided up by day of the week. Sometimes we mix the tasks up so that they fit better with other things that are going on with that day.

Maybe you will only schedule these things on two other days, plus Cleaning Day. For instance, we don't do window washing on Town Day. Often we don't do Deep Cleaning on Kitchen Day, especially if we have a lot of kitchen projects going on. Typically, we do the Deep Cleaning tasks during Afternoon Chore Time.

When everyone works together, it goes fast. If you don't have a lot of big kids to help divide the work with yet, then just do your best at pecking away at it. Use our family's Deep Cleaning schedule to brainstorm and devise a schedule that works best for your home situation.

Monday

Decluttering and cleaning are ongoing processes. The less you have, the less you have to take care of. "You don't own your stuff, your stuff owns you," the saying goes. Take care of all the clutter in the Focus Area. This includes clutter in drawers and cupboards. Evaluate everything in the area:

- ☐ Is it useful?

- ☐ Is it needed?

- ☐ Is it loved?

- ☐ Is it beautiful?

☐ Does it promote your family values?

☐ Do you have more of this item than necessary?

☐ Is it taking up needed space?

☐ Do other people need this item more than you do?

☐ Does it create problems in your house?

If you have a lot of clutter, just work on it for ten or fifteen minutes in one area of your home, and then stop until you come around to this area of the house again next month. In the meantime, do not add more clutter to this Focus Area. Load the clutter into boxes. Take the boxes to the vehicle to drop off at charity on Town Day.

Tuesday

Catch cobwebs (elementary age kids can do this). Kill the spiders! Dust lights and ceiling fans and replace light bulbs (a job for your tallest family members). Dust base boards (a good job for preschoolers). Assign tasks to the children, and race the clock. Put on music and have fun.

Wednesday

Straighten one drawer or cupboard (elementary age kids can do this). If it goes fast, do another one. Stop after fifteen minutes.

Thursday

Wash windows and curtains, as necessary. Wash area rugs. Wipe grime from light switches (a preschooler's job).

Friday

Vacuum in the corners and around the edges *in* and *under* the furniture. This counts as an exercise workout for today. If there are Deep Cleaning tasks for the specific Focus Area that you didn't get done earlier in the week, do them today.

Saturday

Putter and pretty, this is the fun day! Look around and think about how to add a little something special to the room, but be sure that you aren't adding clutter that will increase the work load. There's a fine line here. Does the Focus Area need a new furniture arrangement? Should you start shopping for something that will fit a certain wall area? Write it down and put it in your wallet to remind you when you're out shopping. A simple vase of garden flowers or a bowl of fruit will add a dash of pizzazz to a room.

Do not feel that you must get every single task done; you will be cleaning in the same Focus Area of the house next month. Your home will slowly become decluttered and cleaner as each month goes by. By focusing on one area of the house at a time, you are less likely to be distracted and running around cleaning a bit here and a bit there. This approach also creates a great sense of satisfaction to see an area of the house clean and well-managed.

WINDOW CLEANING

Do not be intimidated by window cleaning. Clean windows will brighten and cheer your day! A Focus Area might have one window or eight. Some windows, due to location, don't get that dirty, and a once-a-year cleaning is fine for them. Other windows (like the ones on my front porch) need to be washed once a month during fly season. With the windows for each Focus Area, think about these things: How dirty are they? How much help do I have? How easy are the windows to clean? Do I need to hire a professional to help?

Create a system for window cleaning. If your children are old enough to help, give them each a task. Time it, and see how long it takes you to clean one window. Then you will be better able to judge how much window cleaning will fit in a day.

I have lived in old houses and know full well the trials of trying to clean the worst window situations possible. When we built our house several years ago, new windows were one of the things I was most excited about. I would go to the new house and lift them up and down and open them and imagine how easy it would be to clean these windows! But I should have been just as thankful for the old windows simply because I had them! How many pioneer women were so excited to just get a single pane of glass to let light into their dugout during the winter. God, forgive me for my discontent.

Here's my window washing system in these days with lots of helpful children. When I had only little children, I did it alone. I remember little children liking to play with the bubbles from my bucket.

Child #1 washes the outside window with bucket of soapy water and then sprays the cleaner on and wipes with newspaper (a cheap and effective method of cleaning windows). This step isn't necessarily done during cold weather.

Child #2 washes the screens, either with a hose and rag or a bucket of soapy water for the really dirty screens, or in the bathtub, during cold weather.

Children #3 and #4 clean the grime in the window frame first with a vacuum and then with a rag and little brush and their own bucket of soapy water.

I give directions and clean the inside windows and the outside part of the bottom pane that folds into the house. If I'm hugely pregnant or postpartum, then the children also do this part.

If we're washing upstairs windows, Child #1 also goes out on the roof and cleans out the gutters. He enjoys this task. It's the danger part. He's a thrill seeker; need I say more?

When we are all working together, window cleaning goes very fast. Happy, fast-paced music helps. So does an ice cream treat for when we are finished. I have some windows that don't get that dirty, and I just employ one child to do the screen, and I do the rest with the window cleaner—no soapy buckets necessary. These windows take less than ten minutes for me to do.

If we do a lot of Deep Cleaning in one day, we work on it for an hour and then stop. What we don't get done in that Focus Area of the house in one month, we work on the next month. Like anything else, if the cleaning is kept up with, the windows don't get that dirty and they're fast and easy to clean. If you allow them to go uncleaned for two years, it will be a huge chore and take a lot more time. Keep your window washing tools and buckets collected and in a specific place so you can quickly and easily get them and do the job with ease.

GARDENING DAY

Gardening Day is the scheduled day when we focus on outdoor work. It doesn't mean that we don't do things like sweep the porch or water plants on other days, but by focusing on the outdoor areas of the home one day every week, we keep things nicely kept and groomed.

THE OUTDOOR LIFE

On Gardening Day, I assign each child specific tasks for the day. These tasks are done weekly during certain seasons. If it's a big job, we all work together. In the days when my older children were small, my husband and I did the majority of the work while the children tagged along or played in the yard. By assigning tasks, you are ensuring that the job gets done, and you are teaching skills and building responsibility in your children.

Take a look around your outdoor areas, and list tasks that need done to help keep it tidy and attractive. Think about hospitality and making it easy and pleasant for guests to get to your front door or to find a place to sit on the front porch or in another outdoor eating area.

Here is a basic list of tasks our family does on Gardening Day:

- ☐ Pick up trash and toys from the yard

- ☐ Mow

- ☐ Weed

- ☐ Water plants

- ☐ Sweep the porch and sidewalk (shovel snow in the winter)

- ☐ Sweep the deck

- ☐ Straighten the garage

- ☐ Sweep the garage

- ☐ Clean the vehicles

During the outdoor living season, give serious thought to making your landscape hospitable. Do you have an outdoor sitting or eating area? Think about other yards that you admire, and jot down ideas that you would like to incorporate into your landscape. It can be as simple as two chairs and a drink table placed beside the sandbox for you and friend to sit at while your children play. Do you have a front porch? Then put a couple of chairs there for evenings so that you can enjoy listening to the night sounds. When you look at your yard, think of it in terms of hospitality.

My personal favorite part of gardening is growing flowers and food. It is not complicated. Seeds are life in suspension—a beautiful thing! Add soil, water, and sun, and amazing things happen. If you are intimidated by what it takes to garden, then start with plants from the garden center rather than seeds. Flowers will beautify your landscape and vegetables are nearly free food.

Even if you learn to grow only one vegetable, you will save money and bolster the health of your family. My sister-in-law likes to save money by growing onions. She uses them daily, and finds them easy to grow. When she has to buy them in the spring because her supply is used up, she is shocked by the prices.

I am a fan of growing my own salad greens. I am still learning, and one of my life goals is to learn to grow greens all year long. I know it can be done, and every year I get a little smarter about extending the season. Another thing I love to grow is tomatoes. There is nothing like the flavor of a fresh tomato from the garden. My mouth starts watering just thinking about BLT sandwiches with fresh tomatoes or snacking on sun-warmed cherry tomatoes as you walk through the garden. Delicious!

My children frequently get their snacks from the garden. Asparagus spears in early spring, strawberries, lettuce, green onions, peas, green beans, carrots, raspberries and more are all eaten fresh right off the plant throughout the growing season. I like to wrap a basil leaf around a cherry tomato for my garden snack.

Gardening is an extension of the home life, and managing the outdoor work is part of the whole picture.

Selling your beautiful flowers and vegetables is a wonderful experience for everyone involved. Farmer's markets are so fun—you get to know new people, the children learn business skills, and others enjoy food that you and your family worked hard to produce. We have had several fun years taking our garden fare to local markets. I highly recommend pursuing this activity as a family. You won't get rich; it is the experience that brings value.

Gardening is an extension of the home life, and managing the outdoor work is part of the whole picture. Nearly free food, a bouquet for your table, a spot for to have an outdoor tea party, a clean vehicle to drive to church on Sunday—all these things make our lives more beautiful. Plan a day to focus on the tasks that make them happen.

GARDENING 101

You can have a green thumb! A key component is going to your garden frequently and keeping the weeds down. This is great exercise and will save you money from buying exercise equipment and incurring gym fees. It will also help you keep an eye on how ripe your crop is, or if it could use some water.

If you are a beginning gardener, I do not recommend going all out and growing the one-acre market garden with every conceivable vegetable. Tuck that idea away for when you and your children are more proficient gardeners. It's a great idea, but not one for beginners.

From experience, I also know that if you are pregnant and due at the end of summer, do not grow a big garden. Unless, of course, you think five-foot-tall weeds are a thing of beauty. If you are going through the first trimester of pregnancy at the beginning of the gardening year, it also wise to forego a big garden.

If it is the middle of a pregnancy and you're feeling great, go for it, just keep it in moderation. Maybe grow a tomato plant in your flower garden, but no market gardening. If you have a fresh baby, you will not feel up to a large garden. Take it easy and plan a weekly excursion to the farmer's market instead. You will get better prices and higher quality than from shipped-in produce. You can get to know the grower and gain tips on how to prepare the produce you buy for eating, as well as how to grow it for yourself.

If you have big kids excited about growing things and know a little bit about gardening, you can rely on them to be the gardeners, and you can participate from your lawn chair in the shade. Choose cool times of the day to work, and be their cheerleader.

If you feel healthy and wonderful, and you want to start growing food for your family this year, here's what I suggest. First, decide what your family's favorite vegetable is. Study how to grow it in a gardening book, and then make it a family project. You might decide that your family's favorite vegetable looks too touchy, so choose another one to start with. My point with the favorite vegetable strategy is that you will be committed to it, will look forward to the harvest, and the children will have fun in the process.

Another easy beginning strategy is the salad garden. Salad vegetables can be easy to grow. If children grow their own salad, they will also be more apt to start eating salads, if they don't already. Salad gardens can be tucked into existing flower beds around the house or in large pots on your porch, eliminating the need to till up a separate garden plot.

Salsa gardens are also easy to grow. You don't need to put in the super-hot peppers, although you may. If you do, beware that they should only be handled while wearing disposable gloves. Take this into consideration if you have a very curious toddler.

Once you have decided which vegetables you want to grow, decide how much of each vegetable you want to raise. That will determine the size of your garden plot. If you are planning a garden on the large side, you will need to get your garden plot tilled. Look in the local paper or ask around for somebody who does this for hire. If your soil is poor, take steps to enrich it. The how-to of this is well-covered in gardening books. Typically adding manure will give you a great start towards good gardening soil. Another very helpful source of information is your state or county extension service. Extension agents can help you plan your garden and have lots of information that your tax dollars pay for. They will tell you what you need to know or where to find the information you're looking for. They might also know somebody who will till your garden or provide you with a source of manure.

Once you have your vegetables planned, your plot tilled, and the soil adequately enriched, it's time to plant the seeds or plants that you purchased at the local nursery. For easy beginning gardening, buy plants at the nursery rather than seeds (such as tomatoes, peppers, cabbage, broccoli, and herbs). For some vegetables such as beans or peas, this isn't an option. These are easy to start from seed anyway.

Try to minimize disappointments during your first year of gardening. Follow the directions that come with the seed or plant. It might seem a little silly to plant a little itty-bitty seed or plant so far away from the next one, but you will experience one of the beauties of God's creations and that is how a plant can grow in front of your eyes. Don't blink! When the asparagus comes up in the spring, it grows an inch per hour at a temperature of 70 degrees!

Seeds that provide nearly instant gratification are radishes, lettuce, and beans. Vines such as cucumbers, squash, and pumpkins are also easy to grow. You can buy these as plants, but growing them from seed usually works just as well. Cucumbers, peas, and runner beans will grow up a fence, though one is not necessary. They will also spread all over the ground in a big green tangle, up and over nearby plants. You can call it a ground cover, and it will help prevent weeds from taking over the garden. If you want beans to climb, buy pole beans not bush beans.

A fun thing for children is to plant a teepee garden. "Plant" bamboo stakes in a circle, fastening them at the top with twine. At the base of each pole, plant a couple of bean seeds. Scarlet runner beans have red flowers that are pretty for this project. Children like to hide and play in the teepee.

The easiest garden plan of all—ideal for beginners or for years when you are short on help and/or incapacitated in one way or another—is to plant vegetables among the plants and bushes in the established beds around your house. Tuck a tomato plant here, a cucumber there, or a line of lettuce behind a row of flowers, and you will succeed at growing nearly free food with ease.

GARDENING WITH CHILDREN

Gardening is a huge learning opportunity, and there are so many helpful books to assist you in your effort. Share with your children what you are learning in the gardening books. Every time you go out and putter around in the yard, take them with you and tell them what you are doing.

Little children like to garden, and their sharp eyes will probably be better than yours at distinguishing between which seedlings are weeds and which are the plant you are seeking to grow. They are wonders at spotting bugs too.

Gardening with toddlers, however, is not always fun and can be a real challenge. They walk on the baby plants and will tear them out with their hands. They can be utter and complete destroyers of the work you've done. Toddlers should only be in the garden with complete supervision. If you take your eyes off of them, they can cause serious damage to young, tender plants. Been there, done that.

This being said, please take your toddler to the garden on a regular basis and talk about the plants. Teach respect for what you are growing. Soon the plants will be so huge that the toddler can't do much damage to them. In the meantime, keep your toddler in a playpen outside where he can see you (with special toys only for this time), assign him to an older sibling, or do the gardening during naptime.

Babies are much easier to garden with than a toddler. They take more naps, so it's easier to slip outside and garden then. They don't need to be trained in contentedness for the playpen. My sister-in-law kept an old swing beside her garden for her baby. A stroller or playpen under a tree is also good for little ones. They love to watch moving leaves. You may also need to get a bug net to protect them from bites.

When you are working in the garden, your other children can help with various tasks. They can dig holes for seedlings, water, weed, find pests, carry a harvest basket, and more. Praise them for all their help, talk to them, answer their questions, and ask them questions.

Older children appreciate the business opportunities that a garden can present. Children that don't yet have a driver's license are able to produce something, get paid for it, and have a social opportunity with the community through market gardening. Farmer's markets are something the whole family can contribute to and enjoy together.

Gardening is also an opportunity for ministry through giving your excess produce away. Take your bounty to church, your neighbors, retirement homes, and more.

Gardening is a very healthy endeavor for children in so many ways!

THE LORD'S DAY

Our family takes seriously God's directive to rest and honor him one day each week, and yet Sunday has been the most challenging day to effectively organize our family for many years. It seems that as soon as we get it figured out, we have a baby and start a new learning curve.

GET ME TO THE CHURCH ON TIME

Part of repairing the problem is first identifying it. There are two things that I think are at the root. One is that six days of the week, we have a completely different morning routine; and second, we go to bed with the thought in mind that tomorrow we are going to rest and relax. What I have learned is to treat Sunday morning just like any other day of the week when it comes to getting up on time for getting the family to church—do not sleep in!

Get up and get yourself ready first. The day before, know what you are going to wear and know that it fits. Get completely ready except for putting on your church dress. Any kind of mess can happen before you leave.

Have a simple breakfast planned, or make one on Saturday (such as a breakfast casserole). Get the children up and sitting at the table early. If they have a filling breakfast with protein, they will be happier kids throughout the morning.

Lay out the children's clothes the day before, including their tights, socks, and shoes. Make it a task on Laundry Day to wash and get the Sunday clothes ready. Keep them in a separate place such as the Laundry Room or your closet, so that a child doesn't misplace Sunday attire during the week.

Pack the diaper bag on Saturday; always keep the diaper bag packed but re-check it on Saturday. Also on Saturday, put the Bibles in a spot where they are easy to grab while going out the door, or go a step further and put them into the vehicle.

On Town Day, time how long it takes for your family to get out the door. This time allotment is likely longer than you think. On your Sunday morning routine, allow time for the lost shoe and spit-up mess. Know that your get-out-the-door routine will take longer on Sunday, and plan for it. I suspect that it takes longer because the children are excited that Dad is home, and also because Dad is part of the get-out-the-door routine.

Be sure that everyone uses the toilet before leaving the house.

Know how long it takes for you to feed the baby, and plan this into your Sunday morning routine. Burp her well so that she will not spit up all over her really cute Sunday clothes or on you.

Inspect everyone *before* they get in the vehicle. Too many times we have arrived at church only to discover that some small person is not wearing shoes.

When it comes to honoring the Lord's Day, don't give up, but persevere. And then rest, relax, and have fun the remainder of the day.

SUNDAY DINNER

I love the slow cooker and when I'm at my best, I load it the night before and put the stoneware insert in the refrigerator. The next morning, I put it in the base and turn it on to be ready by the time we get home from church. Side dishes can also be made in the slow cooker.

SUNDAY EVENING SUPPER

Keep it simple: serve sandwiches; popcorn and apples; leftovers; or cheese slices and fruit. Keep this day low stress and restful.

PLAN AHEAD

Take a look at the weekly calendar as a family so everybody has a good idea of what is going on and what is expected. Make adjustments as needed. Doing this will certainly help prevent things from being forgotten or double-booking events. Do your best to have an early night so that the week starts off with a good night's sleep.

CONNECT WITH YOUR CHILDREN

After being away from my family for three-and-half months when our preemie was born, I simply wanted to *be* with my family. It was not in me to get caught up in the tyranny of the urgent. My previous life had come to a screeching halt, and I was able to see with a clear eye what was truly important.

BUILDING RELATIONSHIPS

Without a doubt, the most important things in life are the relationships we have with those closest to us, the ones under our noses—our children who can at times get just as busy as we are with their own little projects and play ideas or with books, sports, and friends. They are the "least of these" (Matthew 25:45). They are the nearest "neighbor" (Galatians 5:14). They are the children we are to be teaching to love God (Deuteronomy 6).

Our primary efforts must be invested in relationships with our children. One way I did this was by hosting tea parties with my family. Everyone loves a tea party because, for that hour, we stop what we are doing, sit still, eat yummy food, drink good tea, talk, and laugh. This is one thing that my children, boys included, have always enjoyed doing. Over the years, we have had many such parties with grandmas, aunts, cousins, friends, or just our family. We did not do them regularly.

When I came home from the hospital with our preemie baby, that is one thing I decided that we were going to do deliberately and consistently every single week, and what a joy. Everybody looks forward to Tea Party Day. It is one of the highlights of our week. We plan it for late in the afternoon, and my husband, Matt, joins us when he gets home from his work. Our Tea Party then transitions into a light supper of soup and story time after the Table Chores are done.

Tea Parties have been a very good thing and have helped bond our family together, and I highly recommend taking the time and effort to have them regularly in your family. Your Tea Parties might not look like ours; you might choose to do something very different; the important thing is to take the time to build relationships through this delightful and relaxing activity.

MAKE IT EASY

I've made a two-page spread of Tea Party Recipes in my Home Management Book so that we can flip it open, divide the tasks, and do it quickly. We have learned how long it takes the kettle to boil, so we know when to put it on for four o'clock tea. We know how long it takes to make scones, mini-quiches, biscotti, and more, so that we can plan backwards and know when to start. Some weeks we go all out; some weeks we just make scones. By making this two-page spread of the tea party recipes, a no-effort soup supper recipe, and learning when to start the production in our day, we are making something that looks hard to be easy.

What good is it to just look at pretty things?

After lunch, we quickly do all of our work so that we can start on our Tea Party production. The faster we get done with the work, the more fun we get to have making the things for the tea party. We always use the pretty china tea cups, saucers, and pretty plates. They require hand washing, and some have broken, but how nice they look is what makes it so charming. It is sad when things break, but that is life. We can't get upset about things like that. What good is it to just look at pretty things? That's no fun! It is wonderful to look closely at the pretty designs, to feel the china, and to use our hands in a very careful way. This also provides our children with an opportunity to learn how they should take care of things.

FUN AND GAMES

Everyone at our tea party must make some effort to arrive at the table looking "proper." Good manners are required! We have improved at ironing and folding napkins. But it's not at all a stiff and formal time. We share all sorts of fun, jokes, stories, and hilarity. Tea Parties offer a special opportunity for us to bond with our children. I recommend that you plan regular times of the extraordinary for enjoyment with your family. Perhaps it will be a ten a.m. coffee hour on Thursdays or picnic snack time on Fridays under a tree in your yard. Think about your family, your uniqueness, your gifts, your setting, and do something that brings you together and connects you with your children.

MORNING
AND EVENING
ROUTINES

If you have ever been camping or slept outdoors, you know the joy that all of nature expresses at the morning. Before the dawn has even broken, the birds begin their morning songs. As dawn nears, sounds of wildlife become louder and more fervent. Then, when the sun begins its rise into the quickly lightening blue, all creation seems to burst into glory. The sky puts on a show of color from the palest yellow-pink to lavender as the last shades of midnight blue disappear to the west.

JOY COMES WITH THE MORNING

This is a revelation from God to us every morning. The mornings are a gift of still, calm, beauty, and majesty. We can see the sun rising over the horizon and get a glimpse of an idea of the glory of God. As the weather and seasons change, the sounds and the sights reveal even more examples of God's majestic order and character. To receive this gift of common grace, all you have to do is be there.

When camping, you have no choice in the matter. There are no thick walls and windows to block out God's wake-up call. In the everyday reality of life, however, you have to deliberately choose to get up, go outside, and praise God for this gift of another glorious day. Spending those dawn moments with God can give real inspiration and energy for the day ahead. Memories of the glorious morning linger as the daylight hours progress, spurring creativity and motivation to foster the same kind of morning the following day. Momentum builds. and soon the days when you can't have that beautiful time become a disappointment. Starting the day with God and with the calm of dawn is a great way to build strength and vigor so that you can, in turn, bless others.

When life has us feeling beat up, pressed down, and anxious, we sometimes wake up cursing the day. We have to *choose* to rejoice and be glad in it. We need to replace the groan with praise, *"This is the day that the Lord has made; we will rejoice and be glad in it"* Psalm 118:24, KJV.

Then, after we choose to rejoice and be glad in it, we choose to commit our works to the Lord. Yes, it may be a bad day for one reason or another, but if we cultivate an attitude centered on bringing glory to God, staying calm and seeking his peace, and doing our work heartily as unto the Lord, that bad day will be looked at with supernatural eyes. The interruptions and things that go wrong—the pressures that build and even explode around us—are serving some purpose that we may never know the reason for. Some moments you just have to pray, "Your will be done," and there are some days that we will have to pray this prayer unceasingly. When we seek God's will first and live gratefully, with our hands out for whatever he gives us, we can make it from dawn to dusk and beyond with his strength.

"The joy of the Lord is your strength."

—Nehemiah 8:10, KJV

Pleasant mornings and good starts depend on our attitudes. If you are having to hurry and scurry to catch up on what you didn't get ready the day before, your stress will likely spill over to the children and cause them to be on edge. If you are yelling, "Move it! Move it!" like a drill sergeant, then you're picking and tearing at the relationships with your children. Love God; love others. This is the goal: to start off your mornings teaching your children wisdom and speaking to your family with kindness.

Here's what I have learned: When I am prepared, both spiritually and physically, then I have no fear or anxiety and I am calm. When we are calm inside, we speak with calmness to our children. On the other hand, if the children wake to no direction at all, and the mess of the previous day still about, they learn to be wasteful with their time and the day starts off with frenzy. When our children wake to quiet, a plan, and a calm, kind mother, then they in turn have pleasant mornings. You can do this!

Children thrive on order; it gives them security. I keep saying that and I'll say it again because I've seen it lived out both ways over the years. Children want to know the plan for the day whether they can verbalize that or not. They want to know what to expect when they get up. They are healthy in a home of order, peace, and security. We can facilitate this. Planning, preparation, and the related action help build a happy heart in yourself which overflows to your family.

A GOOD MORNING STARTS THE EVENING BEFORE

I am convinced that a good morning experience for the whole family starts with the preparations that have been made the previous evening. Think about all the things that need to be done in your home in the morning for your family and home. Write down every little event and start working backwards. Many tasks depend on other tasks. For example, you can't lay out clean clothes to wear if the laundry is not caught up. There will be no clean dishes if the dishwasher did not get loaded and run.

Work on these ideas the day before in order to prepare for the morning:

☐ Gather laundry and sort so that you can start a load first thing in the morning. If you're sure it won't get stinky overnight, start a load in the washer at bedtime.

☐ Prep the kitchen for breakfast. Who wants to wake up to a dirty kitchen? It is so much more pleasant for you and your family to walk into a clean and pleasant kitchen, coffee brewing (load and set the timer), breakfast ready to cook. One of the children can be assigned to set the breakfast table.

☐ Check your calendar. Do not be surprised in the morning! Know when you go to sleep what the agenda is for the following day. If you need to leave right away in the morning, then get the bags and needed things ready the night before, even going as far as putting them in the vehicle.

☐ Lay out your clothes every evening for the appropriate activity scheduled the following day. If it is Cleaning Day, lay out clothes that are comfortable for cleaning. If it is Kitchen Day, choose appropriately. Even if you're not leaving the house, dress in a way that is self-respecting.

☐ Put your bedside lamps on timers to help you and your family go to sleep and awaken at appropriate times. You must get adequate sleep, yet you do not need to be lazy. Light or lack thereof helps the eyes and brain to shut down and to come on again in the morning.

☐ Before the light goes off and you go to sleep, make sure that you have done a bit to straighten your bedroom and bathroom, that you have read a Psalm and have it in your brain to sleep on, and that you have prayed. Give thanks to God for the day that has passed. Thank him for the day to come and make your requests to your heavenly Father; pray the Lord's Prayer.

The next morning when the light comes on and the alarm sounds, do not ignore them. You are prepared. You have a plan for a calm and consistent morning. Get up and get started on your day with focus. If you need help with a plan, write it all out on a note card and lay it on your bedside table the night before. Then pick it up and do the next thing.

Here are some ideas for a Morning Routine:

☐ Stretch and exercise before the brain turns on (lay your workout clothes beside your bed the night before).

☐ Read a Psalm.

☐ Make your bed.

☐ Straighten your bedroom and bathroom.

☐ Get dressed and ready for the day.

☐ Drink water.

☐ Start a load of laundry.

☐ Make breakfast, read the Bible; doing these with your spouse is an even greater start!

☐ Build up your relationship with your spouse by asking each other: "Is there anything I can do for you today?"

☐ Drink your morning coffee on the deck, and watch the sun come up.

☐ Read from Psalms and Proverbs to your children while they eat breakfast.

☐ Go over the plan for the day with your children and pray about it.

☐ Do food prep for lunch and supper while your children do the Table Chores.

☐ Take five minutes to check up on their bedroom and bathroom chores. Inspect what you expect.

Use these ideas as a springboard for what works best for you, your husband, and your family.

BE SPECIFIC

Work on putting your routine in the most efficient order. A portion of mine looks like this:

☐ Thank God for the morning.

☐ Wash face; put in contacts.

☐ Put on deodorant.

☐ Brush teeth.

☐ Moisturize.

☐ Enhance the natural (mascara, etc.).

At times, I have woken up late, gone straight to the kitchen in my robe, drunk coffee, fed the troops breakfast, and started supper for the slow cooker. In the process, I have cut up an onion and then gone back to my bathroom to do the bathroom routine. Do you see a problem with this picture? Have you ever tried to put in contacts after cutting up an onion? It will ruin your day. My thought was, "I'll get back to my bathroom after these hungry kids are fed." The lesson is this: discipline yourself to get up *before* you are rushed and do your Morning Routine in the most efficient order—contacts before onions!

Regular routines help your family start in their day right. Being prepared, serving healthy food, and setting the tone for the day are big responsibilities, and when they are met, you will see big changes in your home life. Of course, there are seasons (such as new baby or illness) when it is very hard to meet these responsibilities, but don't give up. It's okay for a season to call out to our husbands from the depths of the blankets, "Can I do anything for you today?" Just keep in mind that this isn't the ideal way to begin the day. Do your best to keep the same routine every single morning and the stress and anxiety levels will go down. Keep pressing on, and soon you will have great mornings and days again. Commit these things to the Lord and watch as he helps you through it all. Each day is new. Put yesterday behind you and get started today by planning for tomorrow. Do necessary prep work today to make tomorrow a success, and start each day out with joy.

MEAL TIME
ROUTINES

Meal time can be the most hectic point of the day for a family. It can be a challenge getting everyone to the table at the appointed time. Keeping busy, energetic children seated is another challenge. Food preparation can be overwhelming. And, an equally challenging time is cleanup because a big family makes a big mess.

STREAMLINE AND SAVE TIME

Here are some practical ideas I've found to master meal team routines.

A great meal time starts at the end of the previous meal. Do the Table Chores immediately after a meal. There are several reasons for doing the table chores right after you finish eating, besides the germ factor. First of all, it just looks yucky to walk into a kitchen halfway through the afternoon and see lunch dishes, table scraps, crumbs, and petrified gunk on the table. What an ugly picture that can lend itself to an ugly attitude! Second, when the table is clean, you can use it for other projects. If it is still dirty, you might be tempted to not do that craft or game that you were intending to do with the children. Third, it is easier to clean when the food is not dried hard as a rock to the dishes and table. Fourth, and most importantly, prompt action teaches your children discipline. Remember that we are teaching all the time, through our actions and inactions. Discipline yourself and your children to do the work immediately.

My current problem at lunchtime is keeping the children from running off to their next activity instead of waiting for the other members of the family to finish eating. The children *think* they will come back to do their chores, but in reality, someone else ends up doing them, usually their mother. We are working on staying at the table and having polite conversation while waiting for the rest of the family to finish their food.

The ultimate goal is to train your children to work attentively, cheerfully, and promptly. As parents, our job is to train our children to be clean and neat with the daily work of life. Being clean and neat is good manners; it is loving others. Teaching our children good manners is loving them and loving others.

Table Chores include the following, though your household may vary a bit:

☐ Call the family to do the pre-meal Table Chores.

☐ Set table.

☐ Fill water glasses.

☐ Pray, eat, converse.

☐ Scrape dishes.

☐ Carry dishes to sink or dishwasher.

☐ Load dishwasher.

☐ Collect trash from table, put cloth napkins in laundry.

☐ Put away food.

☐ Wipe table, chairs, high chair.

☐ Sweep under table.

☐ Wash dishes.

☐ Dry dishes.

☐ Put clean dishes away, unload dishwasher.

☐ Wipe counters.

Assign these chores to your children. If you have a lot of children, there is more work but also more help to do the work. Set up your work to be done efficiently. If you find that two people are tripping over each other trying to do their jobs, maybe those two jobs need to be combined and made for one person.

Use the timer and race it while doing kitchen chores. Try to get all of the cleaning chores done in 10 minutes or less. When you knock out these chores promptly, the children realize that the reward of doing work quickly is that they can then move on to other pursuits. They do not have to spend prolonged time in the kitchen. They can then go outside, read, do their other work or a favorite activity, or play until the next thing on the schedule. Work every day at getting it done *more* quickly and cheerfully. Keep a chart to record the times; make it fun.

As soon as Table Chore time begins, the person assigned dishwasher duty should go to the sink and fill it with hot, soapy water and begin cleaning the dishes. Everyone else should follow suit and work quickly. You might want to reward your children with a treat occasionally for being diligent or working cheerfully. Always reward them verbally, encouraging them as you see improvement. When the kitchen and table are clean, have them admire their work, and point out to them how pleasant it is to live in a clean home.

If your children are doing all the work, what are you doing? You are helping the little ones, being the cheerleader, looking at what needs done for the next meal, putting little ones down for naps, switching laundry loads. You're doing the next thing—cheerfully, of course, as unto the Lord.

If you don't yet have enough big kids who can be of real help, then you will have to do more of the work. Include your little ones in the work, and cheerfully train them. Soon they will be helping more and even doing it all. Preschoolers *can* do nearly all of the Table Chores, especially if you use lightweight dishes, small glasses and pitcher, and store your table dishes low. They can be taught to wipe the table and sweep the floor. They can unload and load the dishwasher. They can wash dishes. Preschoolers are fun and amazing.

Do not expect little children's work to be of the same quality as that of an adult or older child, but do allow them to do this work. Do not expect one preschooler to do the Table Chores after a meal for eleven people. Spread the Table Chores among the children. Give them ample praise, hugs, and kisses.

WASHING THE DISHES

Dishes should be done at every meal, regardless if there are two or twenty. Allowing dirty things to lie around the kitchen promotes messiness and the growth and spreading of bad bacteria. When you keep up with the dishes, and the kitchen clean, other things in the house tend to stay kept up. This is a truth, the motion of keeping things clean just keeps rolling as you move about and live in your home.

Preparing the next meal is a joy if you can walk into a clean kitchen. If it is a dirty mess, you do not feel like making anything. Creativity dies on the vine. A dirty kitchen is depressing. If you keep up with this one thing, it will make your family's life much more pleasant.

Choose which side of the sink you will keep your dish rack. This will depend on the layout of your kitchen and whether you are right- or left-handed. Put all of your dirty dishes on the opposite side of the sink from the dish rack. Clean the counter around your dish rack, as you do not want to contaminate your clean dishes.

Scrape and rinse the dirty dishes, and place them in the order that you will wash them. Cleanest to dirtiest: glasses first, then silverware, then serving dishes, then plates, and finally cooking pots and pans.

Fill one sink with hot soapy water and the second sink with hot rinse water. The water should be as hot as you or your child can stand it. If you don't have many dishes to do, then do not waste water on filling the sinks; use a dish pan or a large mixing bowl instead. Also, running the water constantly for dishwashing or rinsing is unnecessary and wasteful.

To wash, you will need a dishcloth, a scraper, a bottlebrush for glasses, and a scruffy. Wash the dishes and put them into the rinse water. Have your dishwashing apprentice (this is the person you are training to wash dishes) pull the dishes out of the rinse water and onto the drying rack. Then have her dry them with a fresh, floursack-style drying cloth. The advantage of this kind of towel is that it does not leave lint on the dishes.

When the towel gets wet, the apprentice should get a fresh towel. Lay the wet one over a rack to dry, and once it is dry, put it in the dirty laundry.

Your dishwashing apprentice should put away the dishes as he dries them. If the dishwashing sink gets too dirty, refill it with hot soapy water. If the rinse sink gets too soapy, refill it with clean water.

After you are done with the dishes, take your dishcloth and wipe the counters, the stove, and lastly the sink. At this point, the apprentice should have everything put away. Wash the dish rack and drainer, and place them in the cupboard under the sink. Then scrub the faucet and the crevices around the sink. Next, clean the drain, and wipe the sink itself. Finally, take your last dish-drying towel and dry the sink.

Stand back with your apprentice and admire a job well done. This is true beauty, a necessary work done with excellence. Take time to appreciate it, and pat each other on the back. The next time you walk into the kitchen to prepare the next meal, you will be so much more cheerful and ready to do the work with a good attitude.

I wrote out every little detail I could think of in the process to give you a full picture of all the steps involved. When you are actually doing it, you might have to focus on the details quite a bit until it becomes a regular routine. This system is efficient, and once you have it down, you will whiz through it and have a beautiful kitchen.

If your children are too little to help and you have plenty of other work to do alone, let the dishes air dry. Lay a clean towel over the dish rack full of dishes for a neater appearance in your kitchen.

Do not have a pity party, and do not teach your children to act this way because they will learn from your example.

If you have a dishwasher, use it for all the small things. Large mixing bowls, pots, and pans take up too much room; these can be washed *while* you are preparing the meal by keeping a sink full of hot soapy water and washing it immediately. Or wash those items in the sink after every meal. During the day, train your family to put their dirty dishes into the dishwasher. This means it must be empty. Assign one or two of your children the task of emptying the dishwasher as soon as it is done running, whether this is one time a day or three. If your children are too little to help you, then you will need to empty it as soon as possible. You want it empty so it will be useful in keeping the kitchen clean. Assign this task per meal, per day, per week, or as sometimes happens at our house, "If you complain, you will keep the job until you can do it without complaining."

I like to post Scripture verses that I'm memorizing above my sink. I got this idea from my mother-in-law. A friend told me once that she and her daughter had many precious dish-washing sessions, memorizing Scripture posted above the sink. What a wonderful memory to have! I have also been in Amish homes where a hymnbook was placed above the sink for singing while working.

Do not sigh while you are washing the dishes. Deep breathing, yes; sighing, no. There is a difference. Do not have a pity party, and do not teach your children to act this way because they will learn from your example. Be mindful of where your thoughts go. If you work cheerfully and use the time well, you will teach them to enjoy their work too,

THE DINNER HOUR

Mealtimes offer a unique opportunity for fellowship because the family is gathered together in one place for a common purpose. How do you redeem this time around the table in your home?

Create an event of your family meals. Don't allow it to be just throwing food down the hatch. Eating is not a race against the clock. Enjoy the time, enjoy the food, and enjoy your fellowship together as a family. On a regular basis, set a lovely table for your main meal of the day. Put the food in serving dishes rather than the pot they were cooked in. Keep a vase of flowers or a candle on your table. In doing those things, you are teaching your children to appreciate art and beauty as well as the communion God has with us as part of the spiritual household of faith. Precede the food with a grateful prayer.

Eat slowly and engage your family in conversation that encourages good communication. Discuss the day's events in the home as well as world events. Have your children give personal reports about progress on projects they've been working on, along with interesting episodes that have transpired throughout the day.

Don't let children wander off when they are done eating. Not only is this rude and unmannerly, but by leaving the table when dinner is still in progress, they are going to miss out on important family conversations. Teach them to ask to be excused. As they grow older teach them to pardon themselves with their reason for leaving.

When your children leave the family table is a matter of discretion. If you are planning a long evening at dinner, sometimes a young child who hasn't had a nap will need to be put to bed early for their well-being as well as for the good of the time you have left together with the rest of the family. This said, children will learn patience and the ability to stretch their typically-short attention spans when they sit with the family. Your time at the table is one of the best opportunities you have during the day to teach your children all sorts of things, so do your best to make the most of it.

TABLE TIME

As Christians, God's Word is the foundation of our lives. Gather together your children every morning after breakfast, or whatever meal works best for your family situation, and after Table Chores are finished and read the Bible together. If you have lots of little children, you can sit on the floor for this. For a slightly older crowd that uses pencils and paper, the table usually works best. The point is that you demonstrate to your children to "Seek first the kingdom of God."

STUDYING GOD'S WORD

While the Bible should be the essential component of your study, here are a few ideas of things to do: read the Bible; read a children's devotional; work on Scripture memorization; review catechism questions and answers; go through a Bible study curriculum; sing together.

Teach your older children to always check what they read in a book against God's Word. When they learn something new in a story, go to the passage in the Bible that teaches this lesson so that they will learn to look at a verse within context. Teach them how to use concordances, topical Bibles, and other references materials more fully by studying through topics and have the ability to locate verses as they research. These steps will help your children to be discerning Christians whose thinking is rooted in God's Word.

If your family homeschools, after studying the Bible, work through the rest of your family's school curriculum. Their minds are generally sharpest first thing in the morning, especially after a good breakfast. Use this time wisely by working on subjects that require concentration, such as math, phonics, and language arts.

CATECHIZING YOUR CHILDREN

A catechism is a question-answer method of teaching that is an efficient way to teach children foundational truths found in the Scripture. Choose the catechism which most closely aligns with your family and church's teaching. Catechisms do not replace the Bible. They put all of Scripture into context with the whole and teach elemental truths along with the Scripture proofs. They encourage further study in God's Word as young people learn the Scripture proofs for the various questions and answers.

Learning a catechism takes your children beyond drinking the milk of the gospel and into the meat of the wonder, beauty and depth of who God is and his plan is us. A catechism acts as a filter for all teachings. When our children have that filter instilled in them in their youth, they will be strong and well-equipped to know the difference between truths and false teachings for the rest of their lives.

When your children know what they believe and why they believe it, they will have strength and peace within and equipped for life in this world.

I saw this played out first hand several years ago. I have two sisters-in-law who were taught the Heidelberg Catechism as children. After a church service one Sunday, I had raised eyebrows and red flags about something being taught while they were able to pinpoint exactly what was said in the service and why it was wrong. I was floored by how well they responded and was convicted to teach a catechism to my children so that they could be this discerning when exposed to wrong teaching. There is strength of character and sound mind when a person can hear untruth and stand against it with confidence.

This is what we want for our children: to know the Lord's truths as found in Scripture and be very familiar with the Scriptures that prove those truths. When your children know what they believe and why they believe it, they will have strength and peace within and equipped for life in this world.

FIFTEEN MINUTES
OF PHONICS

This section is not just for homeschool families but for every family with a pre-reader.

When children can read, they can fly. The world is wide open, and they can learn just about anything. To see the reading light bulbs turn on is one of the great joys of parenting. Their faces light up with delight when they read books for the first time. The teaching process to get to that point can arduous, but when they finally get it and are to the point of reading proficiently, it is heartwarming to observe.

If some of your children are a bit slower in learning than others in your family, relax. This is normal. Children's brains develop at different paces. Children also have different learning styles. Some are better auditory learners while others learn better visually. Some children don't care to learn to read until they really want to know something and then the child will put the effort into reading for understanding. Do your best to discern these differences in your children and adjust accordingly how you teach them.

TEACH ME TO READ

Read to your little children, moving your finger under the words. If you're worried that your older child who doesn't read yet is going to lag behind in other academic areas, then have him listen to audio books to keep increasing knowledge.

Every morning, when their minds are sharp, sit down with your nonreaders and do a phonics lesson. Slowly but surely (barring a learning disability), the phonics will sink in, one concept at a time. Some children will want to fly through it. I have seen each of my reading children get stuck on a concept and it seems as though their brain had to catch up developmentally, but once they did, they would fly along again—so don't be discouraged.

Once your children understand the phonics concepts and can correctly sound out words, continue to practice the rules and word examples with them. Repetition helps them remember the rules, and soon they will become ingrained in the child's thinking and flow naturally. The children will be sight-reading instead of sounding words out and will fly through books. Practice makes perfect.

Consistency will take you a long way toward success.

Teaching reading doesn't take lots of time; you just need to do it. Consistency will take you a long way toward success. Just spend fifteen minutes every day on it. Make it part of your daily schedule, and the results will come. Keep the TV off. They can't read if they're watching television.

Make reading fun and interesting by keeping good classic books around that provoke imagination. Keep the conversation going by asking about their current books. Ask for casual oral book reports while you are doing something else such as washing dishes or folding laundry. Encourage children in their interests by getting them books that explore their topics of delight.

Like everybody else, your children will want to talk about what they are interested in. And they can get very excited about their passions at times, so much so that their words race out faster than they can organize their thoughts. Talking is communicating so just as you guide your children's reading habits, guide their conversations so that they learn to express themselves well.

QUIET TIME

Everybody in the house appreciates Quiet Time. It soothes us. It tames the wild out of little children.

REST FOR THE WEARY

If the weather is good, have the little children run around outside for a while after lunch to get the last bit of energy out. Then lay them down for Quiet Hour.

If they are starting to grow out of the need for sleep, give them a stack of books to quietly read. Each child has different sleep needs. I have children who took naps until they were six. I also had a little girl who, if she napped during the day, stayed awake to all hours of the night wandering around the house, playing alone while everyone else slept.

Older children appreciate the quiet for reading on intense subjects. They are often the children who want to be sure that we have Quiet Hour!

The littlest children and babies need to sleep. If they don't sleep during the day, then they are grumpy in the evening, which is their time with Dad. It's a sad thing if their only time with Dad is a grumpy time, so be sure they get a nap in the afternoon.

Toddlers often need to be taught to hold their hands together when they go to sleep. This acts like swaddling does for little babies. When they hold their hands together, the rest of their body holds still, and they are able to relax and go to sleep.

I have fond memories of reading chapter books aloud to preschoolers in front of a fan on hot summer afternoons. The littlest children fell asleep and the rest of us had a peaceful hour or two.

If your mail or delivery people often come during your scheduled Quiet Hour, put a sign over the doorbell so they don't ring it and rouse the whole house.

It may be tempting to use this hour to work but remember that the caregiver needs rest too. Even if you don't sleep, do something quiet that gives your mind and body a break. This is a bit like a calm and consistent morning routine in that it gives a little rest and restart to the day. Take it seriously.

READ-ALOUD TIME

Read-aloud Time is a wonderful time of the day in life with children. Through books, you travel together through time all over the world on all sorts of adventures. After all that learning, look at maps, make projects, and do more reading. You can explore without leaving home.

Reading aloud gives young children the opportunity to learn history stories and great literature that is beyond their reading level. Instead of working at decoding words, they can simply enjoy the story. It's important for the development of their brains to hear and visualize rather than have pictures spooned in as happens with videos. Not that we don't enjoy videos also, I'm talking about brain activity here.

Everybody wants to sit by Mom and the book, so we take turns. Each child is assigned a day at our house when the child gets to sit by Mom during Read-aloud Time and to help Mom in the kitchen and run out to get the mail. It's a day with special privileges.

Depending on your family dynamics, you may want to do Read-aloud Time during Quiet Hour or even in the evening with the whole family. What I find is that if I read right after lunch, I tend to fall asleep. It doesn't matter how great and exciting the story is, I start to fade and then somebody shakes my arm, "Mom! Mom! Mom!"

Sometimes the children get irritated at me and, at other times, they pull funny tricks on me. Eventually I fall over on the couch and sleep for a while, and the kids move on to other things. It works much better if we have Quiet Hour first. I don't normally nap during Quiet Hour, but if I don't have to read aloud in that first hour after lunch, we have a more fruitful time later.

My personal favorite read-aloud books are the Little House books by Laura Ingalls Wilder, the Chronicles of Narnia by C.S. Lewis, and Roald Dahl books.

AFTERNOON CHORE TIME

The key thing to keep your home consistently clean is to have a consistent chore time. This does not mean that you and your family clean and then sit around twiddling your thumbs so that the house doesn't get dirty. You can still be creative and make messes; the children can still play with playdough and Legos—you simply need a system for everyone to clean things up and get them back in place. The key thing to keeping your home consistently clean is a consistent chore time.

Work is not discouraging unless we let it become discouraging. Work is simply the process needed to get to an end point. In this case, the end point is a clean house and its enjoyment.

When a family lives in a home twenty-four hours a day, seven days a week, things get dirty, messes are made, clutter is left lying around, and small children create chaos. Yes, it will be a mess. That's a fact. But don't let it discourage you; just get to work. Make housework a habit that happens without a great deal of thought, and it will become much easier to do. Soon you'll learn to fly through most of your tasks.

Now smile! You want a clean house and you want to do fun things that give life pleasure—these things are living, and living *is* work. Work is fun if you make it fun; and work is a joy and because it is serving the Lord, it gives satisfaction and fulfillment.

BALANCE

While cleaning is an important task we should approach with focus and vigor, it can become an obsession that is destructive to our families. Clean is not the only goal of the homekeeper. The homekeeper also wants her family to live with love, comfort, and happiness. These are intangibles that have more to do with atmosphere and attitude. The pulse of your children's hearts are more important than excess dirt on the floor. While you need to conquer the dirt that builds up so quickly in our homes, don't do it at the expense of your children. Demonstrate to your family that you care more about them personally than you do about keeping the house in perfect order all of the time. And show them that it's because you care about them that you want to keep a tidy home.

This being said, it is hard to create the atmosphere and attitude of love, comfort, and happiness in our homes if they are pigpens. Have you ever watched pigs or seen their pen? Pigs root around with their noses, turning over anything and everything in order to find something to eat. This process is very destructive to the place they are kept. They eat anything and everything. Pigs wallow and move their bodies around in the dirt in order to create a bed. When it rains into their wallow, it becomes a mud bath where they take residence until cold weather comes. And when they pile on top of each other, they can even suffocate the pigs at the bottom of the pig pile. This is not a happy site or a model we should emulate.

Think of the word images that come from the lifestyle of pigs: *pigpen*, *wallow like a pig*, *pig pile*. Imagine a family doing the same thing: rummaging through cupboards looking for food and then wallowing about, doing nothing productive but sleeping in their mess.

DAILY DUTY

Keeping your home tidy and clean is as simple as keeping a daily chore time. We hold Afternoon Choretime every single day so that we can have a restful evening in a comfortable and neat atmosphere. This is the time of day when we restore order. We put away schoolbooks and projects we were working on. If it's a large project that we will come back to the next day, we tuck it away in a safe place and straighten up as much as possible around it. We make the mood relaxing so that family can enjoy a restful evening. We have food cooking that tantalizes the senses for an enjoyable family suppertime. We put on calming music that sets the mood for the evening.

THE PROCEDURE

At a set time, say "Afternoon Choretime! Let's pick up and clean!" Don't be a drill sergeant; be an encourager. Say things that you would want to hear from your parents if you were the child picking up toys and straightening the house. Think about that for a minute. We are all different and what motivates or encourages one child is different from what will influence another. Be sensitive to your children and the words that you use. Be careful when showing mistakes, critiquing work, or demonstrating your disappointment. Be gracious and kind. Sing while you work; make it fun.

Tell the children to quickly put away projects they are working on. While you are instructing them, light a candle (high out of reach of the littlest climbers), and put on music. This helps signal to the children that evening is coming, and it is time to prepare for it.

Assign each person a room to straighten and clean. If you have no big children yet, you will need to do the straightening and cleaning alone. Bring your children along with you to do these chores. This is training for them. They might be a hindrance now, but in this training, they are learning the work and will be soon training their younger brothers and sisters how to do it. Make a list of Daily Chores for each room and laminate it or put it in a sheet protector to be kept in that room.

"An ounce of prevention is worth a pound of cure."

—Benjamin Franklin

As you go to each room, refer to the chart. Show it to the children so that they will know that there is a list of work for the room. Take a photo of the room when it is picture perfect so that the children know what the room should look like when they are done, and attach the photo to the Daily Chore sheet.

Work quickly and efficiently. Pull a basket or wagon around for collecting toys and send the children on little missions to put the toys away. Give a trash bag to a child, and send her around to be the trash collector. Hand out feather dusters or dust cloths, and teach them to dust. By quickly dusting every day, the rooms do not get caked with dirt. Feather dusters are great fun for children, and a quality feather duster does an excellent job.

Teach your children to put things away when they are done with them. Remember to teach them this again while you work at putting things away. They will learn to put things away if you are with them and not in a different part of the house doing your own thing. It is when you become busy with another thing in another room that they will drop the object and move on. If you remind them while you are tidying up, they will learn the value of the habit and eventually do it on their own. When things are picked up on a regular basis, you'll have far less to put away during Afternoon Chore Time.

If your big children can work well at room cleaning, then have them work alone or with a little buddy. Assign them to teach a little child how to clean their assigned room. Train them to be an encouraging teacher, setting the example yourself.

If there is a need for speed, then set the little ones up with an activity that will keep them busy for the clean-up time. Some children and some ages are simply more distracting to the assigned room cleaner than they are helpful. For instance, toddlers seem to delight in following a room cleaner around and undoing what was just done which causes the room cleaner to be working in a never-ending cycle of frustration. Put these children at an activity at the table, in a pack 'n play with special toys only for this time of day, or in a high chair with a snack or with crayons and paper.

Assign a day of the week for a certain activity to be done by the littlest one while the rest of the crew cleans. For example: Monday—playdough; Tuesday—washing dishes (water play); Wednesday—chunky puzzles; Thursday—coloring; Friday—finger paint. Not all of these will work for all children and situations, but come up with your own list of activities for the particular child who is not yet able to clean or be a helpful little buddy.

Have the children choose the room they want to be responsible for cleaning. This adds ownership to it for them, because they care more about what their favorite room looks like. If there is disagreement about who gets what room, then have the children draw straws. Keep the same rooms for a long stretch of time (three to four months) so that the children will get really good at that room's particular chores. This teaches them to do their work with excellence and build muscle memory in cleaning a specific place. By changing room assignments frequently, nobody gets really proficient at doing a particular room. It is also easier to let tasks slide by for the next room-keeper to do next week. In addition, keeping a room assignment for long periods makes it easier for the home manager by not re-training new room-keepers every week.

After the Room Chores are done for the main rooms of the house, then the children do their Bedroom Chores. After the Bedroom Chores, do the Deep Cleaning chore for the day. Sometimes it's a big chore; sometimes it's miniscule. It all depends on the Focus Area of the house and the Deep Clean chores for the specific day.

If a chore doesn't get done one day, it's okay. You can do it next time it comes around in the housecleaning schedule. The system is your tool; you are not its slave.

After the house tidying is done, go to your bedroom and bath and spend five minutes freshening up. This is another little re-start for you to have a consistently calm evening time. Put on a fresh apron, and start the supper work with the assistant chefs.

Once the house is clean, have the children do Sit Time. Assign them a chair and give them a stack of books to look at. If they can read, then Sit Time is the equivalent of Reading Time. If the children have had enough reading time in the day, then you can have them play a game that is easy to set up and tear down before supper, such as checkers, chess, pick-up sticks, UNO, or Skip-Bo. The idea is to offer a quiet activity that is not messy.

At our house, following Afternoon Choretime, the big kids go outside to do their Animal Chores. Sometimes they are done by the time Dad comes home, and sometimes the older children do outside chores with Dad. Each home is a little different; the goal though is to have as much of the work done as possible before supper, so that everyone can have a pleasant evening enjoying each other.

What time you start doing chores is also going to vary with your home, the ages of your children, how big of messes they make with their projects, and other variables. If Afternoon Choretime is a new thing for your house, expect to have a period of fine tuning to iron out details.

When we do daily chores in every room of the house, the house always looks clean and is never more than ten minutes from looking picture perfect. If we skip Afternoon Choretime for a couple of days or a week, then our house looks like a pigpen and will take an extended period of time to straighten and clean. Having a system for doing the regular maintenance chores helps the house run by itself and keeps it beautiful.

BATHROOM MANAGEMENT

Bathrooms in the home of a family with children can get disgusting very quickly. It's simply a volume factor: the more people who use something, the more quickly the clean factor expires. The family must therefore learn some bathroom management techniques in order to keep things under control.

Here's a simple and effective rule to keep a bathroom clean: every time you are in the bathroom, do something to clean it. Teach this rule to everyone in your home. Even teach it to the toddler you are potty training. You'll be surprised at the results.

This is a valuable habit to carry through life. Just doing one thing to improve the room does a lot to keeping it clean. Put a little sticky note sign on your mirrors as a reminder of this for you and your family.

SHOWER CONTROL

After you have showered, wipe down a wall with an old bath scruffy that you keep in there just for cleaning. It only takes a minute or so. For a tub/shower, do one wall and the tub on odd days and the two end walls on even days. You do not need a special cleaner, just agitation. If you have hard water, use a product that takes care of calcium, lime, and rust deposits once in a while. There are good products available to put on the shower walls to keep them clean, but if you wipe it every time you're in it, the buildup shouldn't get too bad. Train your family to do the same with their showers or tubs.

DAILY DUTIES

The main users should be the chief cleaners. Our girls, for example, sleep on the second floor, so the second floor bath is their responsibility. On a daily basis, boys should clean any toilet that is used by boys. This will train them to aim correctly. Make it easy for the children to clean by keeping a bucket of cleaning supplies and paper towels under every bathroom sink. If you have hard water that creates build up, then tackle the heavy duty cleaning when the Deep Cleaning Focus Area for bathrooms comes around.

In each bathroom, post a list of Daily Chores:

☐ Wash the sinks and counters.

☐ Wipe toilet from top to bottom.

☐ Sweep floor.

☐ Spray floor around toilet and wipe.

If you want, go a step further and post the names of the children beside a chore for each day. Do these chores during Afternoon Chore Time.

MULTITASK

While you are in the bathroom watching little bathers, clean it. Rather than browsing a magazine, spruce things up. Get the corners and crevices that the children miss; wash the window. Wipe the cupboard doors, and straighten a drawer. It doesn't take long to do a couple of these tasks. You can get the whole bathroom in tip-top condition while your little ones are playing with the rubber ducky.

LITTLE BATHERS

Little children love water play, but they aren't that wild about water in the face. What I have found helpful is to let toddlers play while showering to get accustomed to water dripping in their face. They don't seem to notice if they are playing. The second thing I've found helpful is to keep the water low in the tub and show them how to do the back float. If they can feel the tub under their back, it is not as scary. Gradually increase the amount of water as their confidence builds. Playtime in the bathtub gives toddlers confidence in the water. Always stay in the room during their bath, of course, and take that opportunity to clean. While shampooing, teach them to hold a dry washcloth on their face. This keeps the water from getting in their eyes, and the washcloth doesn't get soaked until the shampoo is rinsed out of their hair.

Inspect fingernails and toenails during the bath and clip as needed afterward. Soft nails are easier to clip.

Saturday nights are always bath night at our house. In the winter, we also do baths on Wednesday nights. The babies and toddlers often get a bath after a messy diaper. In the summer, because they play outside so much, the little children get a bath or shower every evening before supper.

Conditioner and a tangle-free spray are essential for painless hair-combing. I have five girls, and it seems like each girl has a different hair texture and thickness. Each one also has a preference for the type of brush or comb used on her hair. We're all different; be mindful of preferences.

Cradle cap seems to disappear with coconut oil and scalp stimulation. I think it is also helpful to stay on top of probiotics because it is thought that cradle cap may be caused by a fungal overgrowth in the baby. Probiotics are healthful in many other ways besides helping with cradle cap, so why not take them? When I was in the NICU, the nurses used a soft brush when washing babies' scalps.

It was the same type as a mushroom cleaning brush or corn silk remover brush that you will find in a kitchen store.

Another baby cleaning trick I learned in the NICU is to swaddle the naked baby when bathing him and gently put him in the warm water. The baby feels more secure with his limbs close to his body, and the blanket keeps the water from shocking his senses. It also makes it easier to hold onto the baby during his bath. Uncover each part of the body as you wash him, and then re-cover it as you move on. Wash his face with pure water and the rest of his body with a very mild soap. A baby doesn't need a bath every day; doing so dries out his skin. Do wash the parts that get dirty: face, ears, neck, hands, and, of course, clean his bottom with each diaper change. As soon as you're done bathing the infant, unwrap him from the swaddle and immediately lift him up, out and into a warm towel to swaddle him again.

Before you bathe your baby, get completely set up. If you can, do the bath in a warm room. If you don't have a heater in the bathroom, do your baby's bath after somebody has taken a steamy shower. Lay out clean clothes, diaper, clean swaddling blankets to warm him quickly, and towels to wrap him in as soon as you remove him from the water. Massage the skin with almond oil after a bath because it is so good for their skin. Baby fingernails and toenails are easiest to cut when baby is sleeping.

BEDROOM MANAGEMENT

For easier cleaning, simplify bedrooms to the bare minimum. Do you and your children really want to spend your time taking care of stuff? When there is too much in the room, it gets spread around, trampled on, and lost and can become a supreme nuisance. With fewer things, the stuff is enjoyed more and usually better cared for. Put simply: it's easier to manage a few things than a lot.

BEDROOM STUFF

The overabundance of stuff infringes on better things to do with our lives. It takes time to pick things up and put them away, to wash, to fix, to sort, to organize, and to store stuff. Why do we need so much stuff? If the things you have are not helping in some way, they're a hindrance and a liability. The answer to this over-accumulation is to purge out the unnecessary. Get rid of your extra things. Stuff sometimes looks helpful or beneficial, but if an item saps time from better activities, then get rid of it.

Bless others with your extra stuff. Hold things with a light hand because they are not yours in the first place. They belong to God. Materialism in our current culture is a constant battle to fight. When we redirect our purpose in life to loving and serving others, then we replace materialism—a preoccupation with material things—with a life lived for God's purposes.

CLOSETS

Here are some practical steps to deal with the space shortages that can occur in homes, particularly older homes with small closets.

First, eliminate anything you don't need. Your children do not need a lot of clothes if you are staying caught up with the laundry. They do not need any more clothes than they can wear in a week's time in any given season of the year.

Second, organize your children's clothes so that little children can carry a small basket or wash tub of laundry to their drawers or shelves and put them away. If there is no room in the drawers for their clothes, then you may need to cut the amount again or look at another way to store the clothes. Some dressers are built inefficiently. Perhaps you need a set of shelves or cubbies.

Another option is to keep some of your children's clothes on shelves or hanging in the laundry room. This is what my boys currently do.

If you have built-in closets, put a dowel rod low enough for the children to reach their hanging clothes. Otherwise, they will climb, and that is asking for problems.

For a few years, shelves in my girls' closets held one clothing shelf for each day of the week. When the girls started to shove things onto the shelves, I knew they had too many clothes. Usually somebody grew and had things passed to them without cleaning out the clothing that was too small. The shelves also enabled me to see who was short of clothing. Now they have grown, and we have moved to hanging all of the big girls' clothes and storing the little girls' clothes in drawers placed at the bottom of the closet. Be flexible and aware of problems and seek solutions on a regular basis. The bottom line is to minimize. It will be easier for everyone to manage.

Shoe organizers work well over the door for storing socks, tights, hair bows, and more. Be sure to store articles within their reach so that the children don't tear down the organizers when climbing to get their things.

BEDS

Bunk beds and lofts are essential for saving space. Whenever you need space in your home, look around the edges of the rooms and go *up* with storage. If you have high ceilings, you can even do triple bunks. Trundle beds also save space.

You may have to build in order to get the custom beds that fit a specific rooms' needs. Bunk beds are not hard to build. Our oldest son built all of the loft beds we needed, and he is self-taught at construction. If you want them to be pretty, use hard wood and stain the finished product. We chose to paint the loft frames in our girls' room a baby blue. The boys have a John Deere theme in their room, and the bunks are painted green. The girls' bunks have shelves built in around the head of each bed. There are many creative ideas online for bunk beds and lofts.

CLEANING

To keep bedrooms clean, training is required on two key points. One is to train the children to pick up every night before they hop into bed and every morning after getting ready for the day. The second is to dust and vacuum every week on an assigned day.

If they keep their rooms picked up as a daily habit, then cleaning is easy, just like it is elsewhere in the house. The key is that your children need to be trained to pick up after themselves and that happens when you inspect what you expect. While you pick up your bedroom, instruct them to pick up theirs and then check their work. When they see you keeping your room in order, they will be more likely to keep their rooms in order also. Children will imitate the good and the bad that they see you do.

Daily Bedroom Chores

- ☐ Make the bed. This will take less than a minute and makes a big difference in how the room looks. Go for the big dramatic morale boosting effect of making the bed first.

- ☐ Put dirty clothes into a hamper or take them to the laundry room, whatever your particular home situation calls for. Just get them off of the floor. Work fast and get the dirty clothes to the proper place; this should just take a minute or two. Fast and easy.

- ☐ Put everything else into its proper place. Shelves with baskets, buckets, cubbies, and the like are useful for putting *like* with *like*.

- ☐ Collect trash.

- ☐ Do the happy dance. The room is clean!

Every week on Cleaning Day, wash the sheets, vacuum the floor, and dust the bedrooms.

It's not hard if the bedrooms are kept orderly every day. Divide the bedroom into Focus Areas, and each week of the month, assign a fifteen-minute period on Cleaning Day to clean that area. Make a chart for this, and post it on the bedroom door.

Week 1: Closet

Week 2: Under the bed

Week 3: Shelves and dresser tops

Week 4: Ceiling lights, cobwebs, light switches

If these chores are done consistently, they do not grow to be big, daylong tasks. Use the timer and do the work with the children. The children will match their effort to yours.

EVENING TIME

What happens in your home between the dark and daylight? What is going on when the light lowers? Pause for a moment, close your eyes, and picture it in your mind's eye. Typically, this is when the work of the day is done and the family is home.

As home managers, let's see that this time of the day offers a restful retreat from the world and plenty of happy hearts, comfort food, and time well spent. Let's aim for this goal, recognizing it will look different in each home. We all have unique family personalities. The bottom line is that we love each other and glorify God with our evenings.

How do you set the tone of the home? It starts with your attitude. How do you react to things? Put good things in, and good things will come out.

Work on setting the tone for the evening in the late afternoon by putting on refreshing music. Put a memory verse card above your sink, and review it while you put supper together. Pray over the supper, thank God for the day and for your family, and ask God's blessings on the evening together as a family.

Respond to the needs of the children with kindness. That's easy for me to say, but not so easy for me to do some days. It takes self-discipline and relying on the Holy Spirit that lives within. Help your children be prepared for the evening by having their chores completed by a certain time. If they are piddling and bickering, then stop everything and call a meeting. Explain to them what the family's goals are for the evening—happy hearts, a restful retreat, comfort food, and a good time had by all. You might need to paint a picture of what this looks like in your home for the children. Encourager them. Then, go to work making it happen.

Do you have supper early or late in your home? There is no right or wrong answer, however, it *is* important to have structure and regular meals for small children. Those two things go a long way towards contented and peaceable children. If your family has supper late, then the children will need to have a substantial snack in the late afternoon. Plan for this. Add it to your schedule and grocery list. Plan a suppertime routine that promotes a pleasant evening.

How the evening is spent will depend on each family's priorities. A few alternative choices to watching television include reading aloud, playing games, talking, playing instruments, singing, breathing the fresh air outside on the porch and just talking, playing catch, or watching the sun set. Each family must decide what works best.

Guarding the family evening can be tough when we compete with meetings, extracurricular activities, and sports. Take an account of how much your family separates from each other in the evenings every week. Sometimes we need to say no to one good thing in order to say yes to a better thing.

Family time means interacting with each other. Sitting beside each other does not necessarily mean that you are doing something together. Be deliberate. Every night will not go perfectly and be a beautiful picture. The idea is to have a goal to aim for. Family loves each other unconditionally, family takes care of each other, and family is a safe place.

ARTS AND CRAFTS

Arts and crafts offer opportunities for fun, promote creativity, and may even turn into a home business. By working at various arts and crafts, we make gifts, learn skills in many areas, and keep us occupied on rainy days.

The more people we have in the family, the more varied the individual artistic interests. I am finding this out as my children grow older. We do more and more crafty things, and the projects are becoming larger. It is definitely something they enjoy doing and want to do more of. This has directed more thought into how to accommodate opportunities for growth and development in their artistic endeavors.

As your children grow, their interests will evolve and develop. Watch for their unique interests, and cultivate them by allowing them space, time, and materials for them. Since our oldest was ten, he has spent his gift money and earnings on shop tools. He goes to auctions to get tools for a good price. Our second son has an eye for detail, and has always enjoyed photography. He's also excellent at designing and caring for landscapes and setting up for outdoor parties.

LOCATION, LOCATION, LOCATION

As wonderful as they are, crafts can be messy and take up space. They require storage of an assortment of tools and materials. This has required us to carve out space for crafting. In our home we call it the "Sewing Room." It is our place for all crafting endeavors, though sewing predominates.

In the past, we used the unfinished part of the basement for arts and crafts before we turned it into a Laundry Room. Then we rearranged our house by moving all the girls into one bedroom and using a previous bedroom for a Sewing Room. Then we did more rearranging. We tore out a wall between two bedrooms in the basement, and now we have a bigger Sewing Room. Think creatively for making room for the creative projects. In our case, it was more efficient to move the girls into one room for sleeping. That is all their bedroom is used for anyway. Their toys are in the Playroom, and their craft projects are in the Sewing Room. Their clothes are stored in the Laundry Room. Think about how your particular family lives, their interests, and create your home to fit your family.

WHEN INSPIRATION STRIKES

Our latest arts and crafts time took place every Thursday afternoon before our Tea Party. At other times, we have held art class every day during nap time. Often, we take an afternoon to work on various projects in the Sewing Room. Sometimes a child or two are excused from our homeschool for the day so that they can work on a project all day long.

Once in a while, we will cancel school for a week while we diligently work on sewing projects. During these weeks, we try to prepare ahead with freezer meals or an easy slow cooker menu plan, extra cleaning ahead of time, and specific activities planned for the little children. These are fun and memorable project times.

Because we have a Sewing Room, it works well for us to leave our projects in limbo there and schedule a time period in the day to come back to them. This did not work well when we did our projects at the dining room table. The effort to get out a big project kept us from doing them. The Sewing Room has allowed us the freedom to work on projects a bit every day, and because of that, we get more accomplished. If you would like to have a weeklong project time and are short on space, perhaps you could rearrange your living room and put out a big folding table to work from. Another idea is to eat outside for a week so the food and mess are not on the dining table. In winter, you could lay out a picnic cloth on the living room floor for meals.

LITTLE CHILDREN

We have special things for the little children to do *only* while we are in our Sewing Room. They are not to take these activities and toys to other places in the house, and they are not allowed to be in the Sewing Room unless Mom or a big girl is there to supervise. These activities are:

☐ A jar of buttons and a muffin tin to sort buttons into.

☐ Yarn to thread buttons onto.

☐ Sewing cards of various difficulties.

☐ Very simple children's crafts (things they can do on their own).

Pursue creative and meaningful home crafts with your children, and watch as their artistic gifts come to light and bless others.

HOMESCHOOLING

When our oldest was a baby, I gleaned a lot of baby wisdom from another mom at church who had five children. Her children were sweet, pleasant, well-mannered, intelligent, and homeschooled. We watched and admired those children. As the years went by, they had more babies, and we had more babies. My questions to this mentor-mom changed from baby questions to stubborn toddler questions, and then the prospect of school began to loom on the horizon for our oldest child. I could not bear the thought of putting my sweet tender boy on the school bus to learn what he already knew. We live far enough from town that it would be an hour ride both ways. Two hours on the school bus for a kindergartener.

HOMESCHOOLING: IS IT FOR MY FAMILY?

I remembered my experience on the school bus all too well, so I started asking my mentor questions about homeschooling, and she started handing me materials to read. It didn't take long for my husband and me to decide to homeschool due to several philosophical reasons beyond simply having our son avoid two hours a day on the school bus. There are books written about the why and how of homeschooling. If you're considering homeschooling, seek information and pray for wisdom and guidance for your unique family. Homeschooling is a lifestyle that I really enjoy but after homeschooling for twenty-odd years, we still talk through options.

Each child and each family is different, and things change through the years.

KNOW YOUR CHILD

Each child is unique. We learn to know our children by living and working with them, through building relationships with them. Part of the beauty of homeschooling is that we get to know each one of our children and can tailor a curriculum to meet each child's learning needs.

As the years go by, our children grow and mature, and our teaching styles must change and grow with them—another beauty of homeschooling. As teachers, we consider it is a privilege to know our children and help them with their unique needs. A method that works for one child might not work as well with another. We need to be sensitive to this fact.

TEACHING CHILDREN TO BE SELF-TAUGHT

As a mom with a hundred different hats to wear, I cannot teach all my children like it is done in our culture's idea of the typical classroom. I learned early to let go of this idea.

One of my goals in training my children is to teach them to teach themselves. If children learn how to teach themselves, they will be set for life. Anything they get curious about they will be able to learn. Education is not as simple as stuffing their heads full of facts; it is giving them the ability to learn new things and to develop thinking skills, tools they will use their whole lives.

Any child that can read well is able to pick up a book, read directions, and learn. Once a child can read for comprehension, she can fly. They can self-teach if you encourage them in it. For the younger nonreaders spend your time reading good books and exploring the world. Encourage them to ask questions and demonstrate looking for answers. Ask the child questions about what she sees. This keeps learning fun and it teaches them to have an inquisitive mind.

When starting a child off on a new book, look the whole thing over with him. Read through the contents, the introduction, the index and glossary. Teach him that every time he picks up a new book, he should familiarize himself with it before reading it.

If you think your child is an auditory learner, and that is why she needs you to read her lessons to her, then get more audio books and related curriculum. Audio learning is also a great way to do double duty while driving on Town Day, while mopping, and doing other cleaning.

If your child seems to need constant help and has constant questions, evaluate whether this need for help is really necessary, or if he just has a lazy habit. When he comes to you for help, ask first, "Did you read the directions?" If it's language arts or spelling, ask, "Did you read the rule?" When you are satisfied that he truly doesn't understand what he's reading, then help him. If he is stumbling because of a word, teach him to do his schoolwork and reading with a dictionary in hand and to look up unfamiliar words. Keep dictionaries close so that learning can happen on the run.

Self-teaching is a ball that you start rolling when the children are little, and your job is to keep the ball rolling. Encourage your children to make a project, write a news report, or a letter to Grandma about what they are learning. When they are producing something that is an outgrowth of an interest, they *care* about spelling and grammar and handwriting. These things must be taught as well, but in the simplest and most pain-free way possible.

STEPS TOWARD WORKING INDEPENDENTLY

Evaluate materials or techniques you are using that are causing the most teacher work, and ask if it's worth it, or if other options can do the same thing in a better way.

Reference books are essential for self-teaching. Some can be picked up free at library book sales or thrift stores. Teach the children how to use these reference tools. You will find instructions on how to use reference books at the front.

Reference books are an important and highly useful investment. Leave dictionaries and Bibles in key areas around your house for your family to use. Place them where people often read. Watch for locations where your children read; that's where you will want to place a dictionary. Where do they write? Place a thesaurus at that location. Decorate your house with books.

Evaluate Your Teaching

Perhaps you have inadvertently encouraged your children to rely on you too much for their learning. If so, begin to deliberately encourage them to be problem solvers. When they request help, ask if they have read the directions and to try reading directions out loud to themselves. Sometimes reading out loud helps with comprehension. Urge them to look up words they don't know. Ask them if they have studied the examples.

If you teach your children to read directions, they will soon apply this discipline to everything. They will be cooking from scratch, putting things together for you, hooking up new appliances, building furniture, and much more. Directions aren't just in schoolwork; they are part of life. Beyond formal education, we don't have teachers following us around in life, telling us how to do every little thing.

Give your children access to the world around them and teach them to *see* it and wonder about it. This happens through active conversation between you and your children. It's important that you engage with them. Lie on the sidewalk with them, watch ants build a hill, and talk about it. Ask questions about *everything*. Why is the sky blue? What is that bird doing? How is cheese made? Who invented taxes? Talking and listening—conversation—is education. Children are naturally curious; cultivate a sense of inquisitive wonder in them.

Lesson Plans

Create lesson plans they can follow without your help. For example, my children know that they are supposed to do two pages of math every day, no matter what. I don't have to *tell* them to do it.

For create an easy lesson plan to follow, take a paper and write the child's name at the top. Then write a column for each book that they are to work in or read and another column for how many pages or sections they should do each day. Once they are done with the daily plan, then they can go do other interests. This teaches them to focus.

Let Them Think

Encourage your children that it's okay to sit and think about something and process it and try to figure it out themselves. This builds confidence in problem solving and creative thinking. Tell them that the important thing is not what they get accomplished but what they are *learning*. If your goal is to get through a curriculum by a certain day, then your focus isn't on truly learning. Completing education never happens. Rushing is a hindrance to true learning, internalizing a concept is learning. Teach them to take their time when doing a lesson.

Teach Them Diligence

This might sound contradictory to the last point about allowing time for internalization, but teach them to work diligently and consistently. Teach them that when they get one thing done, to move on to the next thing. When the schoolwork is complete, then they can do whatever project/activity/toy it is that they love to do. "We work before we play!" Sometimes doing something like writing a paper or doing a math lesson means plodding along steadily.

Teach Each Other

Your children can give each other spelling tests. This helps both parties learn spelling. Have the older children read aloud to the younger. This makes the older children better and more expressive readers. Older children can help younger ones with math concepts as well. Both the older and younger children benefit. Teaching something is the best way to learn it.

At the table, when schoolwork is being done, have buddies sit beside each other. The older buddy can help the younger buddy read words or solve problems. Often the older ones are teaching the younger ones without me encouraging them to do so. Over time, it has come naturally for them.

New Curriculum

Using a curriculum to self-teach involves learning how to read the author's style of writing and presentation, learning new vocabulary, and developing new ways of thinking. When learning a new curriculum, encourage your child to self-teach. Have them start by reading the introduction and table of contents, becoming familiar with the book by finding and perusing the glossary and index, and then looking at how the lessons are laid out.

Spend a week simply becoming acquainted with the curriculum. Then, dive into the first lesson. Following this approach, the first of a new year usually takes more time and energy from everyone, but then once the children learn the new curriculum, they can fly along in their new subjects with just a little bit of steering from you. This is also why you shouldn't throw out a new schedule you just created. It might not be working at first because everybody is taking so long learning how to approach the new material, but then things will fall into place, and it will work out.

While it's important to have a system with clear academic goals for your children to accomplish, do not be rigid. Break out of the box on occasion. Take your kids on field trips as a family. Read a history or science book. Plant a terrarium, hatch eggs, or make a timeline of a period in history inserting your own family tree and history into it. At supper talk about what you learned. Make scrapbooks of projects. Don't confine your homeschooling to a plan that stifles learning.

Accountability

I do not sit beside my children checking every single problem as it's done. I occasionally peer over shoulders and check first, to see that they have done their work. Second, I ask the child if they understand what they are doing. Third, I check a few problems to *know* that they understand. I do that for each subject. I'm not sitting there checking every problem of every book that each child is working through.

My goal for them is understanding, and checking every problem isn't necessary to see that they understand. That doesn't mean that I *never* check every single problem of a page but, generally speaking, I do not.

When a child is reading something, such as a history book, I will ask for an oral book report, to tell me what they have read. Then they narrate back to me what they read. I do this at meals, or when we're working in the kitchen, or just relaxing on the deck. I want them to be able to tell me names of people, time periods, and other interesting tidbits. This starts a conversation for all of us. At our school appointment on Office Day, I will ask further questions.

I don't often require an older child to work completely through a grammar text. I'll pick out their problem areas and have the child work through the part of the book that addresses their need. I have them self-check, and then at our appointment on Office Day, I will check to be sure they understand the areas I assigned them to learn.

MULTITASKING ART

Homeschooling moms buy a lot of books. It's a common joke that we are bookaholics and bibliophiles. We browse bookstores, collect catalogs, and ogle old books. Decluttering and organizing books is probably one of the most challenging jobs that we do.

Homeschooling moms: I'm sure that in your library collection, you have art books, how-to books, and gardening books. I would also guess that most of you have taken your children to art shows, art museums, art lessons, and assigned them reading in art.

While these books and activities can be helpful, here is a practical suggestion to give your children some real-life art. Take them to a window and ask them what they see. If they're shorter than you are, then get down on their level and look up. They usually have the best view of trees and sky. The taller they get, the more creative their word choice. Next, ask everyone, "What can we do to improve this view?" Write down their ideas, and make plans to put them into action.

Do you see how this is the most practical art you can do with your children? The window is your frame, and the content is something that you look at all the time. It changes with the weather and the seasons, so as the year goes by, do this activity again. You will want to add more to your notes and make plans to add interest to the view throughout the year.

A view from a window in your house is one of those common things that hold beauty and help us to understand God and his power, creation, and might. This is one way of taking dominion over the earth. God has given us this view of a little spot on this earth, and we can move things, build things, add to it, take away from it, and create order in it.

Inspiring ideas on how to "improve your view" might come from art books, gardening books, and building books. If you don't have these, then I would encourage you to acquire some; they're really inexpensive at the secondhand stores. There are landscape ideas and projects online also. Learn how to divide your plants and spread them around. If you and your children don't know how to build with wood, start with a bird house or a bird feeder. Plant a cutting garden and create bouquets from it all season long. Once you and your children's creative juices start flowing, and you start improving your views, it will just build and build. Soon your Garden Days will be busy with projects, and your art frames will be works of great creativity—from the sky and tree tops down to the lawn and gardens.

By teaching your children to appreciate the window views, they will also start to see the toys and trash that they leave in the yard and be more diligent about picking them up. This works much better than any lecture. Their eyes see more and more, and the children will point out beauty to you that previously went unnoticed. The window view *is* art.

PRESCHOOLERS

Some years, preschoolers aren't trouble at all and fit right into the school plan for the older children. Other years, there seems to be rub in the mix. Personalities, ages, and other issues all play a role in what makes for a peaceful time and what is less than peaceful. The same children that are causing a problem now will peacefully coexist in a few months with another problem to replace the one that was solved.

One very helpful thing that I've done in the past was to train the little children to take one toy or activity at a time to their mat or area at the table. I have done this for the little one in the pack 'n play, for example. If the activity is an imaginative one, the child will do it for a long time. I remember a specific fifteen-month-old in the pack 'n play playing with only a can full of blocks for close to an hour. One toy at a time teaches concentration. Any good activity will keep the child occupied for at least ten minutes.

When the child is doing the activity, she is not to spread the mess all over the place. This is learning discipline and takes just a little encouragement. You can use a placemat or put some blue painter's tape on the table for boundaries. When the child is done with the activity, she puts it away before getting another one out. For the little one in the pack 'n play, I learned to keep an eye on her, and as soon as she started to tire of the activity, I switched it before she became unhappy. She usually settled right into playing with the new thing unless she was tired or hungry. Activities that work well are typically imaginative, self-correcting, and educational.

The children are not to distract each other or mess with another person's activity. They can play together cooperatively at another time of day. This part of the day is schooltime. If there is a time period during the day that you and the children need to work together and the preschoolers are not napping, then using mats and a pack 'n play and the one-activity-at-a-time strategy is a great way to teach the little ones at the same time. The hardest part is that you *have* to be there to help them learn the system (leaving to do the laundry doesn't work very well during this training time).

Sandpaper letters are an easy thing that you and the older children can make for the preschoolers. Simply take an alphabet stencil, trace it onto 220-grit sandpaper, cut out the letters, and glue them onto 3 x 5 cards. The preschooler traces the sandpaper letters with his finger. In doing so, he will get to know the alphabet. By using his fingers on the sandpaper, it will help cement it into his brain. Do it with him for a while so he learns what directions his fingers should go in tracing the letters. You can do this same thing with numbers.

Activities to do at the table are puzzles of all sorts, peg boards, pattern blocks, Cuisenaire rods, and bead stringing. Pull together things that will help them learn classifying, sequencing, and matching. Put your activities together on a shelf or in a cupboard and get them out *only* for school time. Wash tubs are a great size for holding activities; they fit on shelves neatly, are inexpensive, and little hands can carry them.

SURRENDERING THE HOMESCHOOL TO GOD

When you get overwhelmed with a day, week, month, or life in general, try this exercise in your homeschool for a while. We have found this to be a refreshing change which gets us back on the right track.

- ☐ Gather all of your children around the table.

- ☐ Pray for wisdom.

- ☐ Open your Bible and pick a selection. Psalms and Proverbs are good choices for character applications.

- ☐ Read the verse or passage aloud and have your children copy it into a notebook. This is dictation that will sharpen their listening skills.

- ☐ Check their dictation or have them check it.

- ☐ Recopy it correctly in their best handwriting—they can look at the selection now. This is their handwriting lesson.

- ☐ It will also help them learn how to write. Copying the sentences of others is how many great writers learned the skill.

- ☐ Have them copy each misspelled word from dictation five times. This is their spelling lesson.

☐ Define the big words using the dictionary. This is their vocabulary lesson.

☐ Do a grammar lesson with the selection, identifying each part of the sentence and diagramming it. Use one of your children's language arts books to help with the diagramming lesson.

☐ Memorize the selection together and write it from memory. It should be easy by this point.

☐ As a group, come up with project ideas built around this verse—drama, an act of service, a poster. Then write an essay on the selection or write a creative story about the verse in application.

☐ If there is a natural element in the verse, look it up in a science reference book.

☐ Look up the cross references. Take the rest of your school day to work on these ideas.

HEALTH AND WELLNESS

Evaluate your health. How do you feel? What is causing aches and pains? Do you wish you had more energy? Are you tired?

SLEEP

Adequate sleep impacts our health and mental clarity. It is very easy for us as mothers to shortchange ourselves on sleep. At different times we need different amounts of rest to be our best. I know that the more I get up with a baby, the earlier I need to get to bed.

Answer these questions; jot them down: What time do you want to be up in the morning? How much sleep do you need? How much time does the baby take during the night? How much time do you need in bed to unwind before falling asleep?

Figure out the total, and count backwards from your waking hour to learn when you need to go to bed. If you simply cannot get to bed early enough, then be sure to take the Quiet Hour seriously and sleep then.

WATER

Personally, I started feeling dramatically better when I started drinking water instead of soda, hot tea, iced tea, juice, hot cocoa, or coffee. There are too many detriments in those beverages. Changing your beverages will go a long way towards improving your health. If you are nursing, then it is vital that you have a large glass of water each time that you feed the baby. Water makes all of our body systems work better. It helps your brain function, muscles, joints, nerves, skin—everything!

Simply being hydrated improves our health. If you don't like the taste of your water, squeeze a lemon into your pitcher. The lemon is very good for your health also. Or, try lime slices, basil leaves, or cucumber. Get a filter. Do whatever it takes to make water palatable. Drink a tall glass of water first thing in the morning. Fill a pitcher and commit to drinking water regularly throughout the day.

EXERCISE

Exercise is another thing that gives you more energy. It seems a paradox that something that takes effort to do rewards with more energy, but it is true. I confess to being a warm weather exerciser. I love to get outside and walk or be active in the yard. Exercise does not just cause us to burn fat; it also builds the muscles that hold our bones and joints in place. It builds bone strength and makes a healthy heart. We need to be mobile now if we're going to be able and fit grandparents who can help our children and grandchildren. I don't know about you but I want to do more than sit in the rocking chair on the front porch when I'm old. I have a list of things to do yet and that requires being the healthiest I can be.

Have recess with your children—play in the yard. Garden. Plant fruit trees. Hang out your laundry. Take your children on hikes. Make a habit of a daily walk, and take your children with you. Bike as a family. Read a book while you walk on the treadmill. Do an exercise video with your children; I really like T-Tapp videos to strengthen my core (t-tapp.com). Most recently I've been walking stairs at the arena while my children have practices for their horse events.

Exercise is a habit that becomes easier once you start doing it. You will come to love the way it energizes you. Look at your day's schedule, and find the ideal time to do it for the particular season you are in. Ten minutes of walking or stretching is better than nothing. Do more if you can, but do something.

Having babies stretches out the connective tissue and can tear the muscles in the mid-section, and it's not fun going around with a pooch. Exercise programs to repair the ab muscles can be found online.

SUPPLEMENTS

I used to disdain supplements. I have always cooked from scratch and tried to serve balanced meals. I thought a person could get enough nutrients from this alone, but I discovered otherwise. I began to realize that I had better days when I took my doctor-prescribed prenatal vitamin.

I have a daughter who is allergic to milk, and that caused me to read up on nutrition and learn about how much we really don't get in our diet. Now I sing the praises of taking a B complex. It keeps the hormone swings under control. I don't get weepy or short-tempered, nor as tired or low in energy. Taking Cal-Mag-Zinc prevented me from having restless legs, leg cramps, and bone pain in my hands. Vitamin C decreased my varicose veins and the itching and pain that accompanied them. Fish oil improved my skin. These are my short anecdotes; do your own research. Pay attention to your body, listen to it, try keeping a food diary and learn how different foods make your body feel. We're all different; learn to know yourself.

THE PLAYROOM

Toys teach. Choose your toys with this in mind. Playing externalizes what is going on internally. Children have an enormous capacity for creativity and are wildly imaginative. Provide your children with toys that encourage thoughtfulness.

An open-ended toy is one that can be played with for extended periods of time in different ways by each child. For example, a child might use blocks to build a fence for his farm animals one day, the next day he uses the blocks to build a hill for a goat to climb on, the day after that the blocks may be a skyscraper, and then he might use the blocks to throw at a target. When decluttering toys, look at each one and ask if it is open-ended. Is the toy going to promote thinking skills, imagination, and creativity?

Even good, thought-provoking toys can accumulate and overtake the home. I read recently that the average American child receives seventy new toys a year. Keep the toys pared down to a number that can be easily picked up and stored. Children do not need every new thing under the sun. Use that money (and encourage the grandparents to think this way) for gifts such as memberships to a zoo or museum, a child's magazine, or consumables such as paints or coloring books.

Have a place for the toys, and make it a practice to keep them put away when they aren't being played with. There are seasons when this is easy to keep on top of, and there are seasons when there are more important things to take care of. It is important for children to be self-disciplined in putting their things away. But when a mama of only Littles is laid out on the couch with pregnancy exhaustion, it is enough to keep the kitchen, bathrooms, and laundry clean. Been there, done that.

There are many tips and tricks for managing toys in a large family, but I think the best one is to lock toy cupboards. A locked cupboard is like having another adult in the house.

It is not a cruel thing to lock toys away. It is wise management. The toys are not all locked away at once. Locked doors are a method of managing which toys are available. Rotating toys keeps interest high and brains working in different ways with "new" toys. The children have a set amount out at a time and if they want to trade, then they ask and we unlock the cupboard and trade something out. Be flexible and sensitive to their play.

I have one locked cupboard in the playroom for games, crafts, and some homeschooling materials. Two other locked cupboards hold toys. Each activity or toy is assigned a place on the shelves which are labeled so that anyone can put things away or look to see where to find something. Wash tubs and baskets hold stuffed animals, blocks, and puppets.

The locked cupboards have saved an immense amount of trouble. The kids that are old enough to responsibly get into the cupboards can reach the key, which is kept high. We avoid every single toy, craft, and game from being spread stem to stern. Once a month it is on our cleaning schedule to restore order to the toy cupboards.

FEAST NIGHT

Life needs to be celebrated. God is good to us. We have beautiful people around us to love and enjoy. Take the time to celebrate each other. Laugh and live joyfully. Gather your loved ones around regularly, and bless each other with good food, songs, and thanksgiving. Be grateful for every small and large thing in life and celebrate them. Count even trials as joy (James 1). Sometimes we need our people to help us to show us the silver lining and the things to celebrate.

- ☐ Plan a night every week or once a month to celebrate the goodness of God.

- ☐ Make a special menu plan and grocery list.

- ☐ Determine when to make the food and who will make what. Have fun with the food prep.

- ☐ Use a special table cloth reserved for Feast Night.

- ☐ Use your good dishes.

- ☐ Light candles or put on a bouquet.

- ☐ Dress up and celebrate.

- ☐ Encourage each person to share a story or something to be thankful for.

From the youngest to the oldest, everybody likes to have a good time. Love and laughter right many wrongs. We have hope and joy because we are children of God. Share this with your children.

Take the opportunity on Feast Night to praise and thank your children for their contributions to the family. Encourage them as they work on Christian character, and reward them for progress. Praise God for your blessings. Take turns sharing what each is grateful for. Encourage each other to make goals and plot a path to reach the goals.

Serve a delicious and beautiful dessert. Share how God has been good to you. Teach your children that to fear God is to seek his wisdom, and God's wisdom is full of goodness. Yes, God is good to us. Live a life of joy.

MEAL PLANNING

There are one thousand ninety-five meals a year, give yourself a high five for managing them. Now, let's do it even better.

QUANTITY COOKING

Perhaps you have a large family like I do or maybe you just want to freeze meals for later times.

Get out your favorite recipes and do the math to multiply the ingredient amounts and note these in your recipe books—they are yours to personalize! Then write what pan to put the converted recipe into. You will have to use some trial and error with putting converted recipes into the pots, pans, crocks, and bowls that you own. As you go through the year of cooking, keep jotting notes beside your favorite recipes on how to improve it or how it works multiplied.

Keep your eye out for larger kitchen equipment. Since you will be using your equipment a lot more than the typical consumer, consider buying professional grade. Shop at a restaurant supply store for ideas.

MEAL PLANS

There are several ways of planning meals:

- ☐ Look online for free or paid subscriptions to menu plans with grocery lists.

- ☐ Plan menus around sales flyers from your local stores.

- ☐ Plan around seasonal fruits and vegetables.

- ☐ Plan around what is available in your pantry and freezer.

- ☐ Plan around a specific recipe book or diet.

- ☐ Buy what looks good at the store or farmer's market and then make something out of it upon arriving home—typically the most expensive way to menu plan.

Menu planning saves you time and money, things we all can use more of. It blesses the Lord because we are being better stewards of his resources. Menu planning also blesses your family because when thought is given to meals, they are more apt to be delicious, healthy, and presented in a manner that shows love.

If you think about it, menu planning is always done. Food that is haphazardly gathered and slapped on the table is that way because the plan was poor. Your goal should be to have an excellent plan—a plan that blesses the Lord and your family.

THE BASICS OF A MENU PLAN

It's important to have a Basic Menu Plan because it will be the plan you use when you don't know what to make for dinner. It will be your easy reference tool that anyone in the house can reference. You will make other more creative menu plans, but this one will be the Basic Menu Plan, the one you refer to in busy seasons and on bad days.

These will be the meals that don't need a lot of thinking power to make because you know the recipes so well.

The first thing you want to do when making the Basic Menu Plan is to ask your family what their favorite home-cooked meals are and how often they want to eat those meals. Take a typical four-week calendar page, and write these meals down on appropriate days. If you know that you're going to be out of the home every Thursday evening, for example, then save that evening for a meal that can be eaten quickly. If you know that Wednesday evenings you are always home and the day is not hectic, plan your more detailed dinner for Wednesdays. Look at what days are left on the calendar and plan healthy, inexpensive meals. Plan Crock-Pot meals for busy days such as Town Days and Cleaning Days. Plan your Lord's Day meals. Plan what your children will eat on your Date Night. Plan your Feast Night menus. When incorporating new foods to your menu, keep in mind that it often takes several meals before a new food is accepted by picky eaters.

Planning is work. It might not feel or look like work when you are sitting down doing it, but planning is work, and it makes you a more efficient home manager and cook. With increased efficiency, you will have more time for other pursuits.

Once you have a month's worth of dinner menus, go through all the recipes, and write down the ingredients. These are the things you will need to have on hand in your pantry and refrigerator. This is your Basic Grocery List. When you see things from your Basic Grocery List on sale, then stock up your pantry. This is part of how you save money with your menu plan. The other way is by learning which stores have the best prices for your Basic Grocery List. You will want to write down the typical price you pay beside each item on the list. Another way to save a lot is to look at your Basic Menu Plan and think about how many of these items you can grow yourself and freeze or can.

Keep your pantry organized by type of product so that you can check for recipe ingredients at a glance before Town Day. Keep like with like. Store baking ingredients, salad dressing ingredients, canned goods, dry goods, and so forth in the same places all the time so that any member of the family can easily find ingredients and create a recipe from the Basic Menu Plan without trouble.

Take a look at the recipes and their preparation needs. Write down what should be done ahead and when to start the recipe. If the beef roast recipe calls for marinating for three days, then, on the calendar page, write that task three days before the date it is to be served. If you need French loaves for a specific meal, plan when you will make them, and write it on the calendar. Do this for the needs of every meal.

Make three copies of the Basic Menu Plan and Basic Grocery List. Keep one copy at your desk where you will reference it on Office Day when you are planning your route for Town Day. Keep the second copy in your purse/diaper bag. When you are out and need your memory jogged, the Basic Menu Plan and Basic Grocery List will be handy. Hang the third copy of the Basic Menu Plan inside a kitchen cupboard for easy access and the third Basic Grocery List can be laminated and put on a bulletin board for family members to mark ingredient needs.

PIZZA NIGHT

Homemade Pizza Nights are an event at our house. The little children like to get in on the dough making and roll bread sticks, which creates a big mess. We like veggie pizzas, and that means lots of vegetable cutting—more mess. After a few weeks of doing Homemade Pizza Night on our Cleaning Day, I decided this was not efficient arrangement. There was too much busy work going on and important cleaning work was being neglected. Our kitchen isn't tucked away in a corner; it is Grand Central Station. We moved Homemade

Pizza Night—the blizzard of flour and snowballs of dough—to Kitchen Day when we mop the floor. Homemade Pizza Night might work just fine for Cleaning Day at your house. My point is to think about these things while planning your menu. Be flexible and responsive when things don't work perfectly.

THE BASIC LUNCH MENU

Do the same thing for the Basic Lunch Menu. This is a plan for the days when you do not have leftovers to serve. Choose healthy meals that can be prepared in thirty minutes or less. Efficient lunches will allow time for other activities during the day. Prepare nutritious lunches for growing healthy children. Keep a supply of easy and nutritious lunch items on hand, part of the regular grocery list, and a daily lunch plan on the inside of a cupboard or on a kitchen bulletin board.

Create the ritual of eating lunch as a family. When I was a child, growing up on a farm, the big meal was always at noon and called dinner. At meal times, we talked, joked, and teased each other. After dinner, my father then would lie down on the floor for a ten-minute nap, and if the day was a relaxed workday, we would get to play checkers with Dad. My husband, who also grew up on a farm, tells of his father and grandfather following a similar routine.

Family meals are an event. Conversation happens between parents and children, thoughts are expressed about current events, books being read, work that is happening, and interwoven throughout all this is the calling of God on our lives. Create mealtimes where real connection happens and parents are teaching children the Shema— to love the Lord your God with all your heart, with all your soul, with all your mind, and with all your strength (Deuteronomy 6). Make having lunch together an event with the attitude of sharing, helping, and caring.

BREAKFAST

Feed the family nutritious food to fuel the brain for the activities of the day. Again, serving good food will require a plan and having the necessary supplies on hand.

Cold cereal and breakfast bars have little nutrition and do not fill the stomach well or feed the brain. We shouldn't feed our children junk just to fill them up. Take responsibility to provide nutritious food for breakfast each day.

Everybody getting their own breakfast makes for a disorderly kitchen and an each-for-their-own attitude. Been there, done that. It promotes selfishness. Plan ahead for what your family will eat for breakfast, and follow the plan. Be considerate of those who don't like certain foods or of the whole family getting tired of a dish and change it up when these things happen.

Establish a culture for the breakfast meal where the family starts the day together as a team with Scripture and prayer. When the day is started off with God from the littlest to the biggest children, the focus is completely different than the days that start off like a race. Even if it is a busy day, when the family focus is right early on, there is a steadying influence that carries throughout the day.

SNACK TIME

Depending on what times of day meals occur at your house, you will probably find that you also need at least one snack time in order to keep the motors running in your children. At our house, we eat breakfast around 7:30 or 8:00, lunch at noon, and supper anytime from 6:30 to 8:00.

The late supper hour sounds crazy doesn't it? But we like to eat dinner with Dad. He works long hours some seasons, and then there are chores to do on the farm when he comes home from work. As you might suspect, we can't go from noon to eight in the evening without eating, so in the late afternoon, we have a substantial snack.

Here is what we do and don't do concerning snacks.

Junk food is unhealthy and expensive, so we don't eat it, except for the occasional splurge on Oreos or potato chips. Fruits and vegetables are a wonderful source of vitamins and minerals. Keep track of your fruit and vegetable consumption and try to get at least five servings a day into your family. In the summer, I send my children out to graze on what we have growing—peas, cherry tomatoes, grapes, raspberries, apples, pears, peaches, strawberries.

For those times when I need to buy fruit, I like to buy a different fruit for each day of the week, one for each member of our family. For example, if plums are a good price, then I buy nine for one day's snack. Bananas are popular with my family, so if they are a good price, I buy bunches big enough so that each person can have two. To determine if a price is good or not, you will need to know when different fruits are in season. Usually that is when their prices are lowest, and they are at the best quality. Here is a short list to help you as you plan:

- ☐ Fall: apples, grapes, pears, pomegranates.

- ☐ Winter: pomegranates, citrus, kiwi.

- ☐ Spring: strawberries, rhubarb.

- ☐ Summer: apricots, blueberries, cherries, melons, peaches, plums, grapes.

Fruits are generally finger food. For the littlest children, you will need to cut the fruit into bite-sized pieces. Be sure to cut apple pieces small for toddlers, and squirt some lemon juice over them to keep them from turning dark. Cut grapes in half—they are one of the top choking hazards for children (along with hot dogs).

If you have children old enough to help (an older preschooler can do this easy job), assign a Snack Lady or Snack Man for the day with the duty to prepare the fruit snack and do the cleanup.

Do not let your children walk around the house with their snack. It makes the house dirty. They can sit at the table. It teaches them self-control to sit while eating and to keep their mess contained. Require them to wash their hands before and after snack time to prevent germs and to keep the house preserved from grubby mitts. With a bit of persistence on your part, this will soon become a habit.

Assign one of the children to wash the table afterwards; this can also be a preschooler's job. Keep a little bucket and sponge under the kitchen sink just for their use. Preschoolers love to help, so help them learn to contribute to the family. Buy your children fun cutting tools like a banana slicer, egg slicer for strawberries, and a crinkle cutter for carrots. These are inexpensive gadgets that make work fun.

Fresh vegetables are a healthy, inexpensive snack also. If you have them available for snacking from the time your children are little, they will appreciate them. If you start late, you will simply need to be persistent in offering fresh vegetables and saying no to junk. As long as junk food is available, children will choose it over healthy alternatives. It's that simple. They might be hungry for a few days, preferring to eat nothing, but if you keep the good stuff in front of them, they will eventually eat it and learn to like it. Some children are more adventurous about food, and some are stubborn. I've found that it often takes several experiences with a new food before it is accepted. The key is to persevere.

If you garden, when fresh food is in greater abundance is an easy time to get your family started with fresh vegetables for snacking. The children are used to seeing them and probably even like some of it. Get in the habit of having a vegetable tray in the refrigerator to pull out every afternoon. There are trays that you can buy that have a stay-cool bottom. Daily, cut more vegetables to add to the tray or make a dip for the vegetables. Then set it out on the table and call the children. Baby carrots, green onions, and celery are affordable and easy to get all year round. Add a plate of cheese slices or have cheese sticks available for some protein.

Seasonal vegetables good for snacking include:

- ☐ Fall: broccoli, carrots, cauliflower, green onions, snow peas.

- ☐ Winter: broccoli, cauliflower, radishes, snow peas.

- ☐ Spring: asparagus, green onions, English peas, sugar snap peas, radishes.

- ☐ Summer: cucumbers, sugar snap peas, peppers, summer squash, zucchini.

Here's a fresh vegetable dip our family enjoys:

Dip for Fresh Vegetables

- ☐ 8 ounces cream cheese or chèvre (goat cheese)

- ☐ 3 tablespoons olive oil

- ☐ 3 tablespoons yogurt

- ☐ Chopped fresh herbs (if using dry, reduce amount to ¼):

- ☐ 2 tablespoons chives

- ☐ 2 tablespoons Italian parsley

- ☐ 1 tablespoon cilantro

- ☐ 1 teaspoon mint

- ☐ 1 teaspoon thyme

- ☐ ½ teaspoon rosemary

1. Salt and pepper to taste.

2. Blend. Keep refrigerated.

If you think that buying fresh fruits and vegetables is expensive, take a hard look at the alternatives that you are serving. Ask these questions: How is it contributing to the health of my child? Is it tearing down their immune system? Are there long-term consequences for growing up on this food? What is the benefit of feeding this to my child? Serving for serving, is it really cheaper than offering something healthy?

Let's not forget about other foods you can keep handy, such as dried fruits and nuts. These are great to keep in the diaper bag or van. Be careful that the dried fruits you buy are not coated in sugar.

Sometimes we need extra protein in the diet, and snacks can be a way of getting it. Protein really carries you to the next meal. I see a big difference when we have protein for breakfast vs. straight carbohydrates. I have found that a balance of protein and carbs is the best. The second best is complex carbs like oatmeal. And the worst is cold cereal which sends us all into meltdown at about 10 a.m. If your family needs more protein to carry you through the day, boiled eggs (made more fun with an egg slicer) and cheese slices are easy protein snacks to prepare. Older children like beef or deer jerky—but watch for detrimental additives on these snacks. Other easy protein snacks are yogurt, nuts, cottage cheese, nut butters, or hummus.

What would childhood be without cookies? Who doesn't get a little sappy sentimentalism going with the thought of chocolate chip cookies and a tall glass of cold milk? Yum! If you're going to make cookies, search out the healthiest recipes you can find. Avoid white flour, white sugar, margarine, and shortening for the sake of your health. It might take some experimenting and recipe-altering to find the right blend of healthy grains, sweeteners, and fat, but it can be done.

Avoid serving snacks too close to meal time if you want your children to eat well. Your children's balance of appropriate snack consumption will vary. Consider age, how much snack food is involved, and how close you are to the next meal in determining whether or not they will still have room for a regular meal following their snack. This point of deliberation illustrates another reason why snack food must be healthy. Consider the costs of getting filled up on junk and not eating a good meal. If your children are eating healthy snacks, then when they occasionally don't eat a lot during your regular meal time, they will be all right. They are still getting a well-balanced diet spread throughout the day.

Juice is like candy. Even though it might be 100 percent pure fruit juice, it takes a tremendous amount of fruit to get the juice to fill up that sippy cup. All the solids of the fruit that help digest the fruit sugars are removed. Drinking the juice of fruit is like drinking sugar water. It will give the same highs and lows that candy does. It is far better to get fruit juice in the form that God made it—in the fruit itself. Instead of a cup of apple juice, serve a cut up apple and a cup of water. Instead of grape juice, cut a handful of grapes in half and serve with a cup of water. Instead of orange juice, serve orange segments with a cup of water. Instead of flavored milk, serve it white.

Hyper kids with sugar highs and lows are a detriment to your sanity and the peace of your family. Serve your children healthy foods with lots of water, and watch their behavior become more moderated and your visits to the doctor decrease. If they are thirsty, give them water. Water is the easiest health food to serve. They won't die of thirst if you don't have juice and junk in your house. Keep offering the good foods. The children will figure this out pretty quickly, though they may complain at first. Any major change in their life takes about three days of adjustment. Just don't change too many things at once.

In saying all this, I am not suggesting that you should never enjoy a treat, but simply that there will be a price to pay if unhealthy food is a regular part of your family's diet. Choose wisely!

SAVING MONEY AT THE GROCERY STORE

Processed and packaged food is expensive, and there's rarely a need to buy advertised food. Even the store brand's knockoff of the name-brand processed foods is usually not cheap. You will be much further ahead financially by making your food from scratch, whenever possible. It may be that taking some cooking classes will be a good investment, and even though you may pay for them, you'll save money in the long run. Alternatively, you could watch cooking shows on TV to draw inspiration in learning to prepare foods.

Train yourself to buy only what you need and will use. Don't go to the grocery store if you are hungry, and do not take hungry children to the store with you. Shop with a list of the basic necessities, and stick to it. Stay within your boundaries. Limits promote creativity. You will be forced to think and cook in more creative ways when you aren't buying packaged food.

Buy store-brand canned and frozen vegetables. Store brand milk is generally the same milk as the locally processed milk label is.

Buy produce in season. Buy nutritionally rich food that is filling. Eggs are cheap protein. Dry beans and brown rice are nutritionally superior and much more affordable than their processed counterparts. Potatoes are cheap and nutritious but also high on the glycemic index. Buy meat on the bone, and use the bones to make a rich broth. Buy dry goods in bulk. Generally, they cost much less when bought by the twenty-five or fifty-pound bag.

Watch sale fliers, and buy meat cuts when they are on sale, reduce portion sizes, and serve more vegetables. Better yet, buy a side of meat from a farmer. You will get a higher quality meat and a variety of cuts.

Make gourmet food with the ingredients you have and can afford. Save the specialized ingredient meals for an occasional feast that you serve with your best dishes.

Spices are an inexpensive way to jazz up any food. Dry spices will go stale, mark the date on the container.

Don't allow free access to your cupboards and refrigerator. Train your children when they are little to *ask* if they may have a snack. When you have a limited amount of fruit, give each person an assigned portion per day (one banana a day, for example).

Use cloth napkins instead of paper. Use washcloths for napkins at everyday meals. They are great for mopping up spills and washing the baby's face after the meal.

Keep a box of rags under the sink to use instead of paper towels, and wash plastic bags in the sink for reusing.

The number one thing you can do to slash your family's grocery bill is to garden. It is nearly free food. With a garden, you will have plenty of vegetables to eat, juice, and store for the rest of the year. In addition to cultivating a more traditional garden, plant fruit bushes and trees in your landscape. Grow your own herbs and spices. Get to know local gardeners, and learn what they plant and how they grow their produce with success.

PROJECT DAY

Occasionally the need will arise to have a Project Day or a Project Week—a time when you must repaint a room, tear out the carpet, or do something else that will disrupt the regular routine of home life. When doing projects of this magnitude, it is good to give plenty of thought to them and do not do them on a whim.

Here are some lessons I've learned that you can apply the next time you have a big project to tackle.

First, let me make an acknowledgment, some find the idea of working with children impossible. Children do not need constant entertainment and play. They can be learning from you, even on big project days. With the right attitude from you, they will learn that work is satisfying and fun. You just need to plan carefully to make the process conducive to learning and fun.

Now let's cover the basics: food and sleep. These two are very important to the happiness and well-being of your family. With this in mind, don't plan a project right after another big event; recover from the first event by getting plenty of rest and good food, and some down time. This will help the stress level for everyone in the family. Too much stress leads to grumpy, misbehaving children which can lead to a grumpy mom and dad. So plan the timing of your big project wisely!

Next, plan your food. It needs to be healthy for strength and stamina, but fast and easy to prepare. Going out to eat or pizza delivery do not fit the bill, especially if your project is more than a day long. That will also cut into the budget of your DIY project.

Make a list of your homemade quick meals. Then pin your list inside a kitchen cupboard for the next time you need a quick meal on a Project Day. Slow cooker dinners that you can throw together in the morning are great. Keep a supply of paper service on hand for meals.

Finally, get to bed at a decent time the night before your project. You will have more energy and be able to think and move more quickly.

With the right attitude from you, they will learn that work is satisfying and fun.

Have your clothing planned, and do not forget the children's attire. Everybody should wear old clothes—someone may unintentionally lean against the freshly painted door. Make sure that you have all of your clean laundry put away and your dirty laundry sorted and tucked away. You don't want to trip over it going to and fro.

Think about what your children are going to do while you work on your project. Is it something they can and should be involved with? If not, then plan something *special* for them that will keep them occupied while you're working. A new, open-ended activity is great for a Project Day.

If you suspect that your project is especially intriguing to them, then you will want to talk to them about it. Explain everything you are going to be doing, and make clear the things they can do to help you as well as what they absolutely cannot do. Then, give them a boundary, use tape to mark it, and tape some X's on the floor for their assigned seats where they can watch you do the project. Plan your consequences for disobedience.

Spend some special time with the little children at the beginning of the day, reading a story together or playing with them for ten minutes or so. Do this again after your lunch break. Make sure that they have access to food and drink during the day so that their needs are met without interrupting you.

A helpful tip: if you are interrupted while painting, have a plastic bag handy to put your paint brush into. This keeps it from drying out. If you are taking something apart, collect all the little pieces into a ziploc bag, and put it out of reach of the children.

Plan the project shopping list carefully beforehand so that you aren't constantly running to get supplies. Collect your materials and tools at once and put them in safe spot high enough that the littlest ones won't carry fascinating things away. Move quickly and efficiently with your project. Plan your steps, and move things out of the way that will hinder you. A few minutes moving something could keep you from tripping, spilling, or wasting motion.

If your project is a short one, do all the prep work you can before nap time. As soon as the children are laid down, do your project as fast as possible. Be ready for interruptions if they wake before you are finished. Quickly get them settled into their next activity, and then clean up the project mess.

If you assign older children to watch over little ones while you work on the project, it is nice to plan something new and exciting for them to do together. One of your older children could lead an activity for those not involved while the rest work on the project. This is a good way to teach responsibility.

Sometimes it is helpful to have everyone out of the house for a day, except those that are working on the project. Call a friend and work out a trade. You will have her children for a day while she works on a project, and another day she will take yours. It is nice on these days to have a simple supper planned for both families to eat together.

Painting with children around is a challenge, but it can be done. If they have never painted before, they will want to do it very badly. I am a firm believer in teaching children to work while young and to enjoy their work. Give them something to paint. Put a fresh coat of paint on the dog house or stain the play equipment. Older children can do touch-up painting in the house with a small container of paint and small brush. I would highly recommend using latex paint, unless you want your children to look spotted for a couple of weeks and have people ask about the genetic skin disease your family has (yes, that happened to us!).

For mechanically oriented projects, keep your children close, as they will learn through watching. It seems that something in their brain causes them to understand these things easily.

Paper projects such as bookkeeping, filing, and tax prep are more easily done with silence. I have trouble concentrating on numbers when there are constant interruptions. Perhaps this doesn't bother you. One option is to do these projects during naps or save them up and trade childcare days with a friend.

One important thing to keep in mind with projects is the cleanup that needs to be done when the project is done. Sometimes I get so caught up in resting on my laurels of a wonderfully completed project that I don't notice that I've left tools out. Then the everyday life starts up again, people need to be fed and so on, and I find myself tripping over the same box of project materials for a week.

Make a rule for yourself and your house: "A job isn't done until the tools are put away." This applies to so many things we do around the house, like making meals, doing laundry, and completing schoolwork. Say the rule three times right now, and then go write it on a three-by-five-inch index card and post it in a prominent place. Teach it to your family; this will pay off later.

Often while doing a project, we have to tear apart the house to get to the thing that needs worked on. I'm thinking of our family room right now. I have a decorative painting project planned for it, but in order to do it, I will have to move furniture and take down curtains. And while we're at it, I know already that I will also be mending tears in the upholstery, cleaning the curtains and blinds, and then the fly specks on the windows will bother me and I'll want to wash them, and the list goes on.

Simply put, projects can build on each other and take on lives of their own. Pretty soon, the daily routine is blown, we're eating take-out pizza, laundry is piling high, and everyone is irritable. Know when to stop and restore order. Know when to say, "I'll do ___ next month."

You do not need to put projects off forever; you can do them with children around. You simply need to plan carefully with them in mind. Think what a blessing it will be to them seeing you do projects, learning how to do these things together with you, and being instilled with a can-do attitude. In time, you will be handing over the tools, and they will be doing a project to benefit the whole family.

PREGNANCY AND PREPARING FOR BABY

When I look back on my pregnancies, the worst of them were when my diet, both pre-pregnancy and during pregnancy, was poor. Not enough fresh food, way too much sugar and too many carbohydrates, too much bad comfort food, no exercise, not enough water drinking—these factors lead to ill feelings, both physical and emotional.

FEELING YOUR BEST

If you are growing a baby and a placenta and are not eating well, then you will naturally become very drained. It will take huge effort to lift an arm or move a leg forward. I've been there. Last week, for example, we made cookies that had way too much sugar in them (even though I used evaporated cane juice sugar); carbohydrates are carbohydrates no matter the source. I ate way too many. I had the sugar spike and then a really bad crash. As a result, I was pretty much useless the rest of the afternoon.

The point is this: rethink your diet. What you eat before pregnancy and in the early days when you're carrying a child really impacts how you feel. I know from experience and would encourage you to look at your diet and cut out the junk.

I have found that, during pregnancy, I need much more nutrition than prenatal vitamins provide. Learn to pay attention to your body. Personally, my first trimester misery peaks at about nine weeks and is almost over by twelve weeks. At sixteen weeks, I'm feeling normal again. But everyone is different, and each pregnancy can also be different. Listen to your body and make appropriate adjustments to your diet and exercise. The first trimester is when your body is growing the placenta; it is an incredible organ. Good nutrition and sleep will go a long way toward aiding your body in this tremendous task. Don't do things that will hinder yourself.

The following are health tips I have found helpful in general, but especially while pregnant.

- ☐ First, cut out all sugar, even healthy sugar. It is just simply draining. Eliminate corn syrup, sucrose, glucose, maltose, dextrose, lactose, fructose, fruit concentrate, honey, barley malt, Sucanet, cane juice sugar, brown sugar, turbinado sugar. You will feel like a new person.

- ☐ Eliminate products made with white flour.

- ☐ Cut out simple carbohydrates in general.

- ☐ Eat eggs for breakfast. Protein in the morning will make you feel much better and carry you further through the day. Eggs also provide brain food for the baby. As long as you are carrying and nursing the baby, eggs should be part of your daily diet.

- ☐ Protein helps with nausea, along with keeping your energy up. Eat protein throughout your day.

- ☐ Eat regular small snacks or meals of nuts, milk, pudding, custard, cheese, cottage cheese, yogurt, small portions of meat (red meat gives you other needed nutrients also), fish, hard-boiled eggs (try deviled eggs), bacon, and beans (dips such as hummus), and more.

☐ Overeating makes things worse, especially for heartburn. Keep meals small and frequent.

☐ Eat green, leafy vegetables. They provide nutrients like folic acid.

☐ Baked potatoes are full of goodness and easy on a queasy stomach.

☐ Eat orange and yellow vegetables such as squash, carrots, and sweet potatoes.

☐ Whole grains give you fiber and B vitamins.

☐ Eat citrus and other fruits for nutrients. Vitamin C keeps your immune system strong and helps with blood circulation. During pregnancy your blood volume increases dramatically, and Vitamin C contributes to strong healthy vessels.

☐ Drink water—lots of water. Being dehydrated exasperates every other health problem. I like to squeeze a lemon into a two-quart pitcher, and drink lemon water all day long. Pay attention if you discover water tasting bad; this may indicate a nutrient deficiency.

☐ Sea salt is a good way to get micro-nutrients. It must not be white, or else it's not true sea salt.

☐ Take a really good prenatal or multivitamin with folic acid, a B complex, Cal-Mag-Zinc, and Vitamin C.

☐ Red raspberry leaf tea helps to build a strong uterus.

☐ Walking, sunshine, and fresh air really help with nausea and feeling better overall. Keep moving even when you do not feel like it.

☐ Ginger in many forms helps with nausea, but sugar and corn syrup can counteract its effect so be careful about your method for getting ginger. Make a tea with fresh gingerroot.

☐ Repair your intestinal system with probiotics, greens, and lemon water (from fresh lemon, not bottled juice).

☐ When you are laid low with nausea, use a cool wet cloth on your face. It will rejuvenate you so you can make the effort to do the most important things.

☐ Take a shower every morning as soon as you are able. You will feel much better. Before showering eat something because the blood sugars are low in the morning and you may quickly feel faint standing in the shower. If you can, put on athletic shoes early in the day—it does something to your brain that gives you extra zip.

☐ When cooking smells are intolerable, ask for help and have somebody cook meat ahead for you to put in the freezer. Have your husband grill, put the slow cooker outside so you don't have to smell it, cook double on good days, or eat cold food such as salads and sandwiches.

☐ If your supplements are making you feel bad, try a different brand. Try a buffered Vitamin C or a multivitamin without iron.

Study nutrition for your and your baby's health so that you can be strong, both for your baby and for the rest of your family. All of these things will help, some a lot, some just a little, depending on your physical makeup. We are all different. Pay attention to your body all the time, not just when you are pregnant. Pay attention to your health status before you get pregnant and while you are nursing.

HOUSE AND KIDS

During the early days of pregnancy, and for some expecting moms who feel bad the whole way through, the house can fall apart. Big kids can help so much when you're in this position. They aren't perfect (my children don't do everything exactly the way I would like) but with each year, they get better at their work. In times of need, I have to relax my standards of order and cleanliness, knowing that things can be recovered later. When I had only little children, it helped to place limits on the house—closing rooms off and reducing the number of toys. I clearly remember lying on the couch, with everyone kept in the same room, simply waiting it out. I was available to calm squabbles before they escalated. I could read aloud occasionally, show interest in their delights, and give direction from the couch. Remember it's only for a season.

Just accept life in the way it is at this moment, and choose to have a relaxed attitude.

First of all, a person must realize that work cannot get done while sleeping. You cannot do both at the same time. The key is in accepting the fact that growing this baby must take precedence over the house. Frustration, worry, and anxiety do *not* help anything. "This too shall pass," must become the mantra. Take heart, you know how to whip things back into shape. You simply need to wait for the energy to come back and enable you. With systems in place, the work will slowly get done and order will be back up to par again.

The family, of course, should be doing their daily chores as usual, but remember that they won't always get it right. Eventually your home will be clean again. Slowly but surely, one room at a time, one laundry load at a time, the house will return to its normal cleaning system.

It's all in the attitude: grumping, moaning, and crying about it will not help. Just accept life in the way it is at this moment, and choose to have a relaxed attitude. With systems in place that simply need their manager back in the managing role, it will be all right soon. Take notes so that when your daughters and daughters-in-law are at this point in pregnancy, you will know how to help. My mother has always been wonderful about having us all over for supper to take a load off of me at times, and my mother-in-law brings us great food as well as other gestures of encouragement.

When you get that surge of energy, concentrate on the most important things. Bathrooms and the kitchen must be clean. Laundry should be kept up and floors clean. Each time that you get off the couch, do one thing. If you are able, give yourself a little routine to do every hour or two:

- ☐ Change laundry loads.

- ☐ Do one thing to keep the bathroom clean.

- ☐ Do one thing to keep the kitchen clean.

- ☐ Sweep or vacuum one area of the floor.

Use paper plates, plastic cups, and eating utensils for this season. Stock up on paper towels and napkins. Switch from cloth diapers to disposables.

Baby proof your house really well. Lock doors and use baby gates or blockades of some sort to keep the children—and their subsequent mess—contained. Box up knickknacks and other breakables and items that cause extra dusting.

If you homeschool, consider using video and audio curriculum to help you at this time. Without question, have a whole house Quiet Hour. Put your little children in the bathtub to play (and get clean as an afterthought) while you sit with them and rest and slowly clean the bathroom. In the room where you and the children "live," keep a basket for diaper and wipes, the telephone, paper and pen for jotting notes (the brain tends to go fuzzy during these longs days), sippy cups and your water bottle, and easy snacks (dry, not anything wet or goopy) for you and the children.

If you have older children, keep them busy. They can be quite mischievous without mom's eyes on them. Make a list of specific tasks for them to do each day. Do not allow them to be aimless.

BABY COUNTDOWN

When you find out you are pregnant, you are in a race against the calendar. You need to be prepared for the days ahead when you will feel progressively worse. My worst days started at six weeks, peaked at nine weeks, and then gradually get better. The first trimester seems to be a lesson in endurance.

Before you get pregnant, keep your home prepared and take care of your health. When you discover you are expecting a child, start stocking up freezer food for the coming days of exhaustion and nausea.

In the second trimester when you are feeling great (the placenta is doing its job of nurturing the baby), prepare your house for the last trimester (when you are big and awkward) and the post-partum time (when you are busy with your baby).

☐ Declutter, organize, and clean each room.

☐ Put your home management systems in order and get them running smoothly.

☐ Work with the older children toward independence in their chores and schoolwork.

☐ Revamp your Home Management Book, and teach your children how to use it.

☐ Work hard on helping the children develop positive character traits, being sure to connect with each one.

☐ Cook ahead and stock the freezer.

☐ Stock the pantry deep.

☐ Stock up on paper products.

☐ Depending on what time of year the last trimester and postpartum occur, be prepared with the children for a seasonal clothing switch.

☐ In the ninth month, wash baby clothes and blankets.

If it doesn't get done, don't fret. These things will simply make life easier for you and your family. Remember: Mary gave birth in a barn and laid Jesus in a manger.

THE BUDDY SYSTEM FOR LARGE FAMILIES

The mom of a large family quickly gets outnumbered. An extra arm for each child would be useful, but that's not what God gave us. He gave us children that grow and, as they grow in stature, they also grow in wisdom with the grace of God. As they grow bigger stronger and wiser, they become more independent and helpful people.

I have often said that having three children was the hardest stage of parenting. After three, it got much easier. The stage of three for me was a four-year-old, a two-year-old, and a newborn. At the same time I also had a farmer-husband with a traveling job. Your hardest stage might be a different scenario.

A newborn is helpless, of course, completely dependent on Mom for every minutia. A two-year-old can feed himself. That particular two-year-old was potty-trained, but a potty-trained two-year-old might be more work than diapers. A two-year-old can be helpful, but that help is unpredictable. And a two-year-old needs lots of training, direction, instruction, and guidance ad infinitum. God bless the mothers of two-year-olds.

Once, while paying for my groceries, one of my two-year-olds took off running out of the store and directly out into the street. I felt my heart in my throat. His older brother, when he was two, disappeared from the sandbox. About the time I realized it, I spotted him walking down the country road holding hands with our elderly neighbor. These are a couple of the near-misses we have had that cause me to have grace for other parents when bad things happen.

As our family grew, we assigned the children to each other appropriately.

A four-year-old is more helpful compared to a two-year-old. They, at least, know what you're talking about most of the time. They can fetch things. They can actually help quite a bit, but they are four-year-olds after all, and they need training, direction, instruction, and guidance as well.

By the time we had number four, the rest were a step older and a whole lot more helpful. "Many hands make light work," as the saying goes, and our household condition improved. Why I thought I could be a Sunday School superintendent in our church during that time is still a mystery to me. Times might have been a bit easier but four little children is still a very challenging time.

It wasn't until baby number five that I learned about the buddy system from another mother. It was transforming. I assigned the oldest to the baby. Of course he didn't do all the work, but when I needed to take care of a meal or another child, he could keep an eye on the baby.

As our family grew, we assigned the children to each other appropriately. An added benefit to the help I received from the buddy system was the sweet relationships that developed between buddies.

The following is how we work our personal buddy system. Use this as a guide. Adapt the lists to what works best for you.

DUTIES OF THE BIG BUDDY

Get your Little Buddy up in the morning and:

- ☐ Help Little Buddy get dressed for the day.

- ☐ Take Little Buddy to toilet.

- ☐ Brush your teeth together.

- ☐ Get your Little Buddy a drink of water.

When we leave the house:

- ☐ Help your Little Buddy with socks and shoes, jacket, and seat belt.

- ☐ Keep an eye on your Little Buddy and/or hold hands (whatever Mom deems appropriate).

- ☐ Help your Little Buddy get food at potluck gatherings.

Get your Little Buddy ready for bed:

- ☐ Check that the buddy got a fresh diaper or used the potty.

- ☐ Help put on pajamas.

- ☐ Brush teeth.

Other tasks with your Little Buddy:

- ☐ Teach your Little Buddy to do chores by having them help you with yours.

- ☐ Put your Little Buddy's laundry away.

- ☐ Play with your Little Buddy if he needs some direction in what to do.

- ☐ Help your Little Buddy with anything he needs help with.

☐ Read to your Little Buddy.

Bonuses for the Big Buddy:

☐ The Big Buddy gets to finish the food of the Little Buddy when the Little Buddy gets full (desserts, ice cream, treats).

☐ The Big Buddy gets to help the Little Buddy on the Little Buddy's Special Day.

THE LITTLE BUDDY

Little Buddy must respect the Big Buddy. However, the Big Buddy must be kind and gentle, not exasperating, in helping the Little Buddy with his needs. If the Little Buddy is throwing a fit or otherwise not cooperating, the Big Buddy must get Mom or Dad to help the Little Buddy. Sometimes we needed to change buddies if two personality styles weren't meshing well.

SPECIAL DAY PRIVILEGES AND TASKS

Another thing that really helps things go smoothly is to assign each child a Special Day in the week. We did it in birth order, starting with Monday. Child number eight shares a Special Day with child number one, and we start over again. Assigning a Special Day eliminates squabbles and bickering over the seemingly silly things that kids like to do that make them feel special, such as: get the mail out of the mailbox and be the first to see what arrived. Don't laugh—we have had a ridiculous number of fights about the mail. Taking turns by the calendar day might help the amount of bickering in your house too.

Special Day privileges and tasks help the family by accomplishing work, provide learning experiences, give quality time with Mom and Dad, and keep the peace between siblings.

Here are some ideas to get your family started on Special Day privileges and tasks:

☐ Help Mom in the kitchen with meals and salad prep.

☐ Special kitchen day for choosing and making recipes. Make sure and add special ingredients to the grocery list before Town Day.

☐ Sit by Mom or Dad during Read-aloud Time.

☐ Go for a walk or bike ride with Mom.

☐ Help Mom with laundry: sort, switch loads, hang out, fold.

☐ Help Mom with library/office management: straighten books, pick up floor, sort and file papers, put on stamps, mail letters.

☐ Your day for computer games or Wii.

☐ Get the mail and be the first to look at the papers and magazines.

☐ Be the kid to ride along with Dad or Mom to do an errand.

Be creative and use the children God has given you to help others in the family. This is a great way to knit the hearts of your children one to another. To this day, our adult children have fond memories and good laughs of their times with their buddies.

DATE NIGHT

Every week we look forward to Wednesday. All day Wednesday we look forward to the evening. That's our date night. It's the highlight of our week, our time to connect as a couple. It hasn't always been like that. There were a lot of years when our dates were hit or miss but when we made a more concerted effort to a weekly commitment life got a lot better.

COMMIT

In committing to a regular date night with our spouse, we are reaffirming our commitment to each other. We are placing each other in high esteem. No person is perfect, and it doesn't take long in a relationship for that to become apparent. Committing to each other is committing in spite of those faults, and loving the other in spite of them. It's a two-way street of loving and respecting each other. Date Nights are a commitment to not take each other for granted. A regular date night is a way of holding each other in high esteem. We make the time for each other and put the rest of the world aside. It is a tangible time for prioritization. The rest of the world is drowned out and we focus on each other.

CONNECT

Use this time to connect with each other and catch up on what is relevant. We pause and linger over words and thoughts. Even in the silent moments we are together. Even through the good and bad days, months, and years, it is vital to stay connected. In spite of our imperfections we love all of each other and there is freedom in that shared love.

REVIEW

Reviewing the past days since the last Date Night helps to see with fresh eyes what has happened and where we are going. This time of connecting moves us forward with faith and hope in the future. We are a team and, in meeting together, we know each other better and gain strength from each other in making plans for the future. Date Night offers us an opportunity to see things in a different light, clean up messes that we make with each other, to apologize, forgive, and move forward.

DREAMS AND GOALS

On Date Night we share our dreams and goals and that in itself is a commitment to the future together. Dreams and goals are individual and together. Part of being a team, we help and encourage each other. Building each other up and helping each other see things in different ways is part of the value of regularly connecting on Date Night. Moving into the future, we look at the highlights of the past as reference points and plan ahead for more.

HAVE FUN

Date Night can be a hundred different things. We're all different. Our current favorite Date Night is going to a Sushi Restaurant. We have plans for packing sandwiches and going kayaking on a summer evening. We don't know what tomorrow may hold so we make the most of each day and enjoy life together while we have it. What are your favorite things? What do you think would be fun? Make a list, and start doing them together.

CHILDREN

Making a Date Night happen when the children were little was challenging, no doubt. We were short on finances and disrupting the children's bedtime routine seemed more hassle than it was worth. In fact, any time we found ourselves alone in the daylight hours, we called it a date. There were years that we called the drive to church a date because we were the only people in the front of the van and that's when we did our talking and connecting. When our oldest children turned old enough to babysit, we would go to the nearest restaurant where we could eat and be back home within an hour. There was nothing special at all about the restaurant, but the place gave us an opportunity to be alone and talk. There were also times that we sat on the porch in the dark after putting children to bed and called that our Date Night. There were a lot of years that we took the current nursing baby along with us on Date Night.

START

If you don't have a regular date night routine then there's no time like now to start. Choose a night of the week and set a timer in your phone so you remember to do it. Put it on the calendar. Tell your children, plan a simple supper for them and line up a babysitter if you need to. Or plan how you will have a date night at home. Get out of a rut, and put yourselves in a different place, even if that place is a porch stoop or a walk down the down the road.

TEENS AND ADULT CHILDREN IN THE HOME

Today we have three adult children who have been in and out of the house at various times and three teens who have part-time work away from home. These scenarios are challenging because they create work but they aren't home very much to contribute to chores.

What we have done to help with this is to first, have the older children be responsible for their own laundry. Next, we also ask them to help with chores, pitching in where needed. Any chores that are assigned to those working outside the home must be chores that are nonessential to other people's work. One person can't load the dishwasher if the person assigned to unload it isn't present.

Older children and young adults are coming into contact with a lot of ideas and thoughts that are new to them. Be receptive and patient in these conversations and listen. Allow them to process their thoughts out loud. They are also processing their own beliefs, which may be slightly different from yours. Keeping communication open with them is vital to your relationship. Behaving in a condescending or judgmental manner does nobody any good. You may not agree with what they are expressing, and they might not even agree with what they are expressing, but keep calm and cool and listen. Be present with them. Pray for wisdom. These conversations may happen in the late evening when you might find it hard to stay awake for but do your best to be present.

These older children are a joy and blessing. They bring so much fun and stimulating conversation to the home with their new and fresh ideas, ways of seeing things, and big energy. If you haven't come to these years yet, look forward to them because they are good years. They offer a different set of challenges than the previous years of parenting. If you are in them, take a deep breath and stay calm. Reason comes in the calm, not in strife. Strife produces nothing good. Love these years and be the encouraging parent that these children need.

When our family comes home, we want it to provide a warm, loving place of comfort where refreshment happens.

We want our homes to be inspiring places where the family is strengthened and encouraged to go out and do great things in the world. When our family comes home, we want it to provide a warm, loving place of comfort where refreshment happens.

MAKE YOUR BEST DAY EVEN BETTER

Many years ago when I was just a young woman with little children, and still trying to get my act together, I felt the days slipping quickly by. Every morning, my baby was bigger, rolling over, laughing, and expressing his uniqueness. My toddler started to put words together and run... fast. My preschooler told me stories and asked a thousand questions. The days blurred together, one after another.

The older ladies at church stated the obvious, telling me to enjoy these days. But how?

I wanted my days to count for something. I didn't want to merely exist or get by. I wanted to live with purpose, to create each day as a beautiful experience, to love my people through making our days full of the very best. I wanted to lie on my back and eat a popsicle with my three-year-old, letting the sticky juice run down my face as we laughed at the clouds.

I couldn't live that life of freedom if my anxious thoughts were caught up in a web worry over chores undone. I wanted the abundance of joy that comes with the best times, and I imagined better days.

We cannot ignore the realities of managing our homes. The work is always there waiting for us, compounding exponentially at times.

It is a fact of life, a natural law. I eventually learned to embrace it, to appreciate the rhythms of each task, and to anticipate and plan. I worked at that very intentionally, so that there was time—and therefore liberty—to peer into the opening bud of a flower, inhaling the beautiful scent, surrounded, a circle of wondering faces next to mine.

THE ROUTINE

The following are the bare bones items to start you on building your personal home management book. Use one page for each day of the week and write the theme for the day at the top. Add the routines. Put it into action by using your book as a guide each day.

Soon, your best days will be better and you will be creating a more beautiful life. Calm and relaxation result and you can breathe easy knowing that your life is manageable, the work will get done and you will have downtime. There will be time for the creative life, fun times with family and friends, and rest.

THE DAILY AND WEEKLY ROUTINE

Monday: Laundry Day

Tuesday: Kitchen Day

Wednesday: Office Day & Date Night

Thursday: Town Day

Friday: Cleaning Day

Saturday: Gardening Day & Feast Night

Morning Routine

- ☐ Workout and shower

- ☐ Coffee, Bible, Prayer

- ☐ Breakfast, Lunch and Supper preparations

- ☐ Start a load of laundry

Breakfast Routine

- ☐ Table Time

- ☐ Bible, Math, Language Arts, History, Science

- ☐ Fifteen Minutes of Phonics

Lunch Routine

- ☐ Quiet Time

- ☐ Read Aloud Time

Afternoon Chore Time (Friday Cleaning Day & Deep Cleaning)

- ☐ Daily Room Chores

- ☐ Bathroom Chores

Supper Routine

Evening Routine

DEEP CLEANING PLAN

Declutter, cobwebs, dust lights and ceiling fans, replace dead light bulbs, dust baseboards, straighten a drawer or cupboard, wash windows, wash curtains, wash area rugs, wipe light switches and door handles, vacuum corners, edges, furniture, under furniture.

Week 1: First day of month through Saturday

☐ Entryways and stairs

Week 2: First full week of the month

☐ Kitchen and Dining Room

Week 3: Second full week of the month

☐ Bathrooms and Laundry Room

Week 4: Third full week of the month

☐ Bedrooms and Closets

Week 5: Last Monday through the last day of the month

☐ Living Room and Schoolroom

APPENDIX A

COPING WHILE EXHAUSTED AND OVERWHELMED

Many experiences can drag us down. Pregnancy is one of them. Illness is another. And an unexpected trial can put us in a funk that is hard to pull out of.

Don't get resentful about your situation. Resentment breeds bitterness and hopelessness. Start writing down what you are grateful for. Choose to live thankfully.

Scripture promises that we "can do all things through Christ" us (Philippians 4:13). Are you going to our Good Shepherd for strength and wisdom in how to cope through your situation? Pray to God without ceasing, and trust him to give you strength.

Also, I can't say this enough, read the Bible every single day. Read it aloud to your children. Read one psalm and one proverb to them daily. Memorize verses from both together. It's not hard; just sit down with the Bible on one of your breaks from working and say, "Now we are going to memorize Psalm 100." Don't stress about it; make it a fun activity. Little children are usually amazing at memorizing.

Don't stop at reading Psalms and Proverbs; read texts from all over the Bible, read the Gospels. Ask your children what their favorite

Bible stories are and read them from the Bible. Then do the same at another fifteen-minute break.

WATCH WHAT YOU EAT

When you're exhausted is not the time to try new and elaborate dishes, no matter how yummy and fun it looked on that food TV show. You will get started, maybe even complete it, but then have no energy left to clean up the mess.

Focus on whole foods and eat simple. It's easier and better for you. Packaged and processed foods are not worth the ease, and they are too hard on your health. Don't rely on them. Shop from the produce aisle instead. All that you have to do is wash and cut fruit and vegetables, and you can do that a few minutes at a time. A simple meal for lunch and supper is frozen vegetables and a protein.

Your diet is critical to you and your family's well-being. When I look back on my pregnancies, the worst of them happened when I ate poorly prior to my pregnancy and during it. This occurred when I didn't have enough fresh food, took in way too many simple carbohydrates, had insufficient exercise, and wasn't drinking enough water. These poor lifestyle habits led to a myriad of ill feelings, including the lack of ability to cope emotionally.

I encourage an exhausted woman to look at her diet and cut out the junk. I have found that I need a lot more nutrients those in prenatal or multivitamins. I believe we especially need more B vitamins. Our modern diets are dreadfully short on the B vitamins, and when we eat deficient foods such as white flour, white rice, white sugar, our bodies take what is needed to digest the whites from our bodies. Add a growing baby to nutritional deficiencies, and we become further drained. It takes huge effort to lift an arm or move a leg forward. I know; I've been there. Lack of magnesium is another deficiency because we don't eat enough vegetables.

The other thing I have found to be a huge help in my diet, especially when pregnant and nursing, is to eat plenty of protein, especially for breakfast. It provides long stable energy for the day. Find a protein you like, and eat plenty of it: Cottage cheese, cheese, eggs, leftover meat.

We need to be so careful of what we put into our bodies. It affects how we live, how we feel, and that in turn affects everyone that we live with, be it for their good or detriment.

LAUNDRY TIPS

Here's a tried-and-true trick that moms with many children use. The rule is this: if it's not dirty, don't wash it; wear it again. Some children are messier and will go through more than one outfit in a day. Others, especially in the winter months, can wear the same outfit three days before it looks dirty. Don't make life harder for yourself by washing things that aren't really dirty. Little children don't sweat like adults, and their clothes can be worn until they spill food, drink, or arts and crafts gunk on them.

When you fold laundry, do it with your children. Sit on the floor and go slow. Listen to an audio story, watch a show or video, and keep moving forward, one thing at time. Make it fun for them by sending them on little missions to put things away and timing their missions. Have races. Give your children lots of praise for each thing they do. Teach them these verses while you work on folding:

KINDNESS AND LOVE

Children can be a great help with encouragement, love, and praise. Children that are not getting these things, but have to deal with an upset mama, will be cranky in return. Do not wound them.

Yes, children should be obedient, but little children need so much love. They thrive on praise, they crave physical touch, and they love to do things with mama. Make sure that your children have plenty of love to balance any chastisement they receive. Get down to their eye level when you are talking to listening to your children. Put yourself in their place. Ask yourself, "What is the child trying to tell me with these actions?"

This is a verse I use with my children when I hear their tongues get sharp, which always reminds me of my own tongue. What example am I giving them?

Another thing that will help in communicating with children is this simple practice: every single time you talk to them, force yourself to smile. "Fake it 'til you make it," is a common catchphrase. When you speak while you're smiling, your tone of voice changes, and you will find that the words that come out of your mouth are more gracious. I'm certainly not encouraging you to live a fake life, but sometimes forcing that smile helps the rest of the body to relax, let go of tension, breathe, and keep on with kindness. Look into their eyes and see the person the child is.

Talk to your children about this, and help them to do the same thing. Teach them to smile when they speak. It is hard to complain and whine while smiling. Focus on that together for a week, and I expect that you will see a dramatic improvement in speech and attitude. If nothing else, you'll get goofy smiles, silliness, and laughter.

SIMPLIFY AND STREAMLINE

When you are exhausted and/or big and pregnant, and you see a million things that you want to do, but lack the energy to do them, here are some practical steps you can take.

First, stick with simplified routines. Cut out any fluff that is not vital. Identify the part of the day when you feel best and capitalize on it.

Call your children, sweetly, and tell them, "We are going to work on _____ chore for fifteen minutes, and then we are going to sit on the couch and read a book." Now work on that thing as hard and fast as you can, using a timer, if you want. You are doing work *together* and preschoolers *love* this.

Then, sit down with your children and read to them, and be sure to snuggle. Preschoolers love this too. If you need fifteen minutes more for a rest, take it. Make sure that every time you sit down, you have a glass of water in hand and drink it.

Use your timer, and after you have had fifteen to thirty minutes of rest, do fifteen minutes of work. Make sure that the work you are doing is important work; don't clean what doesn't need to be cleaned.

If you are regularly cleaning, it can't be that dirty—not compared to the dirt that a bunch of farm children drag in on a regular basis. Just think about what my mudroom looks like, and it might make you feel better about yours.

One very cold hard winter day, in my mudroom was a small water tank covered with dried manure, a pile of straw, and a newborn calf that had nearly frozen to death. After twenty-four hours of this, the whole house smelled like a barn. That same winter we had a goat penned in the garage. Every time the door opened, barn smell came in. How's that for perspective? Barn smell is nice—when it stays in the barn.

Now, look into the past and think for a minute how your great-great-grandmothers lived. Or catch up on current events, and think about how most of the world lives today.

I love clean, believe me. I think it is a natural God-given womanly attribute to clean. But sometimes we have to let go a bit. Some things in life are more important than clean. Some things in life are more important than organization. Use the best minutes of your day to love your family.

For your fifteen-minute work periods, focus on floors, bathrooms, and kitchen. Those are the dirtiest parts of our homes. Make the work as easy as possible. As a temporary solution, use paper towels for cleaning instead of rags to save on your laundry. Use paper plates, plastic cups, spoons, and forks instead of washing your regular dishes. That will save on cleanup. Paper and plastic are less expensive than household help.

Before you put your children to bed, have a fifteen-minute tidy. Get a basket and go around with your children to pick up and put away. Make it a game to see how fast they are, or count how many things they find.

Cheer when you are done! Say encouraging words, "See how nice this room looks now!" Don't say it in a snarky voice; that is discouraging. Don't destroy your relationships with your children with sarcasm. Be genuinely encouraging.

Another way to keep your home tidy is to shut off certain rooms or cupboards for a time. If you're too tired to keep a certain room tidy, work on that room, fifteen minutes at a time, until it is the way you want it to look and then close it. Shut the door, ban its use, and close it down for a period. We do this with our Sewing Room on occasion. It is a place that can quickly turn into a crafting explosion. I love to see my children being creative, but when I don't have the time or energy to oversee its use or cleaning, then I close the door.

The stress of being overwhelmed and exhausted is real, but it is also temporary. This too shall pass. Look for the bright moments in each day and reflect on those when you are drifting off to sleep for the night. Tomorrow is another day and with God's help, some attitude checks, and strategy, you will get through it.

APPENDIX B

MOVING BEYOND SURVIVAL MODE

I frequently get e-mails from ladies who look around and don't know where to start in managing their homes. "Do the next thing" is a fine saying, but if everywhere you look, you see things to do, you wonder which thing is next.

It's an experience that we all have now and then. Often I spread myself too thin, and that is a recipe for chaos. Friends and family have seen my chaos and will confirm the truth that I am not perfect. This series of steps is not only for those who don't know where to start, but it will help you recover from a chaotic season.

If your home life needs a recovery session, then do each of the following steps daily. Each day check that you have the previous steps under control before moving forward.

STEP ONE: PREPARE SUPPER AND WASH THE DISHES

Pick a one-dish meal that's easy and that you have the ingredients for. If it's not too late, put it in the slow cooker. I specialize in slow cooker meals when I have projects to do. And, moving beyond survival mode *is* a project. Once supper is made, wash every single last dirty dish in the kitchen. Commit to keeping the counters clean and the dishes washed from this day forward

STEP TWO: FIND YOUR CLOTHES

Sort through your clothes and find seven outfits that fit you—one for each of the next seven days. Now your clothes are ready for you to step into each morning. Commit to putting on clothes as soon as you get out of bed in the morning, even go so far as to lay them out the night before. This will help your work attitude and demonstrate to your children that things are changing first thing every morning. Locate Sunday clothes a day or two before for everyone in the family so you can all get to church without a Sunday morning family breakdown.

STEP THREE: MORNING ROUTINE

Write down your morning routine and tape it to your bathroom mirror. The times beside these things are how long it should take when you are in Maintenance Mode (Maintenance Mode is when your home management systems are working, your house is regularly cleaned, and your daily to-do list is maintenance tasks).

- ☐ Read Bible and pray. Write down three things you are thankful for today.

- ☐ Make bed (30 seconds).

- ☐ Straighten bedside tables (30 seconds).

- ☐ Dress for the day. You do not need to stare at your clothes in a fog because you laid them out the night before (2 minutes).

- ☐ Fix hair and face.

- ☐ Straighten and wipe bathroom (1 minute).

☐ Take supplements; drink 2 glasses of water.

☐ Check calendar (30 seconds).

☐ Start laundry (3 minutes) and set your timer to remind you to switch loads.

☐ Check social media and e-mails. Set a timer. Don't sit there all day!

☐ Make breakfast for children. Read a psalm to them. Give them words of encouragement.

☐ Decide what's for lunch and supper.

If your bathroom is a disaster, then "straighten and wipe" will take longer than a minute. Don't take much longer. Save deep cleaning the bathroom for later. Do take one minute to quickly put things away and wipe out the sink.

Stop when the minute is complete and move on. If your children are awake and have not eaten breakfast, then do not check your social media. Feed the children.

Tweak the Morning Routine to fit your life and keep your priorities straight.

Have you done *all* of your Morning Routine? If not, identify why not and then change things so that you can do it all. Will five or fifteen minutes of stretching exercises make your day better? Then slip them into your morning routine in a logical place. I like to exercise first thing before my brain kicks in.

STEP FOUR: EVENING ROUTINE

An Evening Routine gets you to bed at a decent time. Adequate sleep makes for a happy and productive person in the morning.

Part of what makes for a successful Morning Routine is a strong Evening Routine. How is your Evening Routine? Write it down and tape it on your bathroom mirror beside the Morning Routine. Also post it in your kitchen, beside your Morning Routine. Make both of these routines priorities.

Think about what is working well with your Morning and Evening Routines and keep those parts. What is going poorly? Replace a bad habit with a good one. This is why you should *write it down* and refer to it as you establish routines. Refer to your routines every single day for a whole month. It takes twenty-one days to establish new habits. A habit is something that you do automatically without hesitation, without even thinking.

Work on making your Morning and Evening Routines habits that you can do without deliberating:

☐ Check the calendar, make To Do list (3 minutes).

☐ Get out a big pitcher for your daily quota of water: 2 ½ quarts. Either fill now and put in the frig or fill in the morning (1 minute).

☐ Lay out clothes for tomorrow (2 minutes).

☐ Bathe, wipe one shower/bath wall (15 minutes).

☐ Read (Use wisdom in how long you read; don't stay up all night.).

☐ Read the Bible and say your prayers (10 minutes).

☐ Turn out light (Set your bedside lamp on a timer for evening lights-out and morning wake-up light.).

STEP FIVE: "YES, MOM"

After breakfast, spend ten minutes reviewing "How to obey" with your children. Read the Scriptures with them. Tell the children you are sorry for the times you have hurt them with your words and actions. Pray with them and ask God to help you parent better with more wisdom. Next, role-play scenarios that you are working on in your home. This looks like Simon Says. Teach the children to reply with "Yes, Mom" cheerfully. Teach them how to appeal by asking, "May I appeal, Mom?" Make this fun, and reward the children with lots of hugs and kisses. Explain to them that disobedience will result in consequences. This is teaching outside the moment of conflict. When a conflict occurs, everyone's emotions can run crazy and it is not a calm and teachable moment. Role-playing scenarios can be very profitable.

STEP SIX: AFTERNOON CHORE TIME

Afternoon Chore Time (see below) is a very important routine that often gets pushed by the wayside at our house. That is when things start to slide towards ugly. An ugly house makes for ugly attitudes from everyone who lives here. Ugly attitudes rub off on others and bring them down.

Afternoon Chore Time needs to be elevated to one of the most important things that happen in the day. Maybe afternoon doesn't work at all for your family's work or school schedule, and you call it Morning Chore Time. The important thing is to *do* these *regular* chores. For my family, it is a signal that the workday is drawing to a close, and it is time to get ready to have a family meal and evening together.

For the family members who works away from home and walks in on Afternoon Chore Time, it is a welcoming atmosphere. It says, "We're getting ready for the evening, and we're glad you're home!"

Personalize it to suit your individual circumstances. The most important thing on the following list is to tidy the house, so whatever you do, don't drop that.

- ☐ Put on relaxing music and light a candle (1 minute).

- ☐ Set little ones at the table or in the playpen with an activity so they don't undo the work (5 minutes).

- ☐ Children put away schoolwork (5 minutes) and start Daily Afternoon Chore Chart (15-30 minutes).

- ☐ Do a 10-minute tidy. Put everything into its proper place, straighten cushions, clear level surfaces. Assign each child a room and post it on their Afternoon Chore Chart.

- ☐ Freshen up; fix hair; do one thing to clean your bathroom (10 minutes).

- ☐ Start supper; set the table; have an appetizer and drink for those who are just arriving home.

There are many varieties to home scenarios, such as big and little children, only big children, only little children, no children, grown children, small house, big house, work-from-home parent, second shift worker, third shift worker. Be creative and flexible in creating your routines so that they work for your family and make your days better.

Our homes all look different; however, people live in homes and living makes messes. No matter what, daily chores must be done, and it really helps to have a chore routine that happens at the same time every day without fail. Habits become reflexive and routine. When your daily work is so ingrained that you do it automatically, you might have to ask, "Did I do this task?" You don't even realize that you were doing it. You may be singing along to a song or lost in your thoughts or planning something all while your body is automatically going through habitual cleaning work.

Good habits make life easy and beautiful. That is why I don't change my children's chores very often. I want their assigned work to turn into strong habits, and I want them to become very proficient at each one of their chores.

Afternoon Chore Time is one of the pillars of a good day. Your Morning and Evening Routines are two other strong pillars. When those three important routines are running like a smooth machine, the rest of the day will fall into place. Commit to focusing on those three routines until they become an integral part of your daily life. Make them lifelong habits that become hard to unsettle.

STEP SEVEN: EASY MENU PLAN

With focus this little project will take less than an hour. Find a blank calendar page from an old or unused calendar. Pick a month that has 31 days. Another location for a calendar is the spreadsheet program on your computer. Look at templates for a calendar. Alternatively, take a sheet of paper and down the side of it write the numbers 1 to 31. Write an easy supper plan for each day with menus you already know to be tried-and-true.

The reason I like to use a calendar page is that you get a better visual sense of variety in the meal planning. For example: Italian on Mondays; ground beef on Thursdays; fish on Saturdays; roast on Sundays.

Write a corresponding grocery list for each supper plan. Make a couple of copies of the grocery list, keeping one in your purse.

STEP EIGHT: SELF

More than anything else, the one thing that gets in the way of home management is our own self. This can happen in two ways. The first and probably most predominant for busy parents with little children is that we neglect taking care of ourselves. We do not take the time to eat the right food, drink enough water, take supplements, get daily sunshine and fresh air, exercise, or time alone (especially the introverts among us).

By not taking care of these basic needs, we set ourselves up for a health disaster. When our health and resultant energy quota are just enough to get by, we let our family down. They need you alert and able, not a walking zombie.

Most importantly, we need to take care of our spiritual health so that we are not an old grump to our families. Children do not need a short-tempered parent who berates them over every little thing. Get your attitude right by having a quiet time in the Scriptures every morning and every evening. The Psalms have so much to teach us about God, and they are comforting to our souls. Read one daily. Read from Proverbs every morning to your children at breakfast. This is for everyone's character training. Yes, parents need character training too.

When you work through your Morning and Evening Routines, be sure to include things that better your overall health. If exercise and sunshine do not fit into your Morning and Evening Routine, then tack it on to Lunch or your Afternoon Routine. Have recess with your children. Find a good spot in the day, and then make exercise a habit.

Some important things to help with health:

☐ Squeeze a lemon into a pitcher of water for you to drink during the day.

☐ Take B vitamins for emotional stability and feeling good overall.

☐ Eat protein. Eggs are especially good because they are brain food for babies during pregnancy and nursing.

☐ Cut out sugar, corn syrup, and simple carbohydrates. These fast sugars immediately enter the blood system. The highs and lows they create are hard on your system and mood. They also suppress the immune system, are toxic to your body, and feed cancer cells. Cut out sugar for one week, and see how good you feel.

☐ Fish oil is good for your health, your skin, and your unborn baby's eyes.

☐ Avoid processed food because of the salt and additives that come with them. Eat whole foods.

☐ Eat salad daily; it makes you feel so much better.

☐ Hanging out laundry is great for stretching, bending, and getting sunshine and fresh air.

☐ T-Tapp (t-tapp.com) is my favorite exercise. It feels great all over the body. It is not running, jumping, and gasping for air. It provides great stretching in a physical-therapy type way. A fit mama will be able to do things with her grandchildren and maybe even great-grandchildren.

☐ Do a hobby or work that brings you joy; schedule it into your day or week.

The second way that self gets in the way of home management is when we let our own desires take precedence over what we are supposed to be doing. I do not mean that you need to be a doormat to your family or that you as a person should be smothered, but we need to keep things in priority.

When you make decisions moment by moment throughout the day, they need to be filtered through two questions: "Is this activity glorifying and serving God?" and "Are my first priorities taken care of?" Thinking through these questions is a habit that we deliberately need to foster. Write these two questions and put them above your kitchen sink or on a whiteboard in the common area of the house. When our priorities get unbalanced, our spiritual life gets out of balance as well. This affects our emotional and mental health and can cause a negative spiral that can spin us into chaos.

How we take care of ourselves now and the choices we make will impact not only today, but who we and our families become in the future. Pray for wisdom, and commit to changing your small daily habits to be more God-glorifying.

STEP NINE: LAUNDRY

Some people love it, some hate it, and some are ambivalent to it. Wherever you fit on this spectrum, laundry is necessary for a clean life.

You can make the chore more pleasant with these tips:

- ☐ Beautify the laundry area.
- ☐ Install adequate lighting.
- ☐ Make the laundry area as organized and efficient as possible.
- ☐ Smile while you work; choose to enjoy the chore.
- ☐ Fold clothes as a team with an audio story, music playing, or a favorite show.
- ☐ Set limits for each day, depending on your family's size and the size of your laundry. equipment). For example: Once 4 loads are done, you don't have to do any more until tomorrow. This ends the chore and that brings satisfaction.
- ☐ Delegate parts of the work to the children. My older children do their own laundry on scheduled days of the week.
- ☐ Put away all clean and folded laundry every afternoon.
- ☐ Assign one day of the week to catch up on washing, mending, and ironing.

STEP TEN: TAKE CONTROL OF THE CLUTTER

Once a day, take a box and a trash bag and spend fifteen minutes removing trash and clutter from one room. Set the timer and work until it rings. When the time is up, take the trash bag to the trash bin and put the box in the van to take to Goodwill. It is simple to do. What gets in the way are our thoughts and emotions about the extra things we think we need to hold onto. Consider the following questions when looking at your clutter:

- ☐ When was the last time I used this?

- ☐ Do I need this?

- ☐ Is this item taking up space that could be utilized better?

- ☐ Does this item bring me joy? Or annoyance?

Getting unneeded stuff out of our homes frees time and space for better things. Managing and caring for stuff takes time. When it's gone, look around and be at peace.

STEP ELEVEN: TEN MINUTES

Work for ten minutes and then take a ten-minute break. Use a timer and start working through your house, one room at a time, putting things away and cleaning. Get your children involved, and make it a fun race. During the ten-minute work sessions, move as fast as you can. It's amazing what a couple of hours of this will do for your home!

STEP TWELVE: YOUR HOME MANAGEMENT BOOK

Read the part of this book about putting your Home Management Book together. Your Home Management Book is your guide to maintaining order in your home. By referring to it throughout the day, you will be able to keep your home neat, clean, and prepared for anything. It will help you stay on track daily, every week, and every month. When a life event disrupts, your Home Management Book will help you get back on track by telling you what to do next.

THANK YOU

Thank you to Brandt, Brock, Bridgette, BriAnne, Brooke, Brian, Bronwyn, Brielle, and Matthew for your love, forgiveness, resilience, patience, and encouragement in life and with this book project. You are a great joy and I love you to infinity and beyond.

Thank you, Ainsley, for knowing our reality and joining us with your adventurous spirit.

Thank you, Matt, for your constant encouragement, love, and support. We are a great team and I look forward to many more chapters in life with you.

Made in the USA
Lexington, KY
17 December 2017